The Politics of Truth

SELECTED AND
INTRODUCED BY
JOHN H. SUMMERS

The Politics of Truth

Selected Writings of

C. Wright Mills

OXFORD
UNIVERSITY PRESS

2008

OXFORD
UNIVERSITY PRESS

Oxford University Press, Inc., publishes works that further
Oxford University's objective of excellence
in research, scholarship, and education.

Oxford   New York
Auckland   Cape Town   Dar es Salaam   Hong Kong   Karachi
Kuala Lumpur   Madrid   Melbourne   Mexico City   Nairobi
New Delhi   Shanghai   Taipei   Toronto

With offices in
Argentina   Austria   Brazil   Chile   Czech Republic   France   Greece
Guatemala   Hungary   Italy   Japan   Poland   Portugal   Singapore
South Korea   Switzerland   Thailand   Turkey   Ukraine   Vietnam

Copyright © 2008 by Oxford University Press, Inc.

Published by Oxford University Press, Inc.
198 Madison Avenue, New York, NY 10016

www.oup.com

Oxford is a registered trademark of Oxford University Press

Library of Congress Cataloging-in-Publication Data
Mills, C. Wright (Charles Wright), 1916–1962.
The politics of truth : selected writings of C. Wright Mills
/ selected and introduced by John H. Summers.
p.   cm.
Includes bibliographical references and index.
ISBN 978-0-19-534305-2 (hardcover)—ISBN 978-0-19-534304-5 (pbk.)
1. Social sciences.   I. Summers, John, 1971—.   II. Title.
H83.M493 2008   301.092—dc22
[B]   2008011427

9 8 7 6 5 4 3 2 1
Printed in the United States of America
on acid-free paper

For Roy Rosenzweig

ACKNOWLEDGMENTS

I am grateful to Richard Gillam, Kathryn Mills, Nikolas Mills, Pamela Mills, George Scialabba, and Anna Summers for advice and assistance. All writings are reprinted by permission of the Estate of C. Wright Mills.

C. Wright Mills was the most famous American sociologist in the world when he died on March 20, 1962. Yet no biography worth reading has appeared in the four decades since then, nor has a reliable apparatus of scholarship matured around his writings to guide commentary on his legacy. This is the first new collection since 1963; it is only the second collection to appear in English.

The possibilities are as abundant as the collection is necessary. Mills's contemporaries knew him as the author of long books, but also as an aphorist, essayist, reviewer, pamphleteer, and public lecturer. "Books," he once commented, "are simply organized releases from the continuous work that goes into them." The complete bibliography of his published writings runs to more than 200 entries. Add the unpublished writings from his "continuous work" and it runs past 350 entries.

Of the essays, interviews, speeches, and public letters selected for this collection, Mills published all but one in periodicals such as *Dissent*, *Evergreen Review*, *Harper's*, *The Nation*, *New Left Review*, *Saturday Review*, and *politics*. He wrote them for liberally educated, politically aware readers in Europe and America. The same intention accompanies their republication.

What is missing? In 1947, Mills drew up a proposal for a collection of his writings and titled it *The Politics of Truth, and Other Essays*. His proposal included four technical essays in the sociology of knowledge: "Language, Logic, and Culture" (1939); "Situated Actions and Vocabularies of Motive" (1940); "Methodological Consequences of the Sociology of Knowledge" (1940); and "The Professional Ideology of Social Pathologists" (1943). These essays would have been included here but for their availability in digital form to the readers most likely to be interested: the academic social scientists for whom he wrote them. Likewise, the series of autobiographical letters that Mills intended to publish in *Contacting the Enemy* belongs to the theme but not to this collection. Read them in *C. Wright Mills: Letters and Autobiographical Writings*, edited by Kathryn Mills, with Pamela Mills, and published by the University of California Press in 2000.

On December 30, 1959, Mills signed a contact with Oxford University Press for *The Cultural Apparatus, or The American Intellectual*. Tempting though it is to publish fragments from this unfinished manuscript, neither Mills nor his literary executor, William Miller, left a statement of intention. In such cases, it is best to honor the silence by taking the side of discretion.

CONTENTS

The Politics of Truth

Master Tasks for Intellectuals

(1) To define the reality of the human condition and to make our definitions public.
(2) To confront the new facts of history-making in our time, and their meaning for the problem of political responsibility.
(3) Continually to investigate the causes of war, and among them to locate the decisions and defaults of elite circles.
(4) To release the human imagination, to explore all the alternatives now open to the human community by transcending both the mere exhortation of grand principle and the mere opportunist reaction.
(5) To demand full information of relevance to human destiny and the end of decisions made in irresponsible secrecy.
(6) To cease being the intellectual dupes of political patrioteers.

—C. Wright Mills

JOHN H. SUMMERS | New Man of Power

It's been said in criticism that I am too much fascinated by power. This is not really true. It is intellect I have been most fascinated by, and power primarily in connection with that. It is the role of ideas in politics and society, the power of intellect, that most fascinates me as a social analyst and as a cultural critic.

—C. Wright Mills

B EFORE CHARLES WRIGHT MILLS turned twelve, his family moved through five Texas cities and changed residences eight times. For weeks at a spell his father, a traveling insurance agent, left him alone with his mother and older sister. The restless isolation he felt in his boyhood never left him, nor did the special quality of ambition he discovered in his first sustained reading: a collection of little blue books that belonged to his father.

The title was *Applied Psychology*. The author, Warren Hilton, suggested in twelve volumes of epigrams and examples how to turn "the mind into an independent, causal agency." Hilton stressed the plasticity of human nature, the infinite dialectical growth available to any untutored intelligence, properly motivated. *Applied Psychology* was a knock-off edition of the American philosophy of achievement, and Charles read all 1,100 pages in the spring of 1934, as he prepared to graduate from Dallas Technical High School.

Eager to report the powers stirring within him, he began a personal journal. Then, at the end of the summer, he declared his independence in a letter to the editor of the *Dallas Morning News*. The city was a haven for religious fundamentalists. His mother had baptized him in the Catholic Church, and it was she who had persuaded him, when they lived in Sherman and his rebellion was exasperating his teachers, to serve as an altar boy in the local parish. In his letter, however, he squelched the moderate deception that no choice need be made between reason and revelation and left no doubt where his allegiance lay in the conflict.

Published on August 10, 1934, the letter provoked three indignant replies. A business associate passed news of the furor to his father, who quickly ended it. That autumn, not long after he turned eighteen, his parents enrolled him in Texas Agricultural and Mechanical College, a military school. But it was too late. The bias of his temperament was set. "It was thought that A&M would make a man out of me," he later said. "Instead, I became an intellectual."[1]

The experiment at Texas A&M failed before the end of the first year, and young Mills, bucking the anti-intellectualism of military school even as he shuddered to join the "sissies" in Austin, transferred to the state university. There, from 1935 to 1939, he fell under the influence of a group of sociology and philosophy professors trained in the pragmatism of the Chicago School. They taught him a naturalistic approach to self and society that formed the nucleus of his thought. He called the pragmatists his "godfathers."

Mills's first contributions to sociology marked him as a prince in the discipline. "Language, Logic, and Culture," "Methodological Consequences of the Sociology of Knowledge," and "Situated Actions and Vocabularies of Motive" were published to wide notice while he studied for his doctorate at the University of Wisconsin. The articles made an early instance of the linguistic turn in pragmatic social thought and broached the terms for a critical theory of culture that guided his writing for the rest of his career. Mills wanted to jettison the vocabulary of highbrow and lowbrow, advanced guard and establishment, and instead to adopt a radically sociological counter-model. "I should like us to abandon these terms—high, middle, and lowbrow," he said during a speech to the PEN Club in New York. "They stand for fashionably snobbish distinctions and nothing else. I should like to replace them in our vocabulary of criticism by more anarchistic standards of culture."[2] In the "educative interplay" of pragmatic intellectuals and their publics hived democratic sympathies at odds with both the interest-driven logic of capitalist accumulation and the romantic conceit of the advanced guard.[3] The ideal outcome of this "interplay"? To abolish itself in the "self-cultivating man," to create new values from the unity of ideas and action.[4]

Though Mills received his pragmatic inheritance in the late thirties, while it took fire from all sides, he reserved his most serious complaints for its failure to develop a social or political theory by which to secure the "self-cultivating man" in a sensibility. He never filled the theoretical gap, retaining a pragmatic suspicion of concept-mongering, but he did more than anybody to develop and exemplify the sensibility.

In 1941, Mills accepted a position as associate professor of sociology at the University of Maryland. The next summer he submitted his dissertation (a sociological history of pragmatism) at Wisconsin. He dedicated his spare energy to staying out of the war, which turned him toward radical politics. "The Powerless People" (1944), the opening essay in this collection, marked his transition from technical theorist to radical intellectual. *The means of effective communication are being expropriated from the intellectual worker,"* he wrote, sounding a defensive note that echoed through much of his political writing. *"The material basis of his initiative and intellectual freedom is no longer in his hands. Some intellectuals feel these processes in their work. They know more than they say and they are powerless and afraid."* In 1946 he joined his friend and teacher Hans Gerth in publishing *From Max Weber*. The Weber translations, plus a torrent of essays in magazines and journals, brought him to the attention of the Bureau of Applied Social Research in New York, then to the sociology faculty of Columbia College. He won tenure there in 1956, before he turned forty.

At the center of the eleven books Mills published was a trilogy: *The New Men of Power* (1948), *White Collar* (1951), and *The Power Elite* (1956). Cued by Balzac's ambition to build up a total picture of society, the trilogy had a little to say about a great many subjects and a lot to say about a few subjects of great importance. The modern epoch had begun when its ideologies organized the moral energy of Enlightenment against myth, fraud, and superstition. Liberalism and Marxism had developed theories of human beings as secular, rational, peaceable creatures, then had transformed these theories in collective projects. But the institutions built around militarized capitalism and its power-state overwhelmed self and society, according to Mills. In the coming "post-modern epoch," the moral culture of humanist aspiration stood disinherited of the expectation that intelligence and freedom entailed one another.

In 1956 and 1957, visiting Europe for the first time, Mills befriended a group of revisionist communists and socialists in London and Warsaw and began, on the strength of their example, to agitate for a renaissance in humanist values. In the pamphlet resulting from his visit, *The Causes of World War Three* (a chapter is reprinted here), he implored intellectuals on all sides of the Cold War to call "our own separate peace." The failures of conservative liberalism made his case for him in the Americas. The failures of official Marxism in Europe completed his appeal. By 1960, when he wrote the "Letter to the New Left," he stood at the head of an international movement, virtually alone among American intellectuals in carrying none of the metaphysical guilt of a communist past and at the same time exemplifying unbroken radical commitment.

Critics often complained of the war-whooping tone of Mills's writing. But in pronouncing liberalism and Marxism obsolete he absolved himself of their rhetorical conventions as well as their ideological confidence. His anarchism, attuned to the absurd, summoned reserves of semi-conscious knowledge for a pitiless assault upon the decaying legitimations. He was at his most popular while he was mocking "crackpot realists," "advertising maniacs," "technological idiots," and "cheerful robots," laying up perceptions around the margins of the commercial banality. Reading him in *Esquire* "jolted me out of my chair," wrote Hunter S. Thompson. "It's heartening to know that there are still people around with the simple guts to move in on the boobs with a chainmace."[5] Recordings of his addresses in the late fifties show him in command of a mature style, eliciting bursts of laughter and outrage. "You may well say that all this is an immoderate and biased view of America, that this nation also contains many good features," he said on January 12, 1959, at the London School of Economics. "Indeed that is so. But you must not expect me to provide A Balanced View. I am not a sociological book-keeper."[6]

The trilogy presented a panorama of labor leaders, white-collar workers, celebrities, political bosses, corporate chieftains, and "warlords." Mills concluded in each case that those who had the best chance to exercise power were the least well prepared to exercise it responsibly. As he turned to rally the intellectuals as an independent force, he sighted the irony from another direction. Those who were best prepared to exercise power responsibly had the least chance of obtaining it. To complete the predicament, at no time in history were these means of power so concentrated, so consequential to human affairs, as in the age of thermonuclear weaponry and total war. In explaining why this predicament had come about, why it mattered, and how to transcend it, Mills drove his early "fascination with intellect" into a climax as sophisticated as it was enthralling.

The predicament was "structural."[7] The corporate organization of culture tied off the veins of creativity, forcing the craftsman to cater to the formulas and stereotypes of the "overdeveloped supersociety" the United States was becoming. Confined to the roles of "hack" or "star," the craftsman lost contact with the public, which split into "media markets" that trivialized the interests of its individuals into hobbies. The hive of "educative interplay," once a place to practice democratic values, rotted in the commercial transaction. "You cannot 'possess' art merely by buying it," Mills insisted, echoing John Dewey. "You cannot support art merely by feeding artists—although that does help. To possess it you must earn it by participating to some extent in what it takes to design it and to create it. To support it you must catch in your consumption of it something of what is involved in the production of it."[8]

Confronted by the rationalizing model of the factory, most intellectuals underestimated their potential and defaulted on their obligations. Rather than generating counter-symbols and political alternatives, they chased surrogates in religion, cultural nationalism, or professional anticommunism. Public life, rather than occupying the center of moral instruction and political debate, was a leafing of one mood to the next, now anxious, now bored, addicted to crises, partially managed by public relations professionals and shot through by a paradox Mills called "rationality without reason."

Did the supersociety mean that sociology might become a "common denominator" in the culture? In *The Sociological Imagination* (1959), Mills ridiculed academic sociology in a style that appeared to his admirers as an instrument of his subversion and to his critics as disproof of his seriousness. He attacked Robert Merton and Paul Lazarsfeld, his colleagues at Columbia, and transformed the eminent Harvard sociologist Talcott Parsons into stammering apologist for power. Mills accused them of establishing a sort of ecclesiastical guardianship over social knowledge. As the supersociety divested "ordinary men" of the democratic significance of their ideologies, so the research bureaucracy over which Parsons, Merton, and Lazarsfeld presided divested sociology of its political and speculative traditions.

The "sickness of complacency," its sources many and varied, afflicted the craftsman with nothing less than a "spiritual condition."[9]

The sensibility Mills proposed was tolerant and pluralistic, since it recognized the social relativity of canons of value and standards of belief. At the same time, it was politically committed to realizing the ideal content of democracy. The "self-cultivating man" was honor-bound to respect the variety of man-in-society yet committed to overthrowing antidemocratic institutions. Marxism had imparted to the intellectuals of the thirties a theory of history to measure their progress, an ideology to organize their perceptions, a party to discipline their impulses to action, and an interlocking system of political and social thought to coordinate their striving. Mills imparted to the generation of the sixties something more and something less, a "politics of truth" that entailed mutiny and sabotage. "It is easy for intellectuals to talk generously of the need for workers to control the factories in which they work. It is somewhat more difficult for them to begin to take over their own means of work. What we ought now to do is repossess our cultural apparatus, and use it for our own purposes. I mean this personally and literally."[10]

Yet Mills left important questions unanswered. "You advise intellectuals to 'write and speak for these media on their own terms or not at all,' " wrote his friend E. P. Thompson. "O.K. Supposing the answer of those who control the media is 'not at all.' What then?"[11] Theodor Adorno said Mills remained "beholden to what I might call the ruling sociology," since he failed to analyze the economic process while assuming the chance for "personal control of the apparatus of production."[12] Richard Hofstadter suspected that he could say so many astute things about politics only because he had no real politics of his own.

The best responses Mills made to such objections consisted of demonstrations of his own freedom and fullness of mind. He experimented with organic farming, architecture, photography, marriage, and motorcycling. He exhorted his readers to do as he did: to conduct themselves *as if* their biographies could be effective forces in history. Faith in reason counted as one of the factors in its realization. Belief in possibility was the first condition of possibility. This was the method he had discovered as an adolescent in Walter Hilton's little blue books, then, as a young sociologist, in the philosophical psychology of pragmatism. Yet the *as if* method deferred the riddle of power without solving it. In urging his readers to rise against bosses and masters, to unify thoughts and deeds, he never said how to tell the difference between thinking too long and acting too soon.

The Cultural Apparatus, *The New Left*, and *Comparative Sociology*, the manuscripts occupying Mills in the summer of 1960, might have yielded clues. On July 1, however, he had lunch in Manhattan with Raul Roa Jr., Cuba's representative to the United Nations. Roa told him the young men who had made the revolution in Cuba had studied *The Power Elite* at their camps in the Sierra Maestra. "If the American consul should visit me here," Fidel Castro had quipped to a reporter after the book reached him in 1958, "I hide this book under the bed, no?"[13] Roa wanted Mills to visit Cuba to see for himself what his book had helped achieve.

In August, Mills landed in Havana with two cameras and an audio recorder. *Listen, Yankee!*, a series of letters written in the voice of Castro, Che Guevara, and their comrades, appeared ten weeks later. The letters hailed the revolution's experimentalism for stimulating a new relation of man-in-society without capitalist incentives or communist whips. "We are new men," said Mills's Cuban, offering a bitterly ironic comment on American triumphalism.[14] Crevcoeur had asked, "What then is the American, this new man?"[15] *Listen, Yankee!* returned the idea of the New Man to its colonial setting. It embraced the Cubans as brothers under the skin. Were they the only young intellectuals to feel the clean wind of revolution blowing against their backs? "I don't know what you guys are waiting for," Mills said to his students at Columbia. "You've got a beautiful set of mountains in those Rockies. I'll show you how to use those pistols. Why don't you get going?"[16]

Listen, Yankee! was an international sensation, selling more than 400,000 copies, but it also ended Mills's odyssey. On December 10, 1960, the night before he was to debate the Cuban Revolution on NBC television, a heart attack struck. He never completely recovered. As the Bay of Pigs confirmed his worst predictions for American foreign policy, the course of the revolution in Cuba exposed the terrible ambiguities in his thought. In his final year, marked by failing health and a worsening international situation, he wandered around Europe before deciding to return to the United States. On March 20, 1962, he died in his sleep. He was laid to rest in a corner of Oak Hill Cemetery, Nyack, New York. Etched in his tombstone was an aphorism taken from *The Marxists*, his last book: "I have tried to be objective. I do not claim to be detached." He was forty-five.

Edward Shils, a leading figure in the Congress for Cultural Freedom—an organization that practiced its own, state-subsidized politics of truth—once called Mills "a sort of Joe McCarthy of Sociology." Shils also likened him to "a powerful windstorm."[17] The complacency of liberal society in its natural course, rather than any genius Mills possessed, allowed him "to play his rat-catcher's pipe" on a world scale, according to Shils, who settled on the image of the Pied Piper.[18] "Now he is dead," Shils gloated in 1963, "and his rhetoric is a field of broken stones, his analyses empty, his strenuous pathos limp."[19]

Yet Shils warned fellow liberals not to gainsay Mills's importance, arguing that he had aroused a global public greater than any American sociologist in history. The list of friends, correspondents, and readers generated by his travels in the fifties became, in the sixties, a first-class roster and record book of radical thinking, a rallying point in the genealogy of the New Left. He was the elder figure they all knew in common. In 1968, the Central

Intelligence Agency wrote a classified report that identified Mills, along with Herbert Marcuse and Frantz Fanon, as one of three principle leaders of the international Left, though he had been dead for six years already.[20]

"Charlie, to many of us, was an eccentric," Alfred Kazin demurred. "I mean, he was an extraordinary person; I'm aware that he had a certain legend as a radical figure, but it may be my literary inability to take sociologists seriously, but I thought he was what Senator [George] Moses called Son of a Wild Jackass. He was to me very much a Western type from Texas." Although Mills befriended Daniel Bell, Dwight Macdonald, and Richard Hofstadter, his relations with the New York intellectuals were riddled by ambivalence. "I remember once we were having dinner together in the Village," Kazin said. "I was talking about Balzac, and he took notes during dinner because this was all new to him—you know, that sort of thing. On the other hand, a lot of people thought he was great. I thought his mind was very simplistic."[21]

Eccentricity was not the source of Mills's appeal. It was his ability to diffuse the idea of the independent intellectual to those who felt superfluous, or compromised, or orphaned in the maelstrom of the American Century. The gregarious quality of his manner and thought did not impress the Manhattan literati, but it showed in the thousands of citizens who wrote him personal letters, each more earnest than the next. Mills addressed designers, generals, labor leaders, clergymen, scientists, urban planners, and novelists, editors, and journalists from Mexico City to Moscow. Always he denied that intellectual life was an aristocracy or that membership required proof of genius. Always he refused the temptation, so strongly felt in the academic system, to defer to special methods or theories. He returned his public to the ethical and emotional significance of ideas. Reason was not a technical skill but a prayer for salvation, "the most passionate endeavor of which a man is capable."[22]

The variety of style and role in which Mills manifested his passion was the hidden measure of his distinction. Alongside his many academic articles and books he issued pamphlets, public letters, and sermons. He contributed to obscure left-wing magazines and to that stronghold of establishment opinion, the *New York Times*. Speaking as sociologist, satirist, and prophet, as leftist and critic of the left, as Texan and New Yorker, he refused to subdue himself in a false dualism of commitment and withdrawal. He turned up perspectives from which he could criticize obsolete forms and demonstrate that new forms were imaginable. His extravagant indignation, so solemnly regretted by his auditors, called attention to the moral dimension of politics at a time when managerial dimensions dominated. His refusal to efface himself from his prose, so embarrassing to his colleagues, called attention to the personalities concealed in their postures of detachment. By representing no one party, he could speak credibly to many different parties. His greatest achievement was his independence.

Mills's sensibility will inspire dissent for as long as immorality and stupidity inhibit the promise of American life. The estrangement of the craftsman from his calling parallels the estrangement of the public from "the big discourse that has been going on, or off and on, since western society began some two thousand years ago in the small communities of Athens and Jerusalem."[23] Recognizing this common plight is the first condition of our rehabilitation.

Notes

1. Quoted in Lee Jones, "Power Elite's C. W. Mills Challenges Intellectuals," *Daily Texan* (Oct. 1958).
2. Mills, "Power and Culture," speech at PEN Club, May 14, 1956, page 9.
3. "The Cultural Apparatus," this volume.
4. "The Decline of the Left," this volume.
5. Hunter S. Thompson, "Wright Is Right," *Esquire*, v. 53 (Jan. 1960): 18.
6. "Culture and Politics," this volume.
7. Mills used this word "structural" like Lionel Trilling used "actuality"—the frequency of usage signaled an entire train of associations and tendencies.
8. "The Man in the Middle," this volume.
9. "Letter to the New Left" and "The Power Elite—Comment on Criticism," this volume.
10. "The Decline of the Left," this volume.
11. E. P. Thompson to Mills, April 21, 1959, CWM Papers, University of Texas.
12. Theodor W. Adorno, *Introduction to Sociology*, ed. Christoph Godde, trans. Edmund Jephcott (1968; Cambridge, England, 2000), 142.
13. As reported in Jules Dubois, "Report on Latin America," *Chicago Sunday Tribune* (Nov. 20, 1960): 16.
14. "Listen, Yankee!" this volume.
15. Hector St. John Crevcoeur, *Letters from an American Farmer* (1782; Gloucester, Mass., 1968), 49, 47.
16. Arnold Abrams, "C. Wright Mills: Controversial Figure in Conforming Sociology," *Columbia Daily Spectator*, Nov. 29, 1960.
17. Edward Shils, "Imaginary Sociology," *Encounter,* v. 14 (June 1960): 80; and Edward Shils, "Professor Mills on the Calling of Sociology," *World Politics*, v. 13 (July 1961): 606.
18. Shils, "Professor Mills," *World Politics*, 621.
19. Edward Shils, "The Obsession," *The Spectator*, no. 7045 (July 5, 1963): 21.

20. Office of Current Intelligence, "Restless Youth," No. 0613/68, Central Intelligence Agency, Washington, DC, September 1968.

21. Alfred Kazin Interview, Richard Hofstadter Project, Oral History Research Office, Columbia University, 1992, pages 11–12.

22. "On Intellectual Craftsmanship," this volume.

23. "Are We Losing Our Sense of Belonging?" this volume.

ONE

The Powerless People

The Role of the Intellectual in Society

I N JANUARY 1944, Mills wrote to Dwight Macdonald about an essay in the works: "The Politics of Truth." All during the previous year, intellectuals on the Left had been debating another essay, "The New Failure of Nerve," by Sidney Hook. That essay had given rise to a *Partisan Review* series whose contributors included both John Dewey, the subject of Mills's dissertation, and Macdonald, who was beginning a new magazine, *politics*. Mills had sent letters to Hook and Macdonald in praise of their contributions to the "Failure of Nerve" debate. Now he had his own arguments to advance, and he wanted to do so in *politics*, whose name he had been the first to suggest.

Mills was a twenty-seven-year-old associate professor of sociology at the University of Maryland and the author of nearly fifty notes, reviews, and essays in political magazines and academic journals. In "The Politics of Truth" he believed he had exceeded himself. "I believe you will like it," he wrote in his letter to Macdonald; "everybody around here does and I know it's the best prose I've ever written." The essay appeared in the third issue of *politics* as "The Powerless People: The Role of the Intellectual in Society."

Sixteen years later Mills discovered "The Powerless People" in his files. He remembered it as "one of those personal pieces, a sort of lament, mixed up with an attempt to analyze the social conditions of intellectual life, mixed up with political worries and tensions."

———

While the United Nations are winning the war, American intellectuals are suffering the tremors of men who face overwhelming defeat. They are worried and distraught, some only half aware of their condition, others so painfully aware of it that they must obscure it by busy work and self-deception.

Pragmatism was the nerve of progressive American thinking for the first several decades of this century. It took a rather severe beating from the fashionable left-wing of the thirties and since the latter years of that decade it has obviously been losing out in competition with more religious and tragic views of political and personal life. Many who not long ago read John Dewey with apparent satisfaction have become vitally interested in such analysts of personal tragedy as Søren Kierkegaard. Attempts to reinstate pragmatism's emphasis upon the power of man's intelligence to control his destiny have not been taken to heart by American intellectuals. They are obviously spurred by new worries and are after new gods.

Rather than give in to the self-pity and political lament which the collapse of hope invites, Arthur Koestler proposes, in the *New York Times,* a "Fraternity of Pessimists" who are to live together in "an oasis." Melvin Lasky, writing in *The New Leader,* responds to Koestler by urging intellectuals "neither to cry nor to laugh but to understand." The president of the American Sociological Society, George Lundberg, ascribes contemporary disasters, and disasters apparently yet to come, to the fact that the social sciences have not developed as rapidly nor along the same lines as physical science. Malcolm Cowley, of *The New Republic*, wonders why the war years have produced so little that may be considered great American literature. As for live political writing, intellectuals from right of center to revolutionary left seem to believe that there just isn't any. In a feeble attempt to fill the gap, Walter Lippmann's *The Good Society,* originally published in 1937, is reprinted and even acclaimed by at least one anxious reviewer. Many writers who are turning out post-war plans to suit every purse and taste busily divert the attentions of their readers from current political decisions and bolster their hopes by dreams of the future. Stuart Chase and other proponents of a brave new post-war economic world achieve a confident note at the expense of a political realism which worries even John Chamberlain.

Dwight Macdonald has correctly indicated that the failure of nerve is no simple retreat from reason. The ideas current are not merely fads sweeping over insecure intellectuals in a nation at war. Their invention and distribution must be understood as historical phenomena. Yet what is happening is not adequately explained by the political defeat of liberal, labor, and radical parties—from the decision in Spain to the present.

To understand what is happening in American intellectual life we have to consider the social position of its creators, the intellectuals. We have to realize the effect upon them of certain deep-lying trends of modern social organization.

I

We continue to know more and more about modern society, but we find the centers of political initiative less and less accessible. This generates a personal malady that is particularly acute in the intellectual who has labored under the illusion that his thinking makes a difference. In the world of today the more his knowledge of affairs grows, the less effective the impact of his thinking seems to become. Since he grows more frustrated as his knowledge increases, it seems that knowledge leads to powerlessness. He feels helpless in the fundamental sense that he cannot control what he is able to foresee. This is not only true of the consequences of his own attempts to act; it is true of the acts of powerful men whom he observes.

Such frustration arises, of course, only in the man who feels compelled to act. The "detached spectator" does not know his helplessness because he never tries to surmount it. But the political man is always aware that while events are not in his hands he must bear their consequences. He finds it increasingly difficult even to express himself. If he states public issues as he sees them, he cannot take seriously the slogans and confusions used by parties with a chance to win power. He therefore feels politically irrelevant. Yet if he approaches public issues "realistically," that is, in terms of the major parties, he has already so compromised their very statement that he is not able to sustain an enthusiasm for political action and thought.

The political failure of nerve has a personal counterpart in the development of a tragic sense of life. This sense of tragedy may be experienced as a personal discovery and a personal burden, but it is also a reflex of objective circumstances. It arises from the fact that at the centers of public decision there are powerful men who do not themselves suffer the violent results of their own decisions. In a world of big organizations the lines between powerful decisions and grass-root democratic controls become blurred and tenuous, and seemingly irresponsible actions by individuals at the top are encouraged. The need for action prompts them to take decisions into their own hands, while the fact that they act as parts of large corporations or other organizations blurs the identification of personal responsibility. Their public views and political actions are, in this objective meaning of the word, irresponsible: the social corollary of their irresponsibility is the fact that others are dependent upon them and must suffer the consequences of their ignorance and mistakes, their self-deceptions, and their biased motives. The sense of tragedy in the intellectual who watches this scene is a personal reaction to the politics and economics of irresponsibility.

Never before have so few men made such fateful decisions for so many people who themselves are so helpless. Dictatorships are but one manifestation of this fact. Mass armies all over the world are its living embodiment, and the Cairo and Teheran conferences are its most impressive symbols. The soldier may face death yet have no voice in the network of decisions which leads him to recapture Burma or garrison India. Power is an impersonal monster; those who do the taking understand only its technique and not its end.

The networks of military decision may be traced further up the line to the centers of political power. There plans are made by the older men who do not face the chance of violent death. This contrast between the elder statesman and the young soldier is not a popular topic to stress during war, but it is nevertheless one foundation for the modern man's urgently tragic sense of life. When the man who fights and dies can also make the decision to fight in the light of his own ideals, wars can be heroic. When this is not the case, they are only tragic.

Contemporary irresponsibility may be collective; no one circle of men may make the most fateful decision; there may, indeed, be no single fateful decision, only a series of steps in a seemingly inevitable chain, but these considerations do not relieve the resulting tragedy. On the contrary, they deepen it.

The centralization of decision and the related growth of dependence are not, however, confined to armies, although that is where they may be seen in their most immediate form. Organized irresponsibility is a leading feature of modern industrial societies everywhere. On every hand, the individual is confronted with seemingly remote organizations and he feels dwarfed and helpless. If the small business man escapes being turned into an employee of a chain or a corporation, one has only to listen to his pleas for help before small business committees to realize his dependence. More and more people are becoming dependent salaried workers who spend the most alert hours of their lives being told what to do. In climactic times like the present, dominated by the need for swift action, the individual feels dangerously lost. As the *London Economist* recently remarked, "The British citizen *should be* an ardent participant in his public affairs; he is little more than a consenting spectator who draws a distinction between 'we' who sit and watch and 'they' who run the state."

Such are the general frustrations of contemporary life. For the intellectual who seeks a public for his thinking—and he must support himself somehow—these general frustrations are made acute by the fact that in a world of organized irresponsibility the difficulty of speaking one's mind has increased for those who do not speak popular pieces.

If the writer is the hired man of an "information industry," his general aims are, of course, set by the decisions of others and not by his own integrity. But the freedom of the so-called free-lance is also minimized when he goes to the market; if he does not go, his freedom is without public value. Between the intellectual and his potential public stand technical, economic, and social structures which are owned and operated by others. The world of pamphleteering offered to a Tom Paine a direct channel to readers that the world of mass circulations supported by advertising cannot usually afford to provide one who does not say already popular things. The craftsmanship which is central to all intellectual and artistic gratification is thwarted for an increasing number of intellectual workers. They find themselves in the predicament of the Hollywood writer: the sense of independent craftsmanship they would put into their work is bent to the ends of a mass appeal to a mass market.

Even the editor of the mass circulation magazine has not escaped the depersonalization of publishing, for he becomes an employee of a business enterprise rather than a personality in his own right. Mass magazines are not so much edited by a personality as regulated by an adroit formula.

Writers have always been more or less hampered by the pleasure and mentality of their readers, but the variations and the level to which the publishing industry has been geared made possible a large amount of freedom. The recent tendency towards mass distribution of books—the 25 cent "pocket books"—may very well require, as do the production and distribution of films, a more cautious and standardized product. It is likely that fewer and fewer publishers will pass on more and more of those manuscripts which reach mass publics through drug stores and other large-scale channels of distribution.

Although, in general, the larger universities are still the freest of places in which to work, the trends which limit the independence of the scholar are not absent there. The professor is, after all, an employee, subject to all that this fact involves. Institutional factors naturally select men for these universities and influence how, when, and upon what they will work and write. Yet the deepest problem of freedom for teachers is not the occasional ousting of a professor, but a vague general fear—sometimes politely known as "discretion," "good taste," or "balanced judgment." It is a fear which leads to self-intimidation and finally becomes so habitual that the scholar is unaware of it. The real restraints are not so much external prohibitions as control of the insurgent by the agreements of academic gentlemen. Such control is naturally furthered by Hatch Acts, by political and business attacks upon "professors," by the restraints necessarily involved in the Army's program for the colleges, and by the setting up of committees by trade associations of subjects, like history, which attempt to standardize the content and effects of teaching. Research in social science is increasingly dependent upon funds from foundations, and foundations are notably averse to scholars who develop unpopular theses, that is, those placed in the category of "unconstructive."

The United States' growing international entanglements have subtle effects upon some American intellectuals: to the young man who teaches and writes on Latin America, Asia, or Europe and who refrains from deviating from acceptable facts and policies, these entanglements lead to a voluntary censorship. He hopes for opportunities of research, travel, and foundation subsidies.

The means of effective communication are being expropriated from the intellectual worker. The material basis of his initiative and intellectual freedom is no longer in his hands. Some intellectuals feel these processes in their work. They know more than they say and they are powerless and afraid.

In modern society both freedom and security depend upon organized responsibility. By "freedom" and "security," I do not mean independence for each individual; I mean merely that men have effective control over what they are dependent upon. The ethics and politics of democracy center on decisions which vitally affect people who have no voice in them. Today, everywhere, such decisions are central to the lives of more and more people. A politics of organized irresponsibility prevails, and because of it, men in high places must hide the facts of life in order to retain their power.

When irresponsible decisions prevail and values are not proportionately distributed, you will find universal deception practiced by and for those who make the decisions and who have the most of what values there are to have. An increasing number of intellectually equipped men and women work *within* powerful bureaucracies and *for* the relatively few who do the deciding. And if the intellectual is not directly hired by such organizations, then by little steps and in many self-deceptive ways he seeks to have his published opinions conform to the limits set by them and by those whom they do directly hire.

II

Any philosophy which is sensitive to the meaning of various societies for personal ways of life will give the idea of responsibility a central place. That is why it is central in the ethics and politics of John Dewey and of the late

German sociologist, Max Weber. The intellectual's response to the tragic fact of irresponsibility has a wide range but we can understand it in terms of where the problem is faced. The tragedy of irresponsibility may be confronted introspectively, as a moral or intellectual problem. It may be confronted publicly, as a problem of the political economy.

Along this scale there are (1) simple evaluations of our selves; (2) objective considerations of events; (3) estimates of our personal position in relation to the objective distribution of power and decision. An adequate philosophy uses each of these three styles of reflection in thinking through any position that is taken.

(1) If ethical and political problems are defined solely in terms of the way they affect the individual, he may enrich his experience, expand his sensitivities, and perhaps adjust to his own suffering. But he will not solve the problems he is up against. He is not confronting them at their deeper sources.

(2) If only the objective trends of society are considered, personal biases and passions, inevitably involved in observation and thought of any consequence, are overlooked. Objectivity need not be an academic cult of the narrowed attention; it may be more ample and include meaning as well as "fact." What many consider to be "objective" is only an unimaginative use of already plotted routines of research. This may satisfy those who are not interested in politics; it is inadequate as a full orientation. It is more like a specialized form of retreat than the intellectual orientation of a man.

(3) The shaping of the society we shall live in and the manner in which we shall live in it are increasingly political. And this society includes the realms of intellect and of personal morals. If we demand that these realms be geared to our activities which make a public difference, then personal morals and political interests become closely related; any philosophy that is not a personal escape involves taking a political stand. If this is true, it places great responsibility upon our political thinking. Because of the expanded reach of politics, it is our own personal style of life and reflection we are thinking about when we think about politics.

The independent artist and intellectual are among the few remaining personalities equipped to resist and to fight the stereotyping and consequent death of genuinely lively things. Fresh perception now involves the capacity continually to unmask and to smash the stereotypes of vision and intellect with which modern communications swamp us. These worlds of mass-art and mass-thought are increasingly geared to the demands of politics. That is why it is in politics that intellectual solidarity and effort must be centered. If the thinker does not relate himself to the value of truth in political struggle, he cannot responsibly cope with the whole of live experience.

III

If he is to think politically in a realistic way, the intellectual must constantly know his own social position. This is necessary in order that he may be aware of the sphere of strategy that is really open to his influence. If he forgets this, his thinking may exceed his sphere of strategy so far as to make impossible any translation of his thought into action, his own or that of others. His thought may thus become fantastic. If he remembers his powerlessness too well, assumes that his sphere of strategy is restricted to the point of impotence, then his thought may easily become politically trivial. In either case, fantasy and powerlessness may well be the lot of his mind. One apparent way to escape both of these fates is to make one's goal simply that of understanding.

Simply to understand is an inadequate alternative to giving in to a personal sense of tragedy. It is not even a true alternative; increased understanding may only deepen the sense of tragedy. Simply to understand is perhaps an ideal of those who are alienated but by no means disinherited— i.e., those who have jobs but don't believe in the work they are doing. Since "the job" is a pervasive political sanction and censorship of most middle class intellectuals, the political psychology of the scared employee becomes relevant. Simply understanding is an ideal of the man who has a capacity to know truth but not the chance, the skill, or the guts, as the case may be, to communicate them with political effectiveness.

Knowledge that is not communicated has a way of turning the mind sour, of being obscured, and finally of being forgotten. For the sake of the integrity of the discoverer, his discovery must be effectively communicated. Such communication is also a necessary element in the very search for clear understanding, including the understanding of one's self. For only through the social confirmation of others whom we believe adequately equipped do we earn the right of feeling secure in our knowledge. The basis of our integrity can be gained or renewed only by activity, including communication, in which we may give ourselves with a minimum of repression. It cannot be gained nor retained by selling what we believe to be our selves. When you sell the lies of others you are also selling yourself. To sell your self is to turn your self into a commodity. A commodity does not control the market; its nominal worth is determined by what the market will offer. And it isn't enough.

We insist upon clarity and understanding in order to govern our decisions by their consequences. Clear understanding of the political world and of our place within it is also indispensable if we are to keep an appropriate distance from ourselves. Without this distance men collapse into self-pity and political lament. We must constantly shuttle between the understanding which is made possible by detachment and the longing and working for a politics of truth in a society that is responsible. The problems which make a difference, both personally and politically, arise in the active search for these goals. The solutions which may be truthful and adequate require episodes of detachment from political morality and from considerations of self.

The phase of detachment may be isolated from its political context and in the division of labor become an end in itself. Those who restrict themselves to work only such segments of intellectual endeavor may attempt to generalize them, making them the basis for political and personal orientation. Then the key problem is held to rise from the fact that social science lags behind physical science and technology, and political and social problems are a result of this deficiency and lag. Such a position is inadequate.

Alienation must be used in the pursuit of truths, but there is no reason to make a political fetish out of it. Much less may it serve as a personal excuse. Certainly more secure knowledge is needed, but we already have a great deal of knowledge that is politically and economically relevant. Big businessmen prove this by their readiness to pay out cash to social scientists who will use their knowledge for the ends of business. Many top economic brains are now hired by big business committees; and a good social scientist is often fired from government, under business pressure, only to be hired by business or by one of its front organizations.

The political man does not need to wait upon more knowledge in order to act responsibly now. To blame his inaction upon insufficient knowledge serves as a cheap escape from the taking of a political stand and acting upon it as best he can. If one-half of the relevant knowledge which we now possess was really put into the service of the ideals which leaders mouth, these ideals could be realized in short order. The view that all that is needed is knowledge ignores the nub of the problem as the social scientist confronts it: he has little or no power to act politically and his chance to communicate in a politically effective manner is very limited.

There are many illusions which uphold authority and which are known to be illusions by many social scientists. Tacitly by their affiliations and silence, or explicitly in their work, the social scientist often sanctions these, rather than speak out the truth against them. They censor themselves either by carefully selecting safe problems in the name of pure science, or by selling such prestige as their scholarship may have for ends other than their own.

IV

The above acceptances of the *status quo* proceed directly. The present may also be accepted—and made spuriously palatable—by unanchored expectations of the future. This method is now being used in the production and publicity of hundreds of "post-war plans."

The big business man sets the technological trap by dangling his baubles before the public without telling precisely how they may be widely distributed. In a similar manner, the political writer may focus attention away from the present and into the several models of the future. The more the antagonisms of the actual present must be suffered, the more the future is drawn upon as a source of pseudo-unity and synthetic morale. Intellectuals and publicists have produced such a range of "plans" that there is now one to satisfy every one. Most of these commodities are not plans with any real chance to be realized. They are baits for various strata, and sometimes for quite vested groups, to support contemporary irresponsibilities. Post-war "planning" is the "new propaganda."

Discussions of the future which accept the present basis for it serve either as diversions from immediate realities or as tacit intellectual sanctions of future disasters. The post-war world is already rather clearly scheduled by authoritative decisions. Apparently, it is to be a balance of power within the collective domination of three great powers. We move from individual to collective domination, as the nations which have shown themselves mightiest in organizing world violence take on the leadership of the peaceful world. Such collective dominance may lead either to counter-alliances and bigger wars, or to decisions not effectively responsible to the man who is born in India or on an island of the Caribbean.

There is very little serious public discussion of these facts and prospects, or of the causes of the current war. Yet the way to avoid war is to recognize its causes within each nation and then remove them. Writers simply accept war as given, refer to December 7 when it all began, and then talk of the warless future. Nobody goes further in the scholarly directions of the inter-war investigations of the causes of modern wars. All that is forgotten, hidden beneath the rather meaningless shield, "Isolationist." It is easier to discuss an anchorless future, where there are as yet no facts, than to face up to the troublesome questions of the present and recent past.

In the covenants of power the future is being planned, even if later it must be laid down in blood with a sword. The powerless intellectual as planner may set up contrary expectations; he will later see the actual function of his "planning." He is leading a prayer and such prayer is a mass indirection.

Discussion of world affairs that does not proceed in terms of the struggle for power within each nation is interesting only in the political uses now made of it by those in power. Internal power struggles are the only determinants of international affairs which we may influence. The effective way to plan the world's future is to criticize the decisions of the present. Unless it is at every point so anchored, "planning" disguises the world that is actually in the works; it is therefore a dangerous disguise which permits a spurious escape from the anxieties surrounding the decisions and happenings of the present.

V

The writer tends to believe that problems are *really* going to be solved in *his* medium, that of the word. Thus he often underplays the threat of violence, the coercive power always present in decisive political questions. This keeps the writer's mind and energies in general channels, where he can talk safely of justice and freedom. Since the model of his type of controversy is rational argumentation, rather than skilled violence or stupid rhetoric, it keeps him from seeing these other and historically more decisive types of controversy. These results of the writer's position, his work and its effects, are quite convenient for the working politician, for they generally serve to cover the nature of his struggles and decisions with ethically elaborated disguises. As the channels of communication become more and more monopolized and party machines and economic pressures, based on vested shams, continue to monopolize the chances of effective political organization, his opportunities to act and to communicate politically are minimized. The political intellectual is, increasingly, an employee living off the communicational machineries which are based on the very opposite of what he would like to stand for. He would like to stand for a politics of truth in a democratically responsible society. But such efforts as he has made on behalf of freedom for his function have been defeated.

The defeat is not at the hands of an enemy that is clearly defined. Even given the power, no one could easily work his will with our situation, nor succeed in destroying its effects with one blow. It is always easier to locate an external enemy than grapple with an internal condition. Our impersonal defeat has spun a tragic plot and many are betrayed by what is false within them.

	The Intellectual and
TWO	the Labor Leader

MILLS DRAFTED THIS ESSAY on April 8, 1946, working from remarks he had made in January at a meeting of the Inter-Union Institute (IUI) for Labor and Democracy in New York. The occasion was his first
meeting as a member of the Institute, which soon became a political and civic
equivalent to his technical work as head of the Labor Research Division of the
Bureau of Applied Social Research at Columbia University. Mills participated in IUI projects and often wrote for its magazine, *Labor and Nation*. As he
explained in a letter to Carey McWilliams, "It is one of the very few places
where labor leaders and 'intellectuals' get together in print and as a public."

"The Intellectual and the Labor Leader" was retitled "No Mean-Sized
Opportunity" and published in *The House of Labor: Internal Operations of
American Unions*, edited by J. B. S. Hardman and Maurice F. Neufeld (1951).

Labor leaders shy at the word "intellectual." It makes them feel uneasy. Yet
there are men in and around the unions who can't very conveniently be called
anything else. Intellectuals are people who are pretty well educated and who
spend their time using that education in talking and writing, and sometimes
thinking, about various problems. They are always trying to find problems,
and the problems they deal with do not have to be "theirs."

Most men are geared into a job with rather fixed duties. But many intellectuals have jobs that allow them to be a little freer. You will find them
doing all sorts of work in order to earn a living, but one job you are not very

likely to find intellectuals doing is running labor unions in the United States. Nevertheless, many pro-labor intellectuals have ideas about how labor unions ought to be run. This is the center of the problem.

We must distinguish at least four types of intellectual, who in one way or another are concerned with trade unions and their leaders. These four differ in the kinds of skill they possess and in the relations they have to the policy-making decisions made by union leaders. Each type tends to have different aims so far as labor unions are concerned; in trying to achieve these aims, they tend to use different means; and each of them tries to influence the policy-making leaders of the trade union.

1. The first type of intellectual—*the official or the active member of a radical or third party*—has been in and around unions since unions began in this country. Labor leaders are not only aware of this type, but many of them tend to generalize their experience with him, and to think of all intellectuals as being the same.

The radical-party intellectual naturally follows the "line(s)" of his party in working within unions. He is not usually skilled in research techniques. He turns toward the factory workers and the unions in which they are organized. He is out to gain power within the unions by organizing "party cells" or developing party followers within various locals and plants, quite often directed against the majority leadership of the union. And he does so in the name of an ideology.

Sometimes he operates at quite a distance from the organized source of power, thus trusting the magic of his own speech and the "spontaneous will of the class-conscious worker" to win out in the end. As a party intellectual, however, he actually directs struggles for power within unions: He acts as a publicist and a politician within the union.

2. Labor leaders have been using *professionally trained intellectuals* as staff members for some time now. They have had to. Big business and big government have employed such men, and the unions have had to follow suit in order to do battle in the way battle is now done.

The union staff intellectual of this type may be a research or educational director, an economist, or a lawyer. He is concerned with the week-to-week problems the labor leader faces, and which he is able to help solve. And in his business relations with the leader, the staff intellectual tries to influence the leader by presenting phases of a problem that the leader himself does not see. The staff intellectual tries to spot problems in advance and, by setting them up in one way rather than in another, he often does exert some influence over the leader. To have influence on policy, he has to be an expert in spotting and in presenting concrete problems that are in line with those in which the leader is interested but which go somewhat beyond the range of the leader's own perception. He is often a man quite skilled in research; but such power to influence affairs as he may possess depends upon the leader's attitude toward him and his proved usefulness.

This personal dependency on the leader means that the staff intellectual is typically in a quite insecure position. The caution with which such men proceed when policy-relevant issues arise is an aspect of the strong tendency among them to become technicians rather than all-around men of ideas. For they are not trusted, and their advice is considered only insofar as they do not go too far beyond the leaders' range of interests and values. Insofar as they do not go beyond these limits, staff intellectuals act as technicians implementing laid-down policy rather than as direct influencers of policy.

3. Such influence as *the intellectual who works in a government agency that deals with labor unions* may have on union policy comes from his governmental position and not from his character as an intellectual or his skill as a research man. He follows the "line(s)" of government policy in dealing with unions. He deals out rights and privileges in whichever way he thinks the law holds or allows. He tends to be an economic technician with legally defined restrictions upon his thinking and research. Most labor leaders are now well acquainted with such types, and know how they work.

4. Not many labor leaders know the fourth species of intellectual—the *free-lance researcher*—and certainly they are not aware of what he can do for them and for labor unions. The facts are that such intellectuals have not been around very long and insofar as their skills have been used by power groups, they have largely been used in the service of big business, and not in the service of labor.

The free-lance research intellectual is "free-lance" only so far as labor unions, government agencies, and political parties are concerned. He is not usually an employee of any of these three, although he may drift in and out of all them. He is perhaps most often a college professor in some social science department; but he may also be a journalist, or perhaps more likely, a research technician for one of the mass media or for their adjuncts. By definition, however, he has no constant foothold in the institutions of labor or in institutions that continuously deal with the unions.

During the last decade or so, American social science has made research advances that are of tremendous practical relevance to the problems the unions now face. The fact that should be stressed about this fourth type of intellectual is that he is very highly skilled in these newer research techniques. However, the free-lance research intellectual who is pro-labor is not usually "merely a technician." Very often he is also an all-around idea-man, whose research imagination is enlivened by the problems of labor.

Such intellectuals have virtually no influence on the policy makers in labor unions, and the simple reason for this is that they have no power within the union and no means of influencing it from without. They are highly skilled and autonomous—and powerless; they are pro-labor, and they want to work in the service of labor, but somehow they seldom do.

Intellectuals and Policy Making

The free-lance is not only powerless, he is often quite naïve about the kind of power needed to influence a labor leader. Such intellectuals do not see that the policy maker in a union has hold of a kind of power, and that this power also has hold of the policy maker. And so the intellectual often fumbles around with uninformed admonitions and is frustrated when nobody pays attention to what he says.

Neither knowledge alone, nor experience alone, leads to the power of policy making in a trade union. And certainly, such power is not often influenced by admonition or the force of logic. Power in a union is determined by voting strength, by manipulation of influence, by strategic and intimate association, or by control of political machines within and among the unions.

The "third party" intellectual and the union staff intellectual are usually much wiser about the facts of power than is the free-lance intellectual. The party intellectual usually knows that the only way he can influence the union official is to organize a power base on party members in specific locals or plants. And it may take the staff intellectual years before he begins to influence policy. The free-lance intellectual seems to want to influence policy without paying the price the third-party professional, the staff intellectual, or the labor leader himself is willing to pay. He often seems to think he can get it by the sheer magic and wisdom of his talk. But that just does not happen.

The pro-labor research man who does not have power and does not intend to get it the hard way ought to recognize his limitations. If he is also a political-minded person, he must recognize that this alone does not make him a politician. And he should get the difference clear: he has no power with which to act; the trade union leader does. If the intellectual doesn't like the situation, then he ought either to go all out for leadership and shoulder the responsibility this stand involves, or go about his own work as best he can. But he ought not to expect power to be given to him by labor leaders.

The labor leader often puts his question to the intellectual in this way: "Why shouldn't you who *have no practical experience* in my line of work try to sell your ideas and your research to me? And why should you try to tell me what I'm supposed to do?" These are fair questions. The labor leader has the power to ask them that way. I think they are really at the bottom of many labor leaders' objections to free-lance intellectuals, and I want to tackle them. First, what does the term "practical experience" mean today in the field of labor action?

Practical Experience and Social Research

A lot that labor leaders say about their own practical experience and its absence among intellectuals is pretty much beside the point. Trade union leaders are constantly grappling with day-to-day facts and realities, but most of the facts they know and the realities they handle are specific facts and realities. These facts wouldn't necessarily be true for other industries or other unions or for similar unions in other types of communities. You have to "locate" and organize specific experiences in order to make further practical use of them. And many labor leaders don't see the particular experience as just one kind of experience faced by one kind of wage worker or one kind of labor leader in one kind of situation. Thus his very experience often blinds the labor leader to facts and realities that happen to lie outside his immediate domain.

In his emphasis on practical experience, the labor leader often assumes that to be of practical value, experience has to be direct; that it must be had by the man who is going to make use of it. That is the notion of experience the labor leader assumes every time he uses "practical experience" to beat the intellectual over the head. But this is not an adequate notion of practical experience. The figures in an industrial census or in an opinion poll or in a common analysis of a radio script are based on experience just as much as is the report of a business agent to a union vice-president. Today, the really effective labor leader has to know how to get and to use such systematic and over-all experiences. And these are the kinds of experience that the research intellectual has the skill to organize for practical use.

The practical experience available in any one union no longer provides the most practical guide line for running even that one union. The scene in which any union operates today is big and highly complicated. And this means that a wider and bolder and more skillful approach is necessary on the part of the leader than what he can derive from his personal and direct experience. That is true economically and socially and politically—as a lot of labor men have learned during the late war.

The union leader must act on the basis of experiences that are much broader than any one leader usually has had, for three reasons:

1. The opposition—organized big business—operates more and more on over-all plans and over-all labor policies. And those plans and policies are more and more based on *research*.

2. With its improved public relations methods and techniques, organized big business is telling the public a rounded-out story, not just the story of one plant or one industry. And these public relations are based on careful *research*.

3. The government's intervention in business-labor affairs has become very wide in scope and very decisive in character. And government, too, has its arsenal of *researched* facts.

The labor leader is up against these three big facts, and to meet them practically, he is going to have to adopt more over-all plans and long-range policies. He is in a situation where the only practical approach to his problem is to go beyond his immediate practical experience. The experience of one man in one type of spot must be enlarged by the kind of thinking that draws upon the experiences of many men, each trying to get out of particular spots. And that kind of experience and thinking is another name for good research.

The U.S. worker has to depend upon the labor leader to see that his interests are protected. That puts a large responsibility upon the labor leader, and he cannot shoulder up to that responsibility all by himself. He has got to learn to use the experience of the research man if he wants to do the job in the optimum manner.

The skills of the research intellectual of which I speak have not been and are not now used in the service of labor. They have been used and are being used more and more in the service of big business. Now, you can make that statement in two ways: "in the *service* of business" or "in the service of *business*." If you agree that you can say it the first way, then you have to admit that the research intellectual is no mere impractical theorist. Make no mistake about it: the intellectual who is the kept man of big business usually earns his keep: he is of service to business. If you say it the second way, you have to ask yourself why the research intellectual serves business. There are a lot of reasons, of course, but there are plenty of intellectuals now serving business who don't want it that way, who would gladly place their skills in the service of labor.

Part of this situation is the fault of the labor leader who shies away from the intellectual. And yet, it's not really his fault either. He simply doesn't know what the intellectual can do; he doesn't know how to use the intellectual to the top advantage of his organization. If labor leaders have been much slower than big businessmen to see the value of the research intellectual, the latter has been deficient in making out a convincing case for his latent, unused ability to render valuable service. He ought not to neglect this exercise in self-revealment. It is the key to no mean-sized opportunity.

THREE ‖ Sociological Poetry

THIS LETTER TO Dwight Macdonald concerns *Let Us Now Praise Famous Men*, by James Agee and Walker Evans. The book was a critical and commercial flop when it appeared in 1941. Macdonald, seven years later, tried to revive it by distributing unsold copies directly through his magazine and by circulating it to friends. He published Mills's response in *politics* in 1948.

———∞∞∞———

Dear Dwight:

I approached Agee's book with very definite expectations and needs in mind: From what you said when you gave it to me, I thought I might get some answers to a problem that has been consciously bothering me for six or seven years:

How can a writer report fully the "data" that social science enables him to turn up and at the same time include in his account the personal meanings that the subject often comes to have for him? Or: How can the writer master the detaching techniques necessary to modern understanding in such a way as to use them to feel again the materials and to express that feeling to the readers?

I put this question in terms of "social science" because every cobbler thinks leather is the only thing, but it is a problem faced by any writer on social and human topics. Social scientists make up a rationale and a ritual for the alienation inherent in most human observation and intellectual work today. They have developed several stereotyped ways of writing which do away with the full experience by keeping them detached throughout their operation. It is as if they are deadly afraid to take the chance of modifying themselves in the process of their work.

This is not a merely technical problem of analysis or of exposition. It is part of a much larger problem of style-as-orientation. And this larger issue, in turn, seems to arise from the bewildering quality and pace of our epoch and the unsureness of the modern intellectual's reaction to its human and inhuman features. We are reaching a point where we cannot even 'handle' any considerable part of our experience, much less search for more with special techniques, much less write it within the inherited styles of reflection and communication.

I bring all this up, because on the surface, Agee's text is a report of a field trip to the South during the middle thirties; but underneath, it is an attempt to document his full reactions to the whole experience of trying as a reporter to look at sharecroppers. As a report on the sharecropper south, it is one of the best pieces of "participant observation" I have ever read. As a document of how a man might take such an experience big, it is something of a stylistic pratfall.

We need some word with which to point, however crudely, at what is attempted here and at what I have tried to describe above. Maybe we could call it sociological poetry: It is a style of experience and expression that reports social facts and at the same time reveals their human meanings. As a reading experience, it stands somewhere between the thick facts and thin meanings of the ordinary sociological monograph and those art forms which in their attempts at meaningful reach do away with the facts, which they consider as anyway merely an excuse for imaginative construction. If we tried to make up formal rules for sociological poetry, they would have to do with the ratio of meaning to fact, and maybe success would be a sociological poem which contains the full human meaning in statements of apparent fact.

In certain passages, Agee comes close to success. Observe how he reports in a sentence or two the human significance of authority between landlord and tenant, white and Negro. Observe how he handles associations in descriptions, never letting them get in the way of the eye which they guide to the meanings. I think the best things in the volume are the sections on work (320ff) and on the summer Sunday in a small southern town (375ff). In some of these pages imagination and painstaking reporting become one and the same unit of sharp sight and controlled reactivity: they are visions.

But of course the quality about Agee that is best of all is his capacity for great indignation. Printed less than a decade ago, the book in its fine moral tone seems to be a product of some other epoch. For the spirit of our immediate times deadens our will very quickly, and makes moral indignation a rare and perilous thing. The greatest appeal of this book comes from Agee's capacity for indignation.

The motive and the frustration that lift his work above the plain sociological report is his enormous furiosity at the whole arrangement that sent him to the south and his crying terror at being personally estranged from the sharecroppers. This fury is what makes him take it big. He is furious with the magazine people who sent him into the south "to spy," and he is furious at himself for not being able to break through into the human relation that he wants with the sharecroppers he is studying, or rather whom he is trying to love.

If I ask myself, why on the whole it just doesn't come off, the only answer I can find is that in taking it all so big, Agee gets in his own way. Instead of easing himself into the experience in order to clarify the communication of how it really is, he jumps into it, obscuring the scene and the actors and keeping the readers from taking it big. And underneath this is the fact that Agee is overwhelmed and self-indulgent; almost any time, he is likely to gush. He lacks, in this book, the self-discipline of the craftsman of experience: When you get through, you have more images of just Agee than of the southern sharecroppers, or even of Agee in the south among the sharecroppers.

This failure is most apparent when we contrast the magnificent Walker Evans photographs with Agee's prose. These photographs are wonderful because the cameraman never intrudes in the slightest way upon the scene he is showing you. The subjects of the photographs . . . family groups of sharecroppers, individuals among them, children, a house, a bed in a room . . . are just there, in a completely barefaced manner, in all their dignity of being, and with their very nature shining through. But Agee often gets in the way of what he would show you, and sometimes, romantically enough, there is only Agee and nothing else.

Given the difficulties of sociological poetry, however, I think that what is important about the book is the enormity of the self-chosen task; the effort recorded here should not be judged according to its success or failure, or even degree of success; rather we should speak of the appropriateness and rarity of the objective, remembering that Agee has himself written: "The deadliest blow the enemy of the human soul can strike is to do fury honor."

If you can think of any other examples of sociological poetry, let me know of them.

Yours,
Wright Mills

FOUR

Contribution to "Our Country and Our Culture: A Symposium"

T HIS ESSAY APPEARED in the second of three installments of "Our Country and Our Culture," a symposium by *Partisan Review* in 1952. The editors put to the symposium four questions:

1. To what extent have American intellectuals actually changed their attitude toward America and its institutions?

2. Must the American intellectual and writer adapt himself to mass culture? If he must, what forms can his adaptation take? Or, do you believe that a democratic society necessarily leads to a leveling of culture, to a mass culture which will overrun intellectual and aesthetic values traditional to Western civilization?

3. Where in American life can artists and intellectuals find the basis of strength, renewal, and recognition, now that they can no longer depend fully on Europe as a cultural example and a source of vitality?

4. If a reaffirmation and rediscovery of America is under way, can the tradition of critical non-conformism (going back to Thoreau and Melville and embracing some of the major expressions of American intellectual history) be maintained as strongly as ever?

Your questions direct me first, to an assessment of changes in the attitudes intellectuals hold of America, and, second, to my own attitudes toward this country. I take the questions in this double way because I do not believe they are answerable on the first interpretation without the second intruding. It's a matter of whether or not you're aware of their inevitable interpenetration. Nevertheless, I am going to try to keep them distinct.

One

(1) American intellectuals do seem quite decisively to have shifted their attitudes toward America. One minor token of the shift is available to those who try to imagine "the old PR" running the title "Our Country . . . ," etc. in 1939. You would have cringed. Don't you want to ask from what and to what the shift has occurred? From a political and critical orientation toward life and letters to a more literary and less politically critical view. Or: generally to a shrinking deference to the status quo; often to a soft and anxious compliance, and always a synthetic, feeble search to justify this intellectual conduct, without searching for alternatives, and sometimes without even political good sense. The several phases of this development I've recently tried to document and explain elsewhere.

(2) Of course intellectuals *need* not adapt themselves to "mass culture" as it is now set up; but many of them have, doubtless others will, maybe some won't. We must remember that this is a tricky question to answer, because some might exclude from "the intelligentsia" those who do "adapt" to these media contents, believing that they thereby become technicians, maybe brilliant ones, but technicians.

One key thing about American mass culture, as Hans Gerth once commented, is that it is not an "escape" from the strains of routine, but another routine, which in its murky formulations and pre-fabricated moods (Type one: Hot, Type two: Sad) deprive the individual of his own fantasy life, and in fact often empty him of the possibilities of having such a life. So if your questions mean should intellectuals adapt to *that*, I suppose I have to say they can't, because as they do, they cease in any meaningful sense to be intellectuals or artists. Of course, just as intellectuals may also practice medicine or tend a piece of machinery, they may make a living on part-time nonsense. But there is no reason to confuse all that with serious intellectual work.

As for whether or not a democratic society necessarily leads to a leveling of culture, it depends upon your working conception of democracy. My conception does *not* include status uniformity or intellectual equality. One must in such matters balance between snobbery and good sense, but my answer is generally No. And I would of course impute the leveling and the frenzy effects of mass culture in this country not to "democracy" but to capitalist commercialism which manipulates people into standardized tastes and then exploits these tastes and "personal touches" as marketable brands.

(3) Your alternatives assume that artists and intellectuals must, or at least should, find either in America or Europe "the basis of strength, renewal, and recognition." I've always thought the source was in themselves, as individuals and as small self-selected circles; in their work, and—above all—in the best intellectual and artistic traditions of the West. These traditions seem to me international, the common property of mankind including historic Russia, even if rich Americans happen to buy up their products. Because this nation is now one of the two greatest powers on earth should I go into a square dance or collect old American glass? Should I think that Curry tops Picasso or that Frank Wright is not part of an international movement? The perspective from which your questions are put seems to be based on a statesman's-like worry about the discrepancy between the enormous military and economic power of the United States and its relatively low cultural level and prestige. I suppose that is a real problem for you; I hope you won't confuse the two, or assign yourselves the task of bringing the latter up to the former.

As for your question concerning *where* in American life, intellectuals can find such a source (of "strength" and "recognition") my answer is I don't know. I have never had occasion to try so to restrict myself in sources of thought and models of inspiration. In view of the whole tenor of your questions, it's interesting that you ask. Why do you strain so?

(4) The "non-conformism" tradition, to which you make reference, has faded, and in my opinion, will continue to fade. Who, as a group or even as a clique, publicly represents it today? Nobody who isn't so genteel and muted about it that it is practically a secret set of beliefs, or so mechanical and untalented about it that it is publicly irrelevant. Besides, I certainly am not aware of any "reaffirmation and rediscovery of America" going on, outside the Voice of America. The attempt to *understand* "America" has, in my opinion, been largely given up by many intellectuals. Of course it's possible, especially for those who have given up the attempt, to "reaffirm" at will.

Two

The Englishman, John Morley, in his profound essay *On Compromise*, distinguished deference to the existing state of affairs in (1) forming opinions, (2) in expressing them, and (3) in trying to realize them. With him, I believe there is no reason for such deference in the first and at least not yet in the second of these three spheres. The third is another matter: choices are often necessary, even if they are morally corrupting. What is happening is that many intellectuals have had to give up some of the ideas that made their impatience for change palatable, and moreover have lived under conditions that affect their freedom in the first and second spheres. What is happening in the United States is that three is out of the question (no movement), so two tends to dry up (no audience), and so in one, people adapt (no individual opinion). Without a movement to which they might address political ideas, intellectuals in due course cease to express such ideas, and so in time, shifting their interests, they become indifferent.

They can no longer take heart by functioning only in the second area (that is, as intellectuals *per se*) because they no longer believe, as firmly as Morley did, that in the end opinion rules and that therefore small groups of thinkers may take the lead in historic change. They no longer believe that existing institutions and policies are held provisionally—until new and better ideas about them are available as replacements. They no longer believe that the prosperity, or even the chance of an idea, depends upon its intrinsic merits, but rather that its medium and conditions are usually more important to its fate. And they now know that ideas and force do not "belong to different elements"—as nineteenth-century liberals were wont to believe; but rather that movements, established and on the make, use force to modify ideas and ideas to justify force. This presence of coercion, actual or threatened or even unconsciously felt to be threatening, is one important meaning of the dwindling of liberty.

What would presumably clear up a lot of "confusion" and "drift" to which many intellectuals publicly "confess," is some urgent moral orientation which they could embrace—and babble over; the sort of thing some of them have found and lost at least three different times—with little intellectual continuity between them—since the middle thirties. But one should not let such people interfere with the serious and important task of understanding the main drift of modern society.

The reason one feels foolish making programmatic statements today is that there is now in the United States no real audience for such statements. Such an audience (1) would have, in greater or lesser degree, to be connected with some sort of movement or party having a chance to influence the course of affairs and the decisions being made. It would also (2) have to contain people who are at least attentive, even if not receptive, to ideas—people among whom one has a chance to get a hearing. When these two conditions are available one can be programmatic in a "realistic" political way. When these conditions are not available, then one has this choice:

To modify the ideas or at least file them and hence, in effect and at least temporarily, to take up new allegiances for which conditions do exist that make working for them realistic.

Or: To retain the ideals and hence by definition to hold them in a utopian way, while waiting. Of course these two ways can be combined, in various sorts of tentative holding actions. Nevertheless, they present a clear-cut choice.

There are reasons for taking the first way: one might judge that dangers are so great one has to fight with whatever means are at hand, so if Truman and company are the only ones around, then support them and try to defeat the Tafts or MacArthurs. Bore from within for so long as you can breathe down in the old wormy wood. Well, my judgment is that world conditions and domestic affairs are not yet that perilous.

"A principle, if it be sound," wrote Morley, "represents one of the larger expediencies. To abandon that for the sake of some seeming expediency of the hour, is to sacrifice the greater good for the less, on no more creditable ground than that the less is nearer. It is better to wait, and to defer the realization of our ideas until we can realize them fully, than to defraud the future by truncating them, if truncate them we must, in order to secure a partial triumph for them in the immediate present. It is better to bear the burden of impracticableness, than to stifle conviction and pare away principle until it becomes hollowness and triviality."

I suppose this is the direction in which I go. In my own thinking and writing I have deliberately allowed certain implicit values which I hold to remain, because even though they are quite unrealizable in the immediate future, they still seem to me worth displaying. They seem worthwhile in another way too: they sensitize one to a clearer view of what is happening in the world. One tries by one's work to issue a call to thinking, to anyone now around, or anyone who might later come into view and who might listen. There are times when clear-headed analysis is more important and more relevant than the most engaging shout for action. I think this is such a time. Of course, "frank presentation of ominous facts," as the late German-trained Joseph Schumpeter once remarked, is open to the terrible charge of "defeatism," but then, as he pointed out, "the report that a given ship is sinking is not defeatist," and ". . . this is one of those situations in which optimism is nothing but a form of defection."

I also believe, as an amateur historian, that one should never allow one's values to be overwhelmed in short runs of time: that is the way of the literary faddist and the technician of the cultural chic. One just has to wait, as others before one have, while remembering that what in one decade is utopian may in the next be implementable. Surely after the thirties and the forties, we have all learned how very rapidly events can occur, how swiftly whole nations can turn over, how soon fashionable orientations, especially as presented in magazines like yours, can become outmoded.

In the meantime, we must bear with the fact that in many circles impatience with things as they are in America is judged to be either mutinous or utopian.

FIVE | On Intellectual Craftsmanship

A FEW YEARS AGO," said Richard Hofstadter in a 1953 lecture in Michigan, "a distinguished sociologist asked me to read a brief manuscript which he had written primarily for students planning to go on to advanced work in his field, the purpose of which was to illustrate various ways in which the life of the mind might be cultivated." Hofstadter said, "I found myself reading a piece of devotional literature, comparable perhaps to Cotton Mather's *Essays to Do Good* or Richard Steele's *The Tradesman's Calling*. My friend was trying to communicate his sense of dedication to the life of ideas, which he conceived much in the fashion of the old Protestant writers as a *calling*. To work is to pray. Yes, and for this kind of man, to think—really to think—is to pray. What he knows best, when he is at his best, is the pursuit of truth; but *easy* truths bore him. What he is certain of becomes unsatisfactory always; the meaning of his intellectual life lies in the quest for new uncertainties."

The title of the manuscript to which Hofstadter referred was "On Intellectual Craftsmanship: In Lieu of a Handbook for Students Beginning Independent Work." Mills wrote it in April 1952 and mimeographed it in February 1955 for distribution to his students in Columbia College. Revised versions were published in *Symposium on Sociological Theory*, ed. Llewellyn Gross (1959) and as an appendix to *The Sociological Imagination* (1959).

⸺

Everyone seriously concerned with teaching complains that most students do not know how to do independent work. They do not know how to read, they do not know how to take notes, they do not know how to set up a problem nor how to research it. In short, they do not know how to work intellectually.

Everyone says this, and in the same breath, asserts: "But then, you just can't teach people how to think," which they sometimes qualify by: "At least not apart from some specific subject matter," or "At least not without tutorial instruction."

There is the complaint and there are the dogmatic answers to the complaint, all of which amount to saying: "But we cannot help them much." This essay is an attempt to help them. It is neither a statement of formal method nor an attempt to inspire. Perhaps there are already too many formal discourses on method, and certainly there are too many inspirational pieces on how to think. Neither seem to be of much use to those for whom they are apparently intended. The first does not usually touch the realities of the problem as the beginning student encounters them; the second is usually vulgar and often nonsense.

In this essay I am going to try candidly to report how I became interested in a topic I happen now to be studying, and how I am going about studying it. I know that in doing this I run the risk of failing in modesty and perhaps even of claiming some peculiar virtue for my own personal habits. I intend no such claims. I know also that it may be said: "Well, that's the way you work; but it's not of much use to me." To this the reply seems quite clear; it is: "Wonderful. Tell me how you work." Only by conversations in which experienced thinkers exchange information about their actual, informal ways of working can "method" ever really be imparted to the beginning student. I know of no other way in which to begin such conversations, and thus to begin what I think needs to be done, than to set forth a brief but explicit statement of one man's working habits.

I must repeat that I do not intend to write about method in any formal sense, nor under the guise of methodology, to take up a statesman-like pose concerning the proper course for social science. So many social scientists nowadays, it seems to me, seem always to be writing about something; and, in the end, to be thinking only about their own possible thinking. This may indeed be useful to them and to their future work. But it seems to me rather less than useful to the rest of those at work in the social studies, to those who are just beginning their studies, or to those who have lived with them for quite a while.

Useful discussions of method and theory usually arise as marginal notes on work in progress or work about to get under way. In brief, "methods" are simply ways of asking and answering questions, with some assurance that the answers are more or less durable. "Theory" is simply paying close attention to the words one uses, especially their degree of generality and their inter-relations. What method and theory properly amount to is clarity of conception and ingenuity of procedure, and most important, in sociology just now, the release rather than the restriction of the sociological imagination.

To have mastered "theory" and "method," in short, means to have become a self-conscious thinker, a man ready for work and aware of the assumptions and implications of every step he will take as he tries to find out the character and the meaning of the reality he is working on. On the contrary, to be mastered by "method" and "theory" means simply to be kept from working, from trying, that is, to find out about some area of reality. Just as the result of work is infirm without insight into the way it was achieved, so is the way meaningless without a determination that the study shall come to an end and some result be achieved. Method and theory are like the language of the country you live in: it is nothing to brag about that you can speak it, but it is a disgrace, as well as an inconvenience, if you cannot.

I

I forget how I became technically concerned with "stratification," but I think it must have been by reading Veblen. He had always seemed to me very loose, even vague about his "business" and "industrial" employments, which are a kind of translation of Marx for the academic American public. Marx himself, I think it must be agreed, is quite unfinished and much too simple about classes; he did not get to write a theory of classes, although Max Weber finished one version which I believe Marx would have liked. When in the early 'forties I began, with Hans Gerth, to translate some of Weber's writings—it was the first essay we published—certain conceptions were cleared up for me.

I then wrote a book on labor organizations and labor leaders—a politically motivated task; then a book on the middle classes—a task primarily motivated by the desire to articulate my own experience in New York City since 1945. It was thereupon suggested by friends that I ought to round out a trilogy by writing a book on the upper classes. I think the possibility had been in my mind; my plans have always exceeded my capacities and energies. I had read Balzac off and on during the 'forties, and been much taken with his self-appointed task of "covering" all the major classes and types in the society of the era he wished to make his own. I had also written a paper on "The Business Elite," and had collected and arranged data about the careers of the topmost men in American politics since the Constitution. These two tasks were primarily inspired by seminar work in systematic American history.

In doing these several articles and books and in preparing courses on different strata of modern society, there was of course a residue of ideas and facts about the upper classes. Especially in the study of social stratification it is difficult to avoid going beyond one's immediate subject, because "the reality" of any one stratum is in large part its relations to the rest. Accordingly, I began to think of a book on "The American Elite."

And yet that is not "really" how the project arose; what really happened is that the idea and the plan came out of my files, for all projects with me begin and end with them, and books are simply organized releases from the continuous work that goes into them. Presently I shall explain what these files involve, but first I must explain the ideal of intellectual craftsmanship that lies back of them and keeps me at work on them.

II

In joining the scholarly community, one of the first things I realized was that most of the thinkers and writers whom I admired never split their work from their lives. They seemed to take both too seriously to allow such dissociation, and they wanted to use each for the enrichment of the other. Yet such a split is the prevailing convention among men in general, deriving, I suppose, from the hollowness of the work which men in general now do.

I recognized that insofar as I might become a scholar, I would have the exceptional opportunity of designing a way of living which would encourage the habits of good workmanship. It was a choice of how to live as well as a choice of career, for whether he knows it or not, the intellectual workman forms his own self as he works towards the perfection of his craft. And so, I came early to the conviction that to realize my own potentialities and opportunities I had to try to construct a character which had as its core the qualities of the good workman.

Somehow I realized that I must learn to use my life experience in my intellectual work: continually to interpret it and to use it. It is in this sense that craftsmanship is the center of oneself and that one is personally involved in every intellectual product upon which one may work.

To say that one can "have experience," means, in part, that past experience plays into and affects present experience, and that it limits the capacity for future experience. But I have to control this rather elaborate interplay, to capture experience and sort it out; only thus can I use it to guide and test my reflection and in the process shape myself as an intellectual craftsman. A personal file is the social organization of the individual's memory; it increases the continuity between life and work, and it permits a continuity in the work itself, and the planning of the work; it is a crossroads of life experience, professional activities, and way of work. In this file the intellectual craftsman tries to integrate what he is doing intellectually and what he is experiencing as a person. Here he is not afraid to use his experiences and, as it were, to cross-classify them with various projects which he has under way. It is the link between life and work; in it the two become one.

By serving as a check on repetitious work, my file enables me to conserve what little energy I have. It also encourages me to capture "fringe-thoughts": various ideas occur, which may be by-products of every-day experience, snatches of conversation overheard on the street, or, for that matter, dreams. Once noted, these may lead to more systematic thinking, as well as lend intellectual relevance to more directed experience.

I have often noticed how carefully accomplished thinkers treat their own minds, how closely they observe their development and codify their experience. The reason they treasure their smallest experiences is because, in the course of a lifetime, a modern man has so very little personal experience and yet experience is so important as a source of good intellectual work. To be able to trust one's own experience even if it often turns out to be inadequate, I have come to believe, is one mark of the mature workman. Such confidence in one's own experience is indispensable to originality in any intellectual pursuit, and the file is one tool by which I have tried to develop and justify such confidence.

If the intellectual workman is a man who has become self-confidently aware of himself as a center of experience and reflection, the keeping of a file is one way of stabilizing, even institutionalizing, this state of being. By the keeping of an adequate file and the self-reflective habits this fosters, one learns how to keep awake one's inner world. Whenever I feel strongly about events or ideas I try not to let them pass from my mind, but instead to formulate them for my files and in so doing draw out their implications, show myself either how foolish these feelings or ideas are, or how they might be developed into articulate and productive shape. The file also maintains the habit of writing. I cannot "keep my hand in" if I do not write something at least every week. In the file, one can experiment as a writer and thus develop one's own powers of expression.

III

Under various topics in this file there are ideas, personal notes, and excerpts from books; there are bibliographic items and outlines of projects—it is, I suppose, a matter of arbitrary habit, but I have found it best to blend all these items into a master file of topical projects, with many sub-divisions. The topics, of course, are frequently changed. For instance, when as a student I was working toward the preliminary oral examination, the writing of a thesis and, at the same time, doing term papers, my files were arranged in these three focal areas of endeavor. But after a year or so of graduate work, I began to re-organize the whole file in relation to the main project of the thesis. Then as I pursued my work I noticed that no one project ever dominated my work, nor set the master categories in which the file was arranged. In fact, the use of this file encouraged an expansion of the categories with which I was actively thinking. And the way in which these categories changed, some being dropped out and others being added—was an index of my own intellectual progress and breadth. Eventually, the file came to be arranged according to several larger projects, having many sub-projects, which changed from year to year.

All this involves the taking of notes. It is my habit to take a very large volume of notes from any book which I read which I feel worth remembering. For the first step in translating experience, either of other men's symbols, or of one's own life, into the intellectual sphere, is to give it form. Merely to name an item of experience often invites us to explain it; the mere taking of a note from a book is often a prod to reflection. At the same time, the taking of a note is an additional mechanism for comprehension of what one is reading.

My notes seem to be of two sorts: in reading certain very important books I try to grasp the structure of the writer's thought, and take notes accordingly. But more frequently, in the last ten years, I do not read whole books, but rather parts of many books, from the point of view of some particular theme in which I am interested, and concerning which I usually have plans in my file. Therefore, I take notes which do not fairly represent the books I read. I am using this particular passage, this particular experience for the realization of my own projects. Notes taken in this way form the contents of memory upon which I may have to call.

IV

But how is this file—which so far must seem to the reader more like a journal—used in intellectual production? Well, the maintenance of this file is intellectual production, one step removed from daily musing, and one step removed from the library and "the field"; it is a continually growing store of facts and ideas, from the most vague to the most finished.

The first thing I did upon deciding on a study of The American Elite was to make a crude outline, based on a listing of the types of people I wished to understand. The next step was to examine my entire file, not only those parts of it which obviously bore on the topic, but also many others which seemed to have no relevance whatsoever. For imagination and "the structuring of an idea" are often exercised by putting together hithertofore isolated items, of finding unsuspecting connections. I made new units in the file for this particular range of problems, which, of course, led to a new arrangement of other parts of the file.

As I thus re-arranged the filing system, I found that I was loosening my imagination. This apparently occurred by means of insight deriving from merely trying to combine various ideas and notes on different topics. It is a sort of logic of combination, and "chance" sometimes plays a curiously large part in it. In a relaxed way, as it were, I tried to engage my intellectual resources, as exemplified in the file, with the new themes.

I also began to use my observations and daily experiences. I thought first of experiences I had had which bore upon such problems, and then I went and talked with those who I thought might have experienced or considered the issues. As a matter of fact, I began now to alter the character of my routine so as to include in it (1) people who were the phenomena, (2) people in contact with the phenomena, and (3) people interested in them. I do not know the full social conditions of the best intellectual workmanship, but certainly surrounding oneself with a circle of people who will listen and talk—and at times they have to be imaginary characters—is one of them. I try, at any rate, to surround myself with all the relevant environment—social and intellectual—which I think might lead me into thinking well along the lines of my work. That is one meaning of my remarks about the fusion of personal life and intellectual work.

My kind of work is not, and cannot be, made up of one clear-cut empirical "research." It is, rather, composed of a good many small-scale studies which at key points anchor general statements about the shape and the trend of the subject. So the decision—what are these anchor points?—cannot be made until existing materials are reworked and general hypothetical statements constructed.

Now of "existing materials" I found in the files three relevant types: several theories having to do with the topic, materials already worked up by others as evidence for those theories; and data already gathered and in various stages of accessible centralization, but not yet made theoretically relevant. Only after completing a first draft of a theory with the aid of such existing materials as these can I efficiently locate my own pivotal assertions and so design researches to test them—and maybe I will not have to, although of course I know I will later have to shuttle back and forth between existing materials and my own research.

I make it a rule—picked up, I suppose, from philosophical reading which led me into the sociology of knowledge—that any final statement must not only cover the data so far as the data is available and known to me, but also in some way, positively or negatively, take into account the available theories. (This is one of the things I mean by the methodological consequences of the sociology of knowledge.) Sometimes this "taking into account" of a theory is easily done by a simple confrontation of the theory with overturning or supporting fact; sometimes a detailed analysis or qualification is needed. Sometimes I can arrange the available theories systematically as a range of alternatives, and so allow their range to organize the problem itself.[1] But sometimes I allow such theories to come up only in my own arrangement, in quite various contexts. At any rate, in The American Elite, I will have to take into account the work of such men as Mosca, Schumpeter, Veblen, Marx, Lasswell, Michel, Pareto, and I am now at work on them.

In looking over some of the notes on these writers, I find that they fall into three general types of statement: (A) I learn directly, by restating systematically, what the man says on given points or as a whole. (B) I accept or refute these statements, giving reasons and arguments. (C) I use the book as a source of suggestions for my own elaborations and projects. This involves grasping a point and then asking: How can I put this into testable shape and then test it? How can I use this as a center from which to elaborate—use it as a perspective from which descriptive details will become relevant? It is in this handling of existing theory, that I feel myself in continuity with previous work. Here are two excerpts from preliminary notes on Mosca, which may illustrate what I have been trying to describe:

In addition to his historical anecdotes, Mosca back up his thesis with this assertion: It's the power of organization that enables the minority always to rule. There are organized minorities and they run things and men. There are unorganized majorities and they are run.[2] But: why not also consider the apparent opposite? In fact why not the full scale of possibilities?

	Elite (Minority)	Mass (Majority)
Organized	1	2
Unorganized	3	4

1 the organized minority
2 the organized majority
3 the unorganized minority
4 the unorganized majority

This is worth full-scale exploration. The first thing that has to be straightened out: just what is the meaning of "organized"? I think Mosca means: capable of more or less continuous and coordinated policies and actions. If so, his thesis is right by definition. He would also say, I believe, that an "organized majority" is impossible because all it would amount to is that new leaders, new elites, would be on top of these majority organizations, and he is quite ready to pick up these leaders in his "The Ruling Class." He calls them "directing minorities," all of which is pretty flimsy stuff alongside his big statement.

One thing that occurs to me is the use of the table (I think it is the core of the problems of definition Mosca presents to us) as a model for trend analysis: Try this: from the 19th to the 20th centuries, we have witnessed a shift from a society organized as 1 and 4 to a society established more in terms of 2 and 3. We have moved from an elite state to an organizations state, in which the elite is no longer so organized nor so unilaterally powerful, and the mass is more organized and more powerful. Some power has been made in the streets, and around it whole social structures and their "elites" have pivoted. And what section of the ruling class is more organized than the farm bloc? That's not a rhetorical question: I can answer it either way at this time; it's a matter of degree; all I want now is to get it way out in the open.

Mosca makes one point that seems to me excellent and worth elaborating further. There is often in "the ruling class," according to him, a top clique and there is this second and larger stratum, with which (A) the top is in continuous and immediate contact, and with which (B) it shares ideas and sentiments and hence, he believes, policies. (page 430) Check and see if anywhere else in the book, he makes other points of connection. Is the clique recruited largely from the second level? Is the top, in some way, responsible to, or at least sensitive to, this second stratum?

Now forget Mosca: in another vocabulary, we have (A) the elite, by which we here mean that top clique, (B) those who count, and (C) all the others. Membership in the second and third, in this scheme, is defined by the first, and the second may be quite varied in its size and composition and relations with the first and the third. (What, by the way, is the range of variations of the relations of B to A and to C? Examine Mosca for hints and further extend this by considering it systematically.)

This scheme may enable me more neatly to take into account the different elites, which are elite according to the several dimensions of stratification. Also, of course, to pick up in a neat and meaningful way the Paretian distinction of governing and non-governing elites, in a way less formal than Pareto. Certainly many top status people would at least be in the second. So would the big rich. The Clique or The Elite would refer to power, or to authority, as the case may be. The elite in this vocabulary would always mean the power elite. The other top people would be the upper classes or the upper circles.

So in a way, maybe, we can use this in connection with two major problems: the structure of the elite; and the conceptual—later perhaps, the substantive—relations of stratification and elite theories. (Work this out).

From the standpoint of power, it is easier to pick out those who count than those who rule. When we try to do the first we select the top levels as a sort of loose aggregate and we are guided by position. But when we attempt the second, we must indicate in clear detail how they wield power and just how they are related to the social instrumentalities through which power is exercised. Also we deal more with persons than positions, or at least have to take persons into account.

Now power in the U.S. involves more than one elite. How can we judge the relative positions of these several elites? Depends upon the issue and the decisions being made. One elite sees another as among those who count. There is this mutual recognition among the elite, that other elites count; in one way or another they are important people to one another. Project: select 3 or 4 key decisions of last decade—to drop the atom, to cut or raise steel production, the G.M. strike of '45— and trace in detail the personnels involved in each of them. Might use "decisions" and decision-making as interview pegs when you go out for intensives.

There comes a time—not as yet reached in this study—when I am through with books. Whatever I want from them is down in my own notes and abstracts, and on the margins of these notes, as well as in a separate file, are further ideas for empirical studies.

Now I do not like to do empirical work if I can possibly avoid it. It means a great deal of trouble if one has no staff, and if one does employ a staff then the staff is often more trouble than the work itself. Moreover they leave as soon as they have been trained and made useful. Besides, in a field like sociology there is so much to do by way of initial "structuring" (let the word stand for the kind of work I am describing) that much "empirical research" is bound to be thin and uninteresting.

In our situation, empirical work as such—so it seems to me—is for beginning students and for those who aren't able to handle the complexities of big problems; it is also for highly formal men who do not care what they study so long as it appears to be orderly. All these types have a right to do as they please or as they must; they have no right to impose in the name of science such narrow limits on others. Anyway, they do not bother me.

Although I shall never be able to get the money with which to do many of the empirical studies I design, it is necessary for me to continue designing them. For once I lay out an empirical study, it leads me to a new search for data which often turns out to have unsuspected relevance for my problems. Just as it is foolish to design an empirical field study if the answer can be got from a library, so it is foolish to think you have exhausted books before an appropriate empirical study has been translated into questions of what facts are needed. So considered, library materials help the researcher who is working outside the research organizations to approach real answers.

Empirical studies necessary to my kind of work must show two characteristics: First, they must be relevant for the first draft, of which I wrote above; they have to anchor it in its original form or they have to cause its modification, or to put it more abstractly, they must have implications for theoretical constructions. Second: the projects must be efficient and neat and, if possible, ingenious. By this I mean that they must promise to yield a great deal of material in proportion to the time and effort they involve.

Now, I have not decided upon the studies necessary for the present job, but here is the beginning of a larger design within which various small-scale studies have begun to arise. Again I excerpt from the files:

> I am not yet in a position to study the upper circles as a whole in a systematic and empirical way. So what I do is set forth some definitions and procedures that form a sort of ideal design for such a study. I can then attempt, first, to gather existing materials that approximate this design; second, to think of convenient ways of gathering materials, given the existing indices, that satisfy it, at crucial points; and third, as I proceed, to make more specific the full-scale, empirical researches that would in the end be necessary.
>
> (1) The upper circles must, of course, be defined systematically in terms of specific variables. Formally—and this is more or less Pareto's way—they are the people who "have" the most of whatever is available of any given value or set of values. So I have to make two decisions: What variables shall I take as the criteria, and what do I mean by "the most"? After I've decided on my variables, I must construct the best

indices I can, if possible quantifiable indices, in order to distribute the population in terms of them; only then can I begin to decide what I mean by "the most." For this should, in part, be left for determination by empirical inspection of the various distributions, and their overlaps.

My key variables should, at first, be general enough to give me some latitude in the choice of indices, yet specific enough to invite the search for empirical indices. As I go along, I'll have to shuffle between conceptions and indices, guided by the desire not to lose intended meanings and yet to be quite specific about their indices. Here are the four Weberian variables with which I will begin:

I. Class refers to sources and amounts of income. So I'll need property distributions and income distributions. The ideal material here (which is very scarce, and unfortunately dated) is a cross-tabulation of source and amount of annual income. Thus, we know that X per cent of the population received during 1936 Y millions or over, and that Z per cent of all this money was from property, W per cent from entrepreneurial withdrawal, Q per cent from wages and salaries. Along this class dimension, I can define the upper circles—those who have the most—either as those who receive given amounts of income during a given time—or, as those who make up the upper 2 per cent of the income pyramid. Look into treasury records and lists of big taxpayers. See if TNEC tables on source and amount of income can be brought up to date.

II. Status refers to the amounts of deference received. For this, there are no simple or quantifiable indices. Existing indices requires personal interviews for their application and are limited so far to local community studies. There is the further problem that, unlike class, status involves social relations: at least one to receive and one to bestow the deference.

It is easy to confuse publicity with deference—or rather, we do not yet know whether or not volume of publicity should be used as an index to status position, although it is the most easily available: (For example: On one of three successive days in mid March 1952, the following categories of people were mentioned by name in The New York Times—or on selected pages—work this out).

III. Power refers to the realization of one's will even if others resist. Like status, this has not been well indexed. I don't think I can keep it a single dimension, but will have to talk (a) of formal authority—defined by rights and powers of positions in various institutions, especially military, political and economic. And (b) power known informally to be exercised but not formally instituted—pressure group leaders, propagandists with extensive media at their disposal, and so on.

IV. Occupation refers to activities that are paid for. Here, again, I must choose just which feature of occupation I should seize upon. (a) If I use the average incomes of various occupations, to rank them, I am using occupation as an index, and as a basis of class. In like manner (b) if I use the status or the power typically attached to different occupations, then I am using occupations as indices, and bases, of power and skill or talent. But this is by no means an easy way to classify people. Skill is not a homogeneous something of which there is more or less. Attempts to treat it as such have usually been put in terms of the length of time required to acquire various skills, and maybe that will have to do, although I hope I can think of something better.

Those are the types of problems I will have to solve in order to define analytically and empirically the upper circles, in terms of these four key variables. For purposes of design, assume I have solved them to my satisfaction, and that I have distributed the population in terms of each of them. I would then have four sets of people: those at the top in class, status, power and skill. Suppose further, that I had singled out the top two per cent of each distribution, as an upper circle. I then confront this empirically answerable question: How much, if any, overlap is there among each of these four distributions? One range of possibilities can be located within this simple chart: ($+ =$ top 2%; $- =$ lower 98%).

Power			*Class*			
			+		−	
			Status		*Status*	
			+	−	+	−
+ Skill	+		1	2	3	4
			5	6	7	8
− Skill	+		9	10	11	12
	−		13	14	15	16

This diagram, if I had the materials to fill it, would contain the major data and the important problems for a study of the upper circles. It would provide the keys to many types of definitional and substantive questions.

I don't have the data, and I shan't be able to get it—which makes all the more important that I speculate about it, for in the course of such reflection, if it is guided by the desire to approximate the empirical requirements of an ideal design, I'll come upon important areas, on which I might be able to get materials that are relevant as anchor points and guides to further imaginative reflection.

There are two additional points which I must add to this general model in order to make it formally complete. Full conceptions of upper strata require attention to duration and mobility. The task here is to determine positions ($1–16$) between which there is typical movement of individuals and groups—within the present generation, and between the last two or three generations.

This introduces the temporal dimension of biography or career-lines, and of history into the scheme. These are not merely further empirical questions; they are also definitionally relevant. For (a) we want to leave open whether or not in classifying people in terms of any of our key variables, we should define our categories in terms of how long they, or their families, have occupied the position in question. For example, I might want to decide that the upper 2 per cent of status—or at least one important type of status rank—consists of those up there for at least two generations. Also (b), I want to leave open the question of whether or not I should construct "a stratum" not only in terms of an intersection of several variables, but also, in line with Weber's neglected definition of "social class," as composed of those positions between which there is "typical and easy mobility." Thus, the lower white collar occupations and middle and upper wage worker jobs in certain industries seem to be forming, in this sense, a stratum.

In the course of the reading and analysis of others' theories, the design of ideal research, and the perusal of the files, I began to draw up a list of special studies. Some of them are too big to handle, and will in time be regretfully given up; some will end as materials for a paragraph, a section, a sentence, a chapter; some will become pervading themes to be woven into the entire book or into parts of it. Here, again, are initial notes for several such special projects, taken from an application I have made for a small research grant:

(1) A time-budget analysis of a typical working day of ten top executives of large corporations, and the same for ten federal administrators. These observations will be combined with detailed "life history" interviews. The aim here is to describe the major routines and decisions, partly at least in terms of time devoted to them, and to gain an insight into the factors relevant to the decisions made. The procedure will naturally vary with the degree of cooperation secured, but ideally will involve first, an interview in which the life history and present situation of the man is made clear; second, observations of the day, actually sitting in a corner of the man's office, and following him around; third, a longish interview that evening or the next day in which we go over the whole day and probe the subjective processes involved in the external behavior we've observed.

(2) A time-budget analysis of upper class weekends, in which the routines are closely observed and followed by probing interviews with the man and other members of the family on the Monday following.

For both these tasks I've fairly good contacts and of course good contacts, if handled properly, lead to better ones. I've done this with labor leaders and in general I believe business and government people are more cooperative.

(3) A study of the expense account and other privileges which, along with salaries and other incomes, form the standard and the style of living of the top levels. The idea here is to get something concrete on "the bureaucratization of consumption," the transfer of private expenses to business accounts.

(4) Bring up to date the type of information contained in such books as Lundberg's America's Sixty Families, which is dated as of the tax returns for 1923.

(5) Gather and systematize, from treasury records and other government sources, the distribution of various types of private property by amounts held.

(6) A career-line study of the Presidents, all cabinet members, and all members of the Supreme Court. This I already have on IBM cards from the constitutional period through Truman's second term, but I want to expand the items used and analyze it afresh.

There are other—some 35 so far—small scale "projects" of this sort, (for example, comparison of the amounts of money spent in the presidential elections of 1896 and 1952, detailed comparison of

Morgan of 1910 and Kaiser of 1950, and something concrete on the careers of "Admirals and Generals"). But, as I go along, I must adjust my aim to what is accessible. I hope that the above list will make clear the kind of thing I want to do.

VI

My sense of form—unskilled though it still is—begins to tempt me into concealment. I feel the tendency to leave my fragmentary notes and round all this out so as to make my ways of working seem more effective than they are, in short, to draw the reader's attention away from my limited discoveries and towards my modes of presentation and persuasion. I want to guard against that. So I must tell you that during the last several months I have been doing a great deal of writing; to be sure it has been writing along the general lines of the big model and in terms of the theories examined, but still it has at times seemed quite free of all that. I can not say for sure whether my imagination has been prompted by having these larger designs before me, although I am aware that I can easily make it look that way. Maybe these designs are a sort of professional ritual I go through; maybe they are more than that, more than psychologically necessary. At any rate, some of this writing leads me to feel uneasy about the assumption that all the skills required to put a book together are explicit and teachable, as are the deadbeat methods of much orthodox social science today.

Anyway, after these designs were written down, I began, with a clearer conscience, and I must say greater zest, to read historical works on top groups, taking random (and unfiled) notes and interpreting the reading. You do not really have to study a topic you are working on; for as I've said, once you are into it, it is everywhere. You are sensitive to its themes; you see and hear them everywhere in your experience, especially, it always seems to me, in apparently unrelated areas. Even the mass media, especially bad movies and cheap novels and picture magazines and night radio are disclosed in fresh importance to you.

From existing sources as well as those that you have fashioned, trying to remain open, as it were, on all sides, you slowly go forward, continually outlining and re-outlining the whole, specifying and elaborating the list of anchor projects, refining and trying to index parts of the master design, writing this and editing that, bringing intellectual neatness for a day or a week or a month to this section or to that part.

VII

But, the reader may ask, how do ideas come? How is the imagination spurred to put all the images and facts together and lend meaning to them? I do not think I can really answer that; all I can do is talk about the general conditions and a few simple techniques which have seemed to increase my chances to come out with something.

I do not believe that workmanlike imagination is an absolute gift. I at least have got to work in order to call it forth, and when I am really in the middle of some set of problems, I am working for it all the time, even when I do not know it. I have to develop and nurse it, and I must live as well as work in such a way as to allow it to occur. In short, I believe that there are techniques of imagination and definite ways of stimulating it, although I do not want to acquire any technique of work that would limit the play of fancy. Naturally I hope that beginning students might gather a few hints for their own ways of work, and some encouragement to pursue them, but I am not suggesting any rigid technique. Yet, there are several ways I have found useful to invite the sociological imagination:

1: The rearranging of the file, as I have already said, is one way. One simply dumps out heretofore disconnected folders, mixing up their contents, and then re-sorts them many times. How often and how extensively one does this will of course vary with different problems and the development of their solutions. But in general the mechanics of it are as simple as that.

2: A second technique which should be part of the intellectual workman's way of life consists of a kind of relaxed browsing in libraries, letting the mind play over books and new periodicals and encyclopedias. Of course, I have in mind the several problems on which I am actively working, and try to be passively receptive to unforeseen and unplanned linkages.

3: Closely related to playing with the file and relaxing in the library is the idea of actively using a variety of perspectives: I will, for instance, ask myself how would a political scientist whom I recently read, approach this, and how that experimental psychologist or this historian? One thinks in multiple-perspectives which are here represented by men of different specialties. I try in this way to let my mind become a moving prism that catches light from as many angles as possible. In this connection, the writing of dialogues is often very useful.

4: One of the things meant by "being soaked in the literature" is being able to locate the opponents and the friends of every available viewpoint. I very often try to think against something, and in trying to understand and advance an intellectual field, one of the first things I do is lay out the arguments. On this point, see, for instance, the book on John Dewey's technique of thought by Bogoslovksy, *The Logic of Controversy*, and C. E. Ayers' essay on the gospel of technology in *Philosophy Today and Tomorrow*, edited by Hook and Kallen.

5: An attitude of playfulness toward the phrases and words with which various issues are defined often loosens the imagination. I look up synonyms for each of my key terms in dictionaries as well as in various scholarly books, in order to know the full range of their connotations. This simple procedure seems to prod me to a conceptual elaboration of the problem and hence to define terms more precisely. For only if I know the several meanings which might be given to terms or phrases can I select the precise ones with which I want to work. As a student, I kept a notebook containing the vocabularies for handling given problem areas.

6: On all work, but especially on existing theory, I try to keep close watch on the level of generality of every key term, and I often find it useful to take a high-level statement and break it down to more concrete levels. When that is done, the statement often falls into two or three components, each lying along different dimensions. I also try to move up the level of generality: remove the specific qualifiers and examine the re-formed statement or inference more abstractly, to see if I can stretch it or elaborate it. So from above and from below, I try to probe, in search of clarified meaning, into every aspect and implication of the theory.

7: Almost any general idea I come upon will, as I think about it, be cast into some sort of types. A new classification is often the beginning of fruitful developments. The skill required to make up types and then to search for the conditions and consequences of each type has, in short, become an automatic procedure with me. Rather than resting content with Democratic vs. Republican voters—I have to make up a classification of voters along the motivational line, and another long the intensity line, and so forth. I am searching for common denominators within Democratic types and Republican types and for differentiating factors within and between all of the types built.

8: The technique of the "cross-tabulating" is not limited to quantitative materials, but, as a matter of fact, is a good way to get hold of new types. Charts, tables, and diagrams of a qualitative sort are not only display-models for work already done; they are very often genuinely productive in their effects.

9: On almost any problem with which I am concerned, I try to get a comparative grip on the materials. The search for comparable cases in one civilization or historical period or several, or in two samples, gives me leads. I would never think of describing an institution in twentieth-century America without trying to bear in mind similar institutions in other types of milieu and structure.

10: In the search for comparable cases, as I have already remarked, I seem to get the best insights from extreme types—from thinking of the opposite of that with which I am directly concerned. If I think about despair, then I also think about elation; if I study the miser, then also the spendthrift. That is also a general characteristic of anchor projects, which, if it is possible, I design in terms of "polar types." The hardest thing in the world for me is to study one object, but when I try to contrast objects, I get a sort of grip on the materials and I can then sort out the dimensions in terms of which the comparisons are made. I find the shuttling between these dimensions and the concrete types very illuminating. This technique is also logically sound, for without a sample, you can only guess about statistical frequencies anyway: what you can do is give the range and major types of some phenomenon, and for that it is more economical to begin by constructing "polar types," opposites along various dimensions. This does not mean of course that I do not strive to gain and to maintain a sense of proportion—for some lead on the frequencies of given types. One continually tries, in fact, to combine this quest with the search for indices for which one might find statistics.

11: I seem automatically to try to put historical depth into my reflection, and I think this is the reason for it: often what you are examining is limited in number, so to get a comparative grip on it, you have got to place it inside a frame with historical depth. To put it another way, the contrasting type approach often requires the examination of historical cases. This sometimes results in points useful for a trend analysis, or it leads to a typology of stages. I use historical materials, then, because of the desire for a fuller range, or for a more convenient range of some phenomena—by which I mean one that includes the variations along some known set of dimensions. Some knowledge of world history is indispensable to the sociologist; without such knowledge, he is simply a provincial, no matter what else he knows.

VIII

From these considerations, I hope the reader will understand that in a way I never "start" writing on a project, I am writing continuously, either in a more personal vein, in the files, in taking notes after browsing, or in more guided endeavors. And I always have, in following this way of living and working, many topics which I want to work out further. After I decide on some "release" out of this work, I try to use the entire file, the browsing in libraries and periodicals, my conversations and my selection of people—all on this topic. I am trying, you see, to build a framework containing all the key elements which enter into the work; then to put each section in separate folders and continually re-adjust the whole framework around changes in them. Merely to lay out such a skeleton is to suggest what flesh is needed: facts, tables, more ideas.

So one discovers and describes, constructing typologies for the ordering of what one has found out, focusing and organizing experience by distinguishing items by name. This search for order pushes one to seek out underlying patterns and trends, and of course, to find relations that may be typical and causal. One searches, in short, for the meanings of what one has come upon, for what seems capable of being interpreted as a visible token of something else that is invisible. One makes an inventory of everything that seems involved in some phenomena, pares it down to essentials, then carefully and systematically relates these items to one another, thus forming a sort of working model. And then one relates this model to the systematically defined phenomena one wants to explain. Sometimes it is that easy; sometimes it just will not come.

But always, among all these details, one searches for indicators that might point to the main drift, to the underlying forms and tendencies of the society of the US in the middle of the Twentieth Century. For that is what, in the end, one is always writing about.

Thinking is a simultaneous struggle for conceptual order and yet at the same time empirical comprehensiveness. You must not close it up too soon— or you will fail to see all that you should; you cannot leave it open forever—or you yourself will burst. It is this dilemma that makes reflection, on those rare occasions when it is more or less successful, the most passionate endeavor of which a man is capable.

Notes

1. See, for example, *White Collar*, ch. 13. I am now trying to do this with Lederer and Gasset vs "elite theorists" as two reactions to 18th and 19th century democratic doctrine.

2. There are also statements in Mosca about psychological laws supposed to support his view. See his use of the word "natural." But this isn't central, and, in addition, it's not worth considering.

SIX | Thorstein Veblen

T HIS ESSAY ON Thorstein Veblen's *The Theory of the Leisure Class* was
first published as an introduction to the New American Library's 1953
edition. Mills had read Veblen with enthusiasm in college and drew much
from *The Theory of the Leisure Class* and *Absentee Ownership* in his own studies of
power and stratification. In *The Marxists*, he concluded that Veblen "probably
was an anarchist and syndicalist."

Lionel Trilling pronounced this introduction "a really first-rate piece of
pedagogy" and said it was the best thing Mills had written. David Riesman
agreed, but took an antipathetic view of Veblen that reflected differences
between liberal and radical social thought in the fifties. In *Thorstein Veblen: A
Critical Interpretation* (1953), Riesman diagnosed his subject as "a somewhat
schizoid person" who suffered from "emotional claustrophobia" and "buried
sadism." Veblen's social criticism "was in reality a projection of his own
multiple alienation, as immigrant's son, farmer's son, unsuccessful husband,
and itinerant barely-tolerated scholar." Mills, rejecting this view, argued for
Veblen as "the best critic of America that America has produced," indeed as
"the only comic writer among modern social scientists."

Thorstein Veblen is the best critic of America that America has produced. His
language is part of the vocabulary of every literate American; his works are the
most conspicuous contribution of any American to American studies; his
style, which makes him the only comic writer among modern social scientists, is an established style of the society he dissected. Even the leisure class,

which has now been reading Veblen for more than a generation, talks a little like him.

Veblen would have appreciated the fate his work has suffered. An unfashionable mind, he nevertheless established a fashion of thinking; a heretic, his points of view have been received into the canon of American social thought. Indeed, his perspectives are so fully accepted that one is tempted to say there is no other standard of criticism than the canon which Veblen himself established. All of which seems to prove that it is difficult to remain the critic of a society that is entertained by blame as well as praise.

Veblen is still read, not only because his criticism is still plausible, but because his style makes it so, even when the criticism is not taken seriously. Style is not exactly a strong point of American social science; in fact, most sociologists avoid style, even as some historians cultivate it. And, in this respect, Veblen is more historian than "social scientist." At any rate, it is his style that has kept this rather obscure and unsuccessful sociologist of the "Progressive Era"—he died in 1929—alive, after the immediate scene he anatomized has become history.

George Bernard Shaw, in his Preface to *Man and Superman,* remarks that "...he who has something to assert will go as far in power of style as its momentousness and his conviction will carry him. Disprove his assertion after it is made, yet his style remains. Darwin no more destroyed the style of Job or Handel than Martin Luther destroyed the style of Giotto. All the assertions get disproved sooner or later; and so we find the world full of a magnificent debris of artistic fossils, with the matter-of-fact credibility gone clean out of them, but the form still splendid."

That is true of Veblen—although in his case we cannot say that all "the matter-of-fact credibility" in his works has "gone clean out of them."

2

In a grim world, Veblen's style is so hilarious that one would wish to see it left intact as a going force for sanity. One may not always be sure of his meaning today, but his animus remains unmistakable and salutary. Whether or not his style in this, his first book, is his best, Veblen's books as a whole do constitute a work of art, as well as a full-scale commentary on American life.

As works of art, Veblen's books do what all art properly should do: they smash through the stereotyped world of our routine perception and feeling and impulse; they alert us to see and to feel and to move toward new images, many of them playful and bright and shrewd.

Veblen creates a coherent world in which each part is soon understandable and which is peopled by fascinating types of men and women who are soon though newly recognizable. We might learn from him that the object of all social study is to understand the types of men and women that are selected and shaped by a given society—and to judge them by explicit standards. Much of Veblen's comedy comes simply from his making his fresh standards explicit.

The form of Veblen's books and their content are one. It is as much the exact way he says things as what he says that one appreciates in his work. His phrases stick in the mind, and his insights, if acquired early, often make a difference in the quality of one's life. No, his thought could not properly be expressed in any other form than the form which he gave it. And that is why, like all works of art, you must "read" his work for yourself.

3

Thorstein Veblen realized that the world he lived in was dominated by what one might call "crackpot realism." That was, and one must use the word, Veblen's metaphysic—his bone-deep view of the nature of everyday American reality. He believed that the very Men of Affairs whom everyone supposed to embody sober, hard-headed practicality were in fact utopian capitalists and monomaniacs; that the Men of Decision who led soldiers in war and who organized civilians' daily livelihoods in peace were in fact crackpots of the highest pecuniary order. They had "sold" a believing world on themselves; and they had—hence the irony—to play the chief fanatics in their delusional world.

No mere joke, however, but a basic element of his perspective caused Veblen to write in 1922 what might with equal truth be written today: "The current situation in America is by way of being something of a psychiatrical clinic. In order to come to an understanding of this situation there is doubtless much else to be taken into account, but the case of America is after all not fairly to be understood without making due allowance for a certain prevalent unbalance and derangement of mentality, presumably transient but sufficiently grave for the time being. Perhaps the commonest and plainest evidence of this unbalanced mentality is to be seen in a certain fearsome and feverish credulity with which a large proportion of the Americans are affected."

The realization of this false consciousness all around him, along with the sturdiness of mind and character to stand up against it, is the clue to Veblen's world outlook. How different his was from the prevailing view is suggested by his utter inability to be "the salesman."

4

We are told that even as a youth Veblen mumbled and so seemed incomprehensible. His students thought him dull, and he did not pretend to be fond of them. Veblen never got a decent academic job. He was not what the 19th century called a decent man. He was a sure-footed old man who hated sham, realistically and romantically protesting against it by his manner of living as well as by his life work. Veblen was one of those lean, masterless men, who are hated by plump flunkies. He was an idle, curious man, watching bustling citizens and pompous spokesmen beat him at games he refused to play.

It has been fashionable to sentimentalize Veblen as the most alienated of American intellectuals, as the Prince outside even the ghetto. But Veblen's virtue is not alienation; it is failure. Modern intellectuals have made a success of "alienation" but Veblen was a natural-born failure. To be conspicuously "alienated" was a kind of success he would have scorned most. In character and in career, in mind and in everyday life, he was the outsider, and his work the intellectual elaboration of a felt condition.

He was almost a foreigner, except if someone had told him, "If you don't like it here, go back where you came from," it would have had to be Wisconsin or Minnesota. He was born in 1857, to Norwegian immigrants in Wisconsin and he was moved to Minnesota by his father, an artisan-farmer, when he was eight years old.

After nine more years on the farm he was packed off to Carleton, a small Congregational school in Northfield, Minnesota, where he was regarded as impressive but likely to be unsound. After graduating with the class of 1880, he tried to teach in a middlewestern academy. The next year he went to Johns Hopkins for graduate work and in 1844 he took his Ph.D. at Yale. No job was available for Thorstein Veblen. He went back to the farm. He married a girl from a family of university administrators. Still no job. For six or seven years he lived in idle curiosity. The farm had no place for a scholar, although on the Veblen farm scholarship was not out of place. Veblen talked much with his father and learned much from him.

In 1891, Veblen went to Cornell for further graduate work, and shortly thereafter finally got his first academic job at the University of Chicago. He lived eccentrically, and his wife kept going away and coming back again. Girls, we are told, liked Veblen, and he did not really object. He was requested to resign. With his wife again, he got a job at Stanford, where the Chicago story was more or less repeated. His wife now gone for good, Veblen began to teach at the University of Missouri, where he wrote four of five of his best books while living in the cellar of a colleague's house.

During World War I, Veblen went to Washington, filling a minor post in the Food Administration. He was not successful. After the Armistice, Veblen went to New York to write for an unsuccessful little magazine and to lecture at that future haven for refugee scholars, The New School for Social Research. He was not a successful lecturer. Then he went to Stanford and lived in a shack in the nearby woods, where he died on August 3, 1929.[1]

There is no failure in American academic history quite so great as Veblen's. He was a masterless, recalcitrant man, and if we must group him somewhere in the American scene, it is with those most recalcitrant Americans, the Wobblies.[2] On the edges of the higher learning, Veblen tried to live like a Wobbly. It was a strange place for such an attempt. The Wobblies were not learned, but they were, like Veblen, masterless men, and the only non-middle class movement of revolt in twentieth-century America. With his acute discontent and shyness of program, Veblen was a sort of intellectual Wobbly.

5

Two schools of sociological study have flourished in America since Veblen's time. One of them makes a fetish of "Method," the other of "Theory." Both, accordingly, lose sight of their proper study.

The Higher Statisticians break down truth and falsity into such fine particles that we cannot tell the difference between them; by the costly rigor of their methods, they succeed in trivializing man and society, and in the process their own minds as well.

The Grand Theorists, on the other hand, represent a partially organized attempt to withdraw from the effort plainly to describe, explain, and understand human conduct and society: they verbalize in turgid prose the disordered contents of their reading of eminent nineteenth-century sociologists, and in the process mistake their own beginnings for a finished result.

In the practice of both these leading schools, contemporary Social Science becomes simply an elaborate method of insuring that no one learns too much about man and society, the first by formal and empty ingenuity; the second, by formal but cloudy obscurantism.

The work of Thorstein Veblen stands out as a live protest against these dominant tendencies of the higher ignorance. He always knew the difference between the trivial and the important, and he was wary of the academic traps of busywork and pretension. While he was a man at thought, he kept the bright eye of his mind upon the object he was examining. Veblen was quite unable to be a specialist. He tried philosophy and he was trained as an economist, but he was also a sociologist and a psychologist. While specialists constructed a world to suit only themselves, Veblen was a professional anti-specialist. He was, in short, a social thinker in the grand tradition, for he tried to do what Hegel and Comte and Marx and Spencer and Weber—each in his own way—had tried to do:

To grasp the essentials of an entire society and epoch,
To delineate the characters of the typical men within it,
To determine its main drift.

The results of Veblen's attempt to do these things exist in some ten books. His first attempt, published in 1899, is the book you hold in your hand. Five years later he published *The Theory of Business Enterprise*, and then, in 1914, *The Instinct of Workmanship*. When World War I occurred, naturally Veblen turned to it, publishing *Imperial Germany* in 1915, and *The Nature of Peace* in 1917. After that, published a few years apart, he produced *The Higher Learning* and *The Vested Interests*; his more technical essays were collected in *The Place of Science in Modern Civilization*. He wrote *The Engineers and The Price System*, published as a book in 1921, and *Absentee Ownership*—which many consider his best single volume—in 1923. After his death, *Essays in Our Changing Order* was published. These constitute the heritage Veblen left for the use of the human community. There is no better set of books written by a single individual about American society. There is no better inheritance available to those who can still choose their own ancestors.

6

Since the intelligentsia, just now, are in a conservative mood, no doubt during the nineteen-fifties Veblen, when he is not ignored, will be re-interpreted as a conservative. And, from one rather formal viewpoint, Veblen was a pro-foundly conservative critic of America: he wholeheartedly accepted one of the few un-ambiguous, all-American values: the value of efficiency, of utility, of pragmatic simplicity. His criticism of institutions and the personnel of American society was based without exception upon his belief that they did not adequately fulfill this American value. If he was, as I believe, a Socratic figure, he was in his own way as American as Socrates in his was Athenian.

As a critic, Veblen was effective precisely because he used the American value of efficiency to criticize American reality. He merely took this value seriously and used it with devastatingly systematic rigor. It was a strange perspective for an American critic in the nineteenth century as it would be in our own. One looked down from Mont St. Michel, like Henry Adams, or across from England, like Henry James. With Veblen perhaps the whole character of American social criticism shifted. The figure of the last-generation American faded and the figure of the first-generation American—the Norwegian immigrant's son, the New York Jew teaching English literature in a midwestern university, the southerner come north to crash New York—was installed as the genuine, if no longer 100 per cent American, critic.

If Veblen accepted utility as a master value, he rejected another all-American value: the heraldry of the greenback, the world of the fast buck. And since, in that strange institution, the modern corporation, the efficiency of the plain engineer and the pecuniary fanaticism of the business chieftain—are intricately confused, Veblen devoted his life's work to clarifying the difference between these two types and between their social consequences.

7

The America Veblen saw seemed split in two. Running through everything Veblen wrote was the distinction between those activities and moods that are productive and useful and those that are ostentatious and honorific, workmanlike as against businesslike, industrial and amiable in contrast to pecuniary and predatory.

In the course of history, his account ran, material labor had become unworthy; predatory exploit had become the very essence of high dignity. Labor, Veblen believed, became irksome because of the indignity imputed to it; it had not become undignified because it was irksome. By "leisure" Veblen really meant everything that is not of the world of everyday, productive work and of the workmanlike habit of mind.

The key event in the modern history of the leisure class was its involvement in private ownership. Originally, Veblen tells us, predatory warlords seized property—especially the women—of an enemy, and hence their ownership of the booty revealed their prowess. This was of course honorific, because it was an assertion of superior force. In due course, the struggle for existence became a competition for pecuniary emulation: to own property was to possess honor; it was to set up an invidious distinction, a better-than-thou feeling on the part of absentee owners: those who own more than they could personally use, against those who did not own enough for their livelihood.

Popular esteem thus came to be based upon property, and accordingly became the basis for "that complacency which we call self-respect." For men judged themselves favorably or unfavorably in comparison to others of their general class in point of pecuniary strength, and this led to an insatiable, restless straining for invidious distinction.

But would not such a pecuniary struggle lead men to industrious and frugal lives? Perhaps for the lower classes, but not for the higher. Being useless in the struggle for status that had succeeded the struggle for existence, productive work was held to be unworthy. The better classes abstained from it while at the same time they emulated one another. It was not enough to possess wealth in order to win esteem; one had to put it into evidence; one had to impress one's importance upon others. Conspicuous leisure, according to Veblen, did just that—it put one's wealth and power on social display. That was the value of leisure for this pecuniary society. When one's group was compact and all its members intimately known, either leisure or consumption served to demonstrate one's wealth. But when one moved among wider circles of urban strangers, it became necessary to advertise one's wealth. Conspicuous consumption was then needed as a means of ordinary decency. With what was obviously expensive and wasteful one could impress all transient and anonymous observers.

So mere idleness was not enough: it had to be the idleness of expensive discomfort, of noble vice, and costly entertainment. It had, in short, to be conspicuous consumption: the obvious waste of valuable goods as a means of gaining reputability.

Opposed to all this, there stand in Veblen's world the industrial interests of the modern community, and the honest, prosaic man who would serve these industrial interests. But such peaceable men, having a "non-emulative, non-invidious interest in men and things," lack what passes for initiative and ingenuity, and end up as amiable good-for-nothing fellows. For what is good for the community is, of course, in a regime of crackpot realism, "disserviceable to the individual."

By his master split, with businessmen on the pecuniary side, Veblen linked the theory of the leisure class with the theory of the business enterprise. For ownership and acquisition belonged to the pecuniary range of employments, to the moneyed life. And the "captain of industry" was misnamed, for his was a pecuniary rather than an industrial captaincy.

This, all too briefly, is the kind of real, never-never world you who are about to read this book for the first time are about to enter. "All this is incredible," Veblen suddenly remarks in the middle of one of his books, "but it is everyday fact." Veblen has made Alices of us all, and dropped us through the looking glass into the fantastic world of social reality.

8

What Veblen said remains strong with the truth, even though his facts do not cover the scenes and the characters that have emerged in our own time. He remains strong with the truth because we could not see the newer features of our own time had he not written what and as he did. Which is one meaning of the fact that his biases are the most fruitful that have appeared in the literature of American social protest. But all critics are mortal, and some parts of Veblen can no longer live for us. In the criticisms of Veblen which follow, I shall examine only his theory of the leisure class.

9

Veblen's theory is not "The Theory of the Leisure Class." It is a theory of a particular element of the upper classes in one period of the history of one nation. It is a criticism of the *nouveau riche*, so much in evidence in Veblen's formative time, the America of the latter half of the nineteenth century, of the Vanderbilts, Goulds, and Harrimans, of Saratoga Springs and Newport, of the glitter and the gold.

Moreover, what he wrote about was mainly Local Society and its Last Resorts, and especially the women of these worlds. He could not of course have been expected in the eighteen-nineties to see the meaning for the *national* status system of the professional celebrities, who have risen as part of the national media of mass communication and entertainment, nor the major change in national glamour, in which the debutante is replaced by the movie star, and the local society lady by the military and political and economic mangers—the power elite—whom crackpot realists now celebrate as their proper chieftains.

10

The spleen of Veblen is due to the assumption, in his own words, that "the accumulation of wealth at the upper end of the pecuniary scale implies privation at the lower end of the scale." He tended always to assume that the pie was of a certain size, and that the wealthy class withdraws from the lower classes "as much as it may of the means of sustenance, and so reducing their consumption, and consequently their available energy, to such a point as to make them incapable of the effort required for the learning and adoption of new habits of thought." Again, the moral edge of the phrase, "conspicuous consumption" lies in the fact that it tends "to leave but a scanty subsistence minimum . . . to absorb any surplus energy which may be available after the pure physical necessities of life . . ." All this, strangely enough, was a sort of survival in Veblen's thought of classic economic conceptions of scarcity, and betrays a lack of confidence in technological abundance which we cannot now accept in the simple terms in which Veblen left it.

Veblen, thinking of the immigrant masses of his time and of the enormously unequal distribution of income and wealth, did not leave enough scope for the economic pie to expand—and what has happened, especially since the second World War, has meant that the majority of the U.S. population can consume conspicuously. In fact, in the absence of "lower classes on a scanty subsistence," the term "conspicuous consumption" becomes a somewhat flat description of higher standards of living because the invidious element is lacking. Of course the aesthetics of Veblen's case remain applicable.

I I

In depicting the higher style of life, Veblen seemed to confuse aristocratic and bourgeois traits. Perhaps this is a limitation of his American viewpoint. He did this explicitly at one or two points: "The aristocratic and the bourgeois virtues—that is to say the destructive and pecuniary traits—should be found chiefly among the upper classes . . ." One has only to examine the taste of the small shopkeeper to know that this is certainly not true.

Conspicuous consumption, as Veblen knew, is not confined to the upper classes. But today I should say that it prevails especially among one element of the new upper classes—the *nouveau riche* of the new corporate privileges—the men and women on the expense accounts, and those enjoying other corporate prerogatives—and with even more grievous effects on the standard and style of life of the higher middle and middle classes generally. And of course among recent crops of "Texas millionaires."

I 2

The supposed shamefulness of labor, on which many of Veblen's conceptions rest, does not square very well with the Puritan work ethic so characteristic of much of American life, including many upper class elements. I suppose, in the book at hand, Veblen is speaking only of upper, not middle classes—certainly he is not writing of wealthy Puritan middle classes. He did not want to call what the businessman does "work," much less productive work. The very term, leisure class, became for him synonymous with upper class; but, of course, there is and there has been a *working* upper class—in fact, a class of prodigiously active people. That Veblen did not approve of their work, and in fact refused to give it that term—work being one of his positive words—is irrelevant. Moreover, in this case it obscures and distorts our understanding of the upper classes as a social formation. Yet for Veblen fully to have admitted this simple fact would have destroyed (or forced the much greater sophistication of) his whole perspective and indeed one of the chief moral bases of his criticism.

13

Veblen was interested in psychological gratification; he tended to ignore the social function of much of what he described. He would not, in fact, have liked the term "function" to be used in this way, because, given his values, the solid word "function" is precisely the sort he would have reserved for workmanlike men and forces. Consider merely as illustrations three close to hand:

Many of the social scenes with which Veblen had so much fun were, in fact, meeting places for various elite of decision, for prestige behavior mediates between various hierarchies and regions. Hence prestige is not merely social nonsense that gratifies the individual ego: it serves a unifying function; leisure activities are one way of securing a coordination of decision between various sections and elements of the upper class.

Such status activities also coordinate high families; they provide a marriage market, the functions of which go well beyond the gratifications of displayed elegance, of brown orchids and white satin: they serve to keep a propertied class intact and unscattered; by monopoly of sons and daughters, anchoring the class in the legalities of blood lines.

And "snobbish" exclusiveness, of course, secures privacy to those who can afford it. To exclude others enables the high-and-mighty to set up and to maintain a series of private worlds in which they can and do discuss issues and decisions and in which they train their young informally for the decision-making temper. In this way they blend impersonal decision-making with informal sensitivities, and so shape the character structure of an elite.

14

There is another function—today the most important—of prestige and of status conduct. Prestige buttresses power, turning it into authority, and protecting it from social challenge.

"Power for power's sake" is psychologically based on prestige gratification. But Veblen laughed so hard and so consistently at the servants and the dogs and the women and the sports of the elite that he failed to see that their military, economic, and political activity is not at all funny. In short he did not succeed in relating their power over armies and factories to what he believed, quite rightly, to be their funny business. He was, I think, not quite serious enough about prestige because he did not see its full and intricate importance to power. He saw "the kept classes" and "the underlying population," but he did not really see the power elite.

15

Perhaps Veblen did not pay appropriate attention to the relevance of status to power because of his theory of history. The members of his "leisure class" are no history-makers; in fact, they have no real function in history. For in modern societies, Veblen held, industrial forces are the motors of history, and the leisure class is a survival and a lag, an anachronism or a parasitical growth. In fact, Veblen explicitly believed that "they are not in the full sense an organic part of the industrial community." For in that matter-of-fact community, it is the innovator who counts, and in the leisure class the innovator is vulgar, and innovation, to say the least, bad form.

Technological innovators are the history makers, and next to them, according to Veblen, those who are forced to change their ways in order to meet new technical conditions. Today, we cannot go along with what seems to us this over-simple view of the relations of technology to the institutions and the men who adapt and guide its developments and uses. This is one of the several Marxist overtones in Veblen, the assumption that those who are functionally indispensable to the community are the men who count and that those who are parasites are doomed. In our time, of course, we have seen too many technically parasitic men gain power and hold it with authority to believe in this rational, optimistic theory of history.

16

Veblen had an inadequate view of the effect of industrial efficiency upon the rationality of the men close to the machine process. He failed to recognize the terrible ambiguity of rationality in modern man and his society. He assumed that the skilled workmen and the engineers and the technicians would increasingly come to embody matter-of-fact rationality—as individuals and as strata. It was, in fact, upon these strata that he rested as he lectured about the "leisure class." And this, again, is a result of his over-simple split between the honorific and the workmanlike.

Veblen failed to appreciate that the increasing rationality of the efficiency-machines does not at all mean that the individuals who are linked together to run these machines are personally more rational or intelligent—even inside the fabulous engine room itself, and certainly not inside the mass society of which it is a part. In fact, the judgment of "the technicians" and their capacity for general intelligence, especially in social and political affairs, often seems quite paralyzed and is no better than that of the pecuniary fanatics. The rational apparatus itself has expropriated the rationality of the individual to the point where we must often assume that those in charge of the big institutions are normally quite stupid. Moreover, the few key individuals who are able rationally to understand the structure of the whole are no more likely to be engineers than workingmen.

What Veblen called industrial efficiency, "the opaque run of cause and effect," does not necessarily increase the substantive rationality of independent judgment. Nor does close contact with the big machine increase in men any of those amiable, sane traits that Veblen stuffed into his "instinct of workmanship." For in truth, Veblen's "workmanship" is an ideal set forth by a man afraid to set forth ideals, and it is more socially at home in some simple artisan society than in the modern social disorder we are trying to live in and understand.

17

Just what does all the pretentious monkey business about status, which Veblen analyzed so well, have to do with the operations of the political economy? I have intimated that the local society of the very rich—about which Veblen wrote—turned out to be too economically unstable and too politically weak to become an enduring center for a national system of prestige. The professional celebrities of the mass media are without power of any stable sort and are in fact ephemeral figures among those we celebrate.

And yet there is an upper-class demand for some sort of organization of enduring and stable prestige, which Veblen's analysis somehow misses. It is a "need" quite consciously and quite deeply felt by the elite of wealth and especially by the elite of power in the United States today.

During the nineteenth century neither the political nor the military elite were able to establish themselves firmly at the head or even near the head of a national system of prestige. John Adams's suggestion—in his *Discourses on Davila*—which leaned in that direction, was not taken up. Other forces and not any official system of distinctions and honors have given such order as it has had to the polity. The American economic elite—and for this very reason it is uniquely significant—rose to economic power in such a way as to upset repeated attempts to found national status on enduring family lines.

But in the last thirty years, with the managerial reorganization of the propertied class, and the political roles assumed by the managerial elite, there have been signs of a merger of economic, political, and military elite in a new corporate-like class. Together, as an elite of power, will they not seek, as all-powerful men everywhere have always sought, to buttress their power with the mantle of authoritative status? Will they not consolidate the new status privileges, popularized in terms of the expense account but rooted deeply in their corporate class? And in view of their position in the cultural world of nations—as they come more fully to realize it, will they be content with the clowns and the queens—the professional celebrities—as the world representatives of their American nation?

In due course, will not those we celebrate come to coincide more closely with those who are the most powerful among us? In due course, will not snobbery become official, and all of us startled into our appropriate grade and rank? To believe otherwise, it seems to me, is to reject all that is available and relevant in our understanding of world history.

18

We must remember that we could not entertain, at least not so easily, such criticisms and speculations had Veblen not written. And that is his real and lasting value: he opens up our minds, he gets us "outside the whale," he makes us see through the official sham. Above all, he teaches us to be aware of the crackpot basis of the realism of those practical Men of Affairs who would lead us to honorific destruction.

Notes

1. Joseph Dorfman, in his *Thorstein Veblen and His America* (Viking, 1934), has written a detailed account of Veblen's life and work.
2. The Industrial Workers of the World (I.W.W.): an industrial labor union, having a syndicalist ideology, founded in 1905.

SEVEN

IBM Plus Reality Plus
Humanism = Sociology

T HIS ESSAY ON "Third Camp" sociology was published in *The Saturday Review* on May 1, 1954. Upon reading Mills's "fine essay," which praised the Institute of Social Research, Leo Lowenthal and Theodor Adorno agreed to invite him to contribute to a *festschrift* for Max Horkheimer.

———

Sociology, judging by the books of its practitioners, is a strange field of learning. In the libraries of its professors you will find books containing announcements like this: p^1 ($=p^2$ij). As well as books, also called sociology, full of mumblings like this: "Sociological theory, then, is for us that aspect of the theory of social systems which is concerned with the phenomena of the institutionalization of patterns of value-orientation in the social system, with the conditions of that institutionalization, and of changes in the patterns, with conditions of conformity with and deviance from a set of such patterns and with motivational processes in so far as they are involved in all of these." As well as (and this is the last sample) assertions of this kind: "Militarily, economically, and politically, there is going on a struggle for the world . . . this struggle has a portentous psychological meaning: we witness and we participate in an historic contest which will decide what types of men and women will flourish on the earth."

It is possible, I suppose, that the same mind might compose all three statements, but it is not very likely. And, in fact, the same mind did not do so; not even the same type of mind. All of which means that American sociology, as it is revealed in books, is now divided into three main camps. Some sociologists, after having drafted a dozen articles and a hundred memoranda to the foundations, believe themselves to be Statesmen of Social Science, and claim to see just how each of the three fit into the orderly progress of a unified field of learning. But I am not one of them.

I hold that only one of the three camps is worthy of the name sociology, and accordingly, I am not even going to mention the names of the leading members of the other two. Some of my best friends are in those camps, but they will have to blow their own horns. This decision allows me to do all that I can honestly do: give growling summaries of the other two camps (exaggerating them slightly, in order the more clearly to reveal their tendencies); pleasantly elaborate the third, to which I belong; and then mention some key books from which one working sociologist has learned something.

The first camp is that of The Scientists, who are very much concerned to be known as such. Among them, I am sure, are those who would love to wear white coats with an I.B.M. symbol of some sort on the breast pocket. They are out to do with society and history what they believe physicists have done with nature. Such a view often seems to rest upon the hope that if only someone could invent for "the social sciences" some gadget like the atom bomb, all our human problems would suddenly come to an end. This rational and empty optimism reveals, it seems to me, a profound ignorance of (1) the role of ideas in human history, of (2) the nature of power and its relations to knowledge, and of (3) the meaning of moral action and the place of knowledge within it.

Among The Scientists, the most frequent type is The Higher Statistician, who breaks down truth and falsity into such fine particles that we cannot tell the difference between them. By the costly rigor of their methods, they succeed in trivializing men and society, and in the process, their own minds as well.

In fact, several men in the social studies now enjoy enormous reputations, but have not produced any enormous books, intellectually speaking, or in fact any contributions of note to the substantive knowledge of our time. Their academic reputations rest, quite largely, upon their academic power: they are the members of the committee; they are on the directing board; they can get you the job, the trip, the research grant. They are a strange new kind of bureaucrat. They are executives of the mind, public relations men among foundations and universities for their fields. For them, the memorandum is replacing the book. They could set up a research project or even a school, but I would be surprised if, now after twenty years of research and teaching and observing and thinking, they could produce a book that told you what they thought was going on in the world, what they thought were the major problems for men of this historical epoch; and I feel sure that they would be embarrassed if you earnestly asked them to suggest what ought to be done about it and by whom. For the span of time in which The Scientists say they think of their work is a billion man-hours of labor. And in the meantime we should not expect much substantive knowledge; first there must be methodological inquiries into methods and inquiry.

Many foundation administrators like to give money for projects that are thought to be safe from political or public attack, that are large-scale, hence easier "to administer" than more numerous handicraft projects, and that are scientific with a capital S, which often only means made "safe" by trivialization. Accordingly, the big money tends to encourage the large-scale bureaucratic style of research into small-scale problems as carried on by The Scientists.

In their practice, as in that of the Grand Theorists which I will now describe, the social studies become an elaborate method of insuring that no one learns too much about man and society, the first by formal but empty ingenuity; the second, by formal and cloudy obscurantism.

The Grand Theorists represent a partially organized attempt to withdraw from the effort plainly to describe, explain, and understand human conduct and society; in turgid prose they set forth the disordered contents of their reading of eminent nineteenth-century sociologists, and in the process mistake their own beginning for a finished result.

To at least some of those who claim to understand their work and who like it, Grand Theory is the greatest single advance in the entire history of sociology.

To many of those who claim to understand it but who do not like it, it is a clumsy piece of irrelevant ponderosity.

To those who do not claim to understand it but who like it very much—and there are many of these—it is a wondrous maze, fascinating precisely because of its often splendid lack of intelligibility.

Those who do not claim to understand it and who do not like it—if they retain the courage of their convictions—will feel that indeed the emperor has no clothes.

And of course there are many who qualify their views, and many more who remain patiently neutral, waiting to see the professional outcome.

Serious differences among sociologists are not between those who would observe without thinking and those who would think without observing. The differences have rather to do with what kind of thinking, what kind of observing, and what kind of link, if any, there is between the two. The nerve of the Grand Theorists' difficulties lies in their initial choice of so general a level of thinking that one cannot logically get down to observation; and secondly, in the seemingly arbitrary elaboration of distinctions which do not enlarge one's understanding of recognizably human problems or experience. Moreover, almost any 500 laborious pages of theirs could be translated into seventy-five straightforward pages of English containing everything said in the 500. Too much of it is a getting ready to get ready, too much more a getting ready, and through it all, there are too many promises and not enough payoffs.

The line between profundity and verbal confusion is often delicate, and no one should deny the curious charm of those who, like Whitman, beginning their studies, are so pleased and awed by the first step that they hardly wish to go any further. Of itself, language does form a wonderful world.

Yet, isn't it time for sociologists, especially eminent ones, to stop thinking about thinking and begin directly to study something?

The third camp is composed of sociologists who are trying to perform three major tasks, which may be stated in this way:

Whatever else sociology may be, it is a result of consistently asking: (1) What is the meaning of this—whatever we are examining—for our society as a whole, and what is this social world like? (2) What is the meaning of this for the types of men and women that prevail in this society? And (3) how does this fit into the historical trend of our times, and in what direction does this main drift seem to be carrying us? No matter how small-scale what he is examining, the sociologist must ask such questions about it, or he has abdicated the classical sociological endeavor.

I know of no better way to become acquainted with this endeavor, in a high form of modern expression than to read in the periodical, *Studies in Philosophy and Social Sciences*, published by the Institute of Social Research. Unfortunately, it is available only in the morgues of university libraries, and to the great loss of American social studies, several of the Institute's leading members, among them Max Horkheimer and Theodore Adorno, have returned to Germany. That there is now no periodical that bears comparison with this one testifies to the ascendency of the Higher Statisticians and the Grand Theorists over the Sociologists. It is difficult to understand why some publisher does not get out a volume or two of selections from this great periodical.

What the endeavor of sociology looks like may also be seen in the many classics of sociology that have become available in English during the last decade. The most important, I believe, are the several works of Max Weber. Do you remember the big literary rush to Vilfredo Pareto during the Thirties? Well, as the general inattention to him nowadays reveals, he wasn't worth it. Max Weber would be: his voice is that of the classical liberal in a world that seemed to him, back in the first quarter of the century, all set against liberalism, and at the same time he is the most sophisticated revisionists of classical Marxism.

Other important classics now available include: Georg Simmel's "Conflict" and "The Sociology of Georg Simmel," Emile Durkheim's "Suicide: A Study in Sociology" and "The Division of Labor and Society," Gaetano Mosca's "The Ruling Class," and Roberto Michels's "Political Parties."

The later volumes of Karl Mannheim do not have the general relevance of his first two—"Ideology and Utopia" and "Man and Society in an Age of Reconstruction." There is now a paper-backed edition of Thorstein Veblen's "Theory of the Leisure Class." (Someone ought to do his other books, especially "Absentee Ownership.") H. Stuart Hughes has recently written an excellent critical estimate of "Oswald Spengler." Francis Cornford, by his magnificent translation and editing, has given us a virtually new "Republic of Plato."

The best attempt, since Weber, to organize key concepts and formulate hunches in a one-two-three manner is Harold D. Lasswell's and Abraham Kaplan's "Power and Society," which draws upon Weber, Michels, and Mosca in a most intelligent way. Robert A. Dahl and Charles E. Lindbloom, in their "Politics, Economics, and Welfare," have recently produced an excellent statement of the integration of total societies.

Books on social structure or on the various institutional domains that compose it include Gunnar Myrdal's two-volume "An American Dilemma," which deals primarily with the Negro, but is also valuable for much else. Franz Neumann's "Behemoth" and E. Herbert Norman's "Japan's Emergence as a Modern State" are models of excellence for any sociological studies of social structure.

Military institutions and their meaning for modern life have been explored by Hans Speier in several important essays, contained in "Social Order and the Risks of War," which also contains excellent pieces on politics. The classical sociological account in English is Alfred Vagts's "A History of Militarism." And there are good materials also in "Makers of Modern Strategy," edited by E. M. Earle.

On the social and political meaning of the economic structure, Schumpeter and Galbraith are perhaps most significant, although Schumpeter—whose work is as much used as ideological material by the Eisenhower Administration as is any economist's—is the more solid and wide ranging. Henry Durant's "The Problem of Leisure" and J. Huizinga's "Homo Ludens" are fine statements about work and play in modern life. The best single volume on religious trends in American of which I know is Herbert W. Schneider's "Religion in Twentieth Century America," and of education practices, A. E. Bestor's "Educational Wastelands." The best sociological statement of international relations is E. H. Carr's "The Twenty Years' Crisis."

William H. Whyte Jr., in "Is Anybody Listening?" does not seem to be aware of—or at any rate doesn't state—the full meaning of what he so penetratingly describes, but he represents the old-fashioned Man Who Goes Into The Field, rather than sending four dozen researchers there, and his work shows it. So does Floyd Hunter's "Community Power Structure," which is the best book on an American community since the Lynds' studies of "Middletown."

It is shameful that sociologists have not celebrated properly the two wonderful volumes of Arnold Hauser, "The Social History of Art." And equally shameful that no American publisher has brought out George Lukács's "Studies in European Realism."

Most recent books of sociological relevance dealing with the individual have been influenced by the psychoanalytic tradition. Harry Stack Sullivan and Karen Horney, with great sensibility, take into account the small group and the general cultural pattern, but neither has an adequate view of social structure. That is not true of Erich Fromm, who in his "Escape From Freedom" skillfully relates economic and religious institutions to the types of personality they select and form. One of the few books I know that really locates Freud's work in a more ample philosophical framework is the wonderful little volume by Paul Tillich, "The Courage To Be."

Perhaps the most influential book of the last decade on types of individuals is "The Authoritarian Personality," by T. W. Adorno, Else Frenkel-Brunswick, D. J. Levinson, and R. N. Sanford, which, although not well organized and subject to quite damaging criticisms of method, still remains of outstanding importance. In the same tradition is the neat monograph by Leo Lowenthal's and N. Guterman's "Prophets of Deceit," which ought to be read widely just now to understand something of what is involved in the Republican Party split. Many of the sociologically most interesting trends in psychiatric circles may conveniently be found in "A Study of Interpersonal Relations," edited by Patrick Mullahy.

The main drift, the historic character of our time, has not been faced up to by many sociologists. Overshadowing all such attempts in scope and in excellence of detail is Arnold J. Toynbee's six-volume "A Study of History," which sociologists of the third camp will be studying for years to come. It should be read along with Gilbert Murray's lovely little essay, "Hellenism and the Modern World," Herbert J. Muller's criticism "The Uses of the Past," and Pitrim Sorokin's comparisons, "Social Philosophies of an Age of Crisis." Karl Löwith's "Meaning in History" and Paul Tillich's "The Protestant Era" are also key items of the historically grounded sociologist.

E. H. Carr, in his "The New Society" lectures has produced an indispensable and commendably brief statement of major trends in modern society. David Riesman writes better essays than books, but his "Lonely Crowd" is within the third camp. A book selling in Germany much better than in America—to the loss of American readers—is Fritz Sternberg's "Capitalism and Socialism on Trial."

All of these, of course, are samples of the kinds of books from which one sociologist has learned something, and which sustain him against The Scientists—who during the decade have moved from marketing research to the foundations, and so from toothpaste and soap to higher mathematics—and against The Grand Theorists—who have moved from textual interpretation of sociological classics to careful thinking about their own possible thought.

In every intellectual age, some one field of study tends to become a sort of common denominator of many other fields. In American intellectual life today sociology could become such a common denominator, and fact, despite everything, it is slowly becoming that. But for such a salutary development to get fully under way, theorists are going to have to do their work with a sense of reality as well as with scope and insight. Research technicians are going to have to go about their work with more imaginative concern for its larger meanings, as well as with mathematical ingenuity. Both are going to have to drop their trivialization of subject matter and their pretensions about method. Both are going to have to face up to the realities of our time. And both are going to have to acquire the humanist concern—which some American historians have retained—for excellence of clear and meaningful expression.

EIGHT | # Are We Losing Our Sense of Belonging?

THIS ADDRESS BEFORE the Couchiching Conference was given on the shores of Lake Couchiching, Ontario, in August 1954. Later in the year, it was published in *Food for Thought,* the magazine of the Canadian Association for Adult Education.

—⊶—

Because you have put to me this question—whether or not we are losing our sense of belonging—I already know your answer to it. Your answer is generally "Yes." Let me say at once that in the sense in which you mean it, my answer too is generally "Yes."

Yet, just because you have raised this question, I also know, or think I know, something else about you. You are among those who are asking serious questions at a time when few people are asking any questions of their own. But this question of yours is not a pre-fabricated question with a pre-fabricated answer built into it. That is why I know that there is something to which you and I do belong, and I do not believe that we are altogether losing our sense of belonging to it, and I know quite well that we ought not to.

Since we belong among those who ask serious questions and try to answer them, we also belong—whether or not we know it—to that minority which has carried on the big discourse of the rational mind, the big discourse that has been going on, or off and on, since western society began some two thousand years ago in the small communities of Athens and Jerusalem. Maybe you think that is a pretty vague thing to which to belong. If you do think that, you are mistaken. It is quite a thing to belong to the big discourse—even if as lesser participants—and, as I hope presently to make clear, it is the beginning of any sense of belonging that is worthwhile. It is the key to the only kind of belonging that free men in our time might have. And I think that we do belong to it, and that we ought to try to live up to what it demands of us.

What it demands of us, first of all, is that we maintain our sense of it. And, just now, at this point in human history, that is quite difficult. For we belong not only to the big discourse of the rational mind. We also belong, although we do not always feel that we do, to our own epoch. Since we are live men and not detached minds, we are trying to live in and with a certain set of feelings, the feelings of political men trying to be rational in an epoch of enormous irrationality.

What is the dominant mood of people like us, who try to think up questions and answer them for ourselves rather than waiting to be fed both questions and answers? What is the tang and feel of our experience as we examine the world about us today? It is clear that these feelings are shaping the way we ask and the way we answer all the questions of this conference. It is also clear—let us admit it—that our mood is not buoyant, not calm, not steady, and not sure.

It is true that we do not panic, but it is also true that the best among us possess the crisis mentality, and none of us can be up to the demands of our time unless we share something of this kind of mind, for it is rooted in an adequate sense of history and of our place in history.

We are often stunned and we are often distracted, and we are bewildered almost all of the time. And the only weapon we have—as individuals and as a scatter of grouplets—is the delicate brain now so perilously balanced in the struggle for public sanity. We feel that common political sense is no longer a sound basis of judgment, for the common sense of the twentieth century is based largely upon an eighteenth-and nineteenth-century experience which is outmoded by new facts of public life with which we have had little to do, except as victims. The more we understand what is happening in the world, the more frustrated we often become, for our knowledge leads to feelings of powerlessness.

We feel that we are living in a world in which the citizen has become a mere spectator or a forced actor, and that our personal experience is politically useless and our political will a minor illusion. For very often the fear of total, permanent war paralyzes the kind of morally oriented politics which might engage our interests and passions.

We sense the cultural mediocrity around us, and in us, and we know that ours is a time when, within and between all the nations of the world, the levels of public sensibility have sunk below sight. Atrocity on a mass scale has become impersonal and official. Moral indignation as a public fact has become extinct or is made trivial.

We feel that distrust has become nearly universal among men of affairs, and that the spread of public anxiety is poisoning human relations and drying up the roots of private freedom. We see that these men at the top tend to identify rational dissent with political mutiny, loyalty with blind conformity, and freedom of judgment with treason.

We feel that irresponsibility has become organized in high places and that clearly those in charge of the historic decisions of our time are not up to them. But, what is more damaging to us, we feel that those on the bottom, the forced actors who take the consequences, that they too are without leaders, without ideas of opposition, and that they make no real demands upon those in power.

We do not, of course, feel all of this all of the time, but we often feel some of it, and in the dark of the night when we are really alone and really awake we suspect that this might very well be an honest articulation of our deepest political feelings. And if we are justified even in half of these feelings, then we have at hand a second answer to the question of whether we are losing our sense of belonging. Our first answer, you will remember, was a general "Yes", except in the sense that we belong to the big discourse. Our second answer reflects our feelings about the sort of world we are living in. In this context, I don't know whether or not you are losing your political sense of belonging, but I should certainly hope so.

The point is that we are among those who cannot get their mouths around all the little "Yes's" that add up to tacit acceptance of a world run by crackpot realists and subject to blind drift. And that, you see, is something to which we do belong: we belong to those who are still capable of personally rejecting. Our minds are not yet captive. Now I believe that, just now, in the kind of political world we are in, rejection is more important than acceptance. For, in such a world, to accept freely requires, first of all, the personal capacity and the social opportunity to reject the official myths and the unofficial distractions. In a moment I shall return to the sense of belonging as a sense of insurgency, but we must now ask and briefly answer how we have gotten into this state of human affairs.

We are, of course, members of many organizations, but that does not mean that we necessarily belong to them. Many adolescents, especially the children of immigrants, are members of families, but are ashamed to belong to them.

Many men attend church, but do not get any sense of belonging out of it. Many acquaintances and friendships lead to no fulfillment. Many men are disciplined members of armies, but belong to them only in the external sense of expediency and fear of deserting them. All of us are members of one or the other of the absolute national states, although most of us never joined one.

When we say that we are losing our sense of belonging we really have in mind a political fact. We have in mind, one, a certain way of belonging; two, to a certain kind of organization.

The way of belonging here implied, rests upon our belief in the purposes and in the leaders of an organization, and thus enables us freely to be at home in it. To belong in this way is to make the human association a psychological center of our self, to take into our conscience, deliberately and freely, its rules of conduct and its purposes, which we thus shape and which in turn shape us.

The kind of organization we have in mind is a voluntary association which has three decisive characteristics; first, it is a context in which reasonable opinions may be formulated, second, it is an agency by which reasonable activities may be undertaken; and third, it is a powerful enough unit to make a difference in the way the world is going. It is because we do not find available such associations—which are at once psychologically meaningful and historically effective—that we often feel uneasy in our political and economic loyalties.

For between the state and the economy on the one hand, and the family and the small community on the other, we find no intermediate associations in which we feel secure and with which we feel powerful. There is little live political struggle. Instead, there is administration above, and the political vacuum below.

The effective units of power are now the huge corporation, the inaccessible government, the grim military establishment. These centres of power have become larger to the extent that they are effective; and to the extent that they are effective, they have become inaccessible to individuals like us, who would shape by discussion the policies of the organizations to which we belong.

It is because of the ineffectiveness of the smaller human associations, that the classic liberal public has waned, and is in fact being replaced by a mass society. We feel that we do not belong because we are not—not yet at least, and not entirely—mass men.

We are losing our sense of belonging because we think that the fabulous techniques of mass communication are not enlarging and animating face-to-face public discussion, but are helping to kill it off. These media—radio and mass magazines, television and the movies—as they now generally prevail, increasingly destroy the reasonable and leisurely human interchange of opinion. They do not often enable the listener or the viewer truly to connect his daily life with the larger realities of the world, nor do they often connect with his troubles. On the contrary, they distract and obscure his chance to understand himself or his world, by fastening his attention upon artificial frenzies.

We are losing our sense of belonging because more and more we live in metropolitan areas that are not communities in any real sense of the word, but unplanned monstrosities in which as men and women we are segregated into narrowed routines and milieux. We do not meet one another as persons in the several aspects of our total life, but know one another only fractionally, as the man who fixes the car, or as that girl who serves our lunch, or as the woman who takes care of our child at school. Pre-judgment and prejudice flourish when people meet people only in this segmental manner. The humanistic reality of others does not, cannot, come through.

In this metropolitan society, we develop, in our defense, a blasé manner that reaches deeper than a manner. We do not, accordingly, experience genuine clash of viewpoint. And when we do, we tend to consider it merely rude. We are sunk in our routines, we do not transcend them, even in discussion, much less by action. We do not gain a view of the structure of our community as a whole and of our role within it. Our cities are composed of narrow slots, and we, as the people in these slots, are more and more confined to our own rather narrow ranges. As we reach for each other, we do so only by stereotype. Each is trapped by his confining circle, each is split from easily identifiable groups. It is for people in such narrow milieux that the mass media can create a pseudo-world beyond, and a pseudo-world within themselves as well.

The political structure of a democratic state assumes the existence of a public, and in its rhetoric asserts that this public is the very seat of sovereignty. But given all those forces that have enlarged and centralized the political order and made our communities less political and more administrative; given all the mass communications that do not truly communicate; given all the metropolitan segregation that is no community, what is happening is the decline of a set of publics that is sovereign, except in the most formal and in the most rhetorical sense. And, moreover, in many countries the remnants of such publics as remain are now being frightened out of existence. They lose their strength; they lose their will for rationally considered decision and action. They are alone and they are afraid. Their members lose their sense of belonging because they do not belong.

I hope I have now made it clear that this question, whether or not we are losing our sense of belonging, cannot be answered with moral sensibility unless we also ask: "To what is it that we ought to belong"? Mere loyalty alone is less a virtue than an escape from freely thought out choices among the many values that now compete for our attention.

My own answer to this question—which may well be different from yours—can be put very simply. If we are men, what we ought to belong to, first of all, is ourselves. We ought to belong to ourselves as individuals. Once upon a time that answer would have seemed clear, for it used to be called "the appeal to conscience," but we now know that this is much too simple an answer, for we now know that there are men whose consciences are perfectly clear and perfectly sincere—and perfectly corrupt, as revealed in their actions towards themselves and others.

So we must add to this answer one further point. To the extent that we are truly human, we should try seriously to participate in that rational discourse of which I have spoken. And to the extent that we do so, our sensibilities will have been shaped by the high points of mankind's heritage of conduct and character and thought. Accordingly, we shall belong, we ought to belong, to mankind, and it is to mankind that we ought most freely to give our loyalties.

All other loyalties, it seems to me, ought to be qualified by these two, loyalty to ourselves and loyalty to the particular cultural heritage of mankind which we allow to shape us as individuals.

This answer is, of course, more a beginning than an end. We ought to use it to judge all principles and organizations that demand our loyalties. No corporation, no church, no nation, no labor union, no political party, no organization or creed is worthy of our loyalties if it does not facilitate the growth of loyalties to ourselves and to the heritage that mankind at its best moments has produced.

Moreover, we ought not to be committed absolutely to any organization. Our loyalty is conditional. Otherwise, it is not loyalty, it is not the belonging of free men. It is a compelled obedience. Let us not confuse the loyalties of free men with mere obedience to authority. When organizations sell out the values of free men, free men withdraw their loyalties. Not with a "Yes, but" or a "Maybe yes, maybe no", but with a big, plain, flat "No."

The positive question for us is not so much whether we are losing our sense of belonging as whether we can help build something that is worth belonging to. Perhaps that has always been the major social question for men and women shaped by the big discourse. For just as freedom that has not been fought for is lightly cast off, so belonging that does not require the building and the maintaining of organizations worth belonging to is often merely a yearning for a new bondage.

To really belong, we have got, first, to get it clear with ourselves that we do not belong and do not want to belong to an unfree world. As free men we have got to reject much of it, and to know why we are rejecting it.

We have got, second, to get it clear within ourselves that we can only truly belong to organizations which we have a real part in building and maintaining, directly and openly and all of the time.

And we have got, third, to realize that it is only in the struggle for what we really believe, as individuals and as members of economic, political and social groups, that the sense of belonging befitting a free man in an unfree world can exist. In such a world, only the comradeship of such a struggle is worth our loyalty; and only to truly human associations, which we ourselves create, do we, as rational men, wish to belong.

WRITING IN *COMMENTARY*, Nathan Glazer pronounced the first issue of *Dissent* magazine "an unmitigated disaster" but for five pieces that "escape the general blight," among them "The Conservative Mood." Mills wrote a reply to Glazer, published as "Who Conforms and Who Dissents?" in the April 1954 issue of *Commentary*. Of the exception Glazer afforded him, Mills said, "I am afraid that I cannot thank him, for he misunderstands: I, too, share many of the moods and ideas against which he directs his spleen."

In the material prosperity of post-war America, as crackpot realism has triumphed in practical affairs, all sorts of writers, from a rather confused variety of viewpoints, have been groping for a conservative ideology.

They have not found it, and they have not managed to create it. What they have found is an absence of mind in politics, and what they have managed to create is a mood. The psychological heart of this mood is a feeling of powerlessness—but with the old edge taken off, for it is a mood of acceptance and of a relaxation of the political will.

The intellectual core of the groping for conservatism is a giving up of the central goal of the secular impulse in the West: the control through reason of man's fate. It is this goal that has lent continuity to the humanist tradition, re-discovered in the Renaissance, and so strong in nineteenth century American experience. It is this goal that has been the major impulse of classic liberalism and of classic socialism.

The groping for conservative ideas, which signifies the weakening of this impulse, involves the search for tradition rather than reason as guide; the search for some natural aristocracy as an anchor point of tradition and a model of character. Sooner or later, those who would give up this impulse must take up the neo-Burkeian defense of irrationality, for that is, in fact, the only possible core of a genuinely conservative ideology. And it is not possible, I believe, to establish such an ideology in the United States.

I

Russell Kirk's "prolonged essay in definition" (*The Conservative Mind*) is the most explicit attempt to translate the conservative mood into conservative ideas. His work, however, does not succeed in the translation it attempts. When we examine it carefully we find that it is largely assertion, without arguable support, and that it seems rather irrelevant to modern realities, and not very useful as a guideline of political conduct and policy.

1: The conservative, we are told, believes that "divine intent rules society," man being incapable of grasping by his reason the great forces that prevail. Along with this, he believes that change must be slow and that "providence is the proper instrument for change," the test of a statesman being his "cognizance of the real tendency of Providential social forces."

2: The conservative has an affection for "the variety and mystery of traditional life" perhaps most of all because he believes that "tradition and sound prejudices" check man's presumptuous will and archaic impulse.

3: "Society," the conservative holds, "longs for leadership," and there are "natural distinctions" among men which form a natural order of classes and powers.

When we hold these points close together, we can understand each of them more clearly: they seem to mean that tradition is sacred, that it is through tradition that the real social tendencies of Providence are displayed, and that therefore tradition must be our guide-line. For whatever is traditional not only represents the accumulated wisdom of the ages but exists by "divine intent."

Naturally we must ask how we are to know which traditions are instruments of Providence? Which prejudices are "sound?" Which of the events and changes all around us are by divine intent? But the third point is an attempted answer: If we do not destroy the natural order of classes and the hierarchy of powers, we shall have superiors and leaders to tell us. If we uphold these natural distinctions, and in fact resuscitate older ones, the leaders for whom we long will decide.

II

It is pertinent to ask Mr. Kirk at what moment the highly conscious contrivances of the founding fathers became traditional and thus sanctified? And does he believe that society in the U. S.—before the progressive movement and before the New Deal reforms—represented anything akin to what he would call orders and classes based on "natural distinctions?" If not, then what and where is the model he would have us cherish? And does he believe that the campaign conservatives—to use the phrase of John Crowe Ransom—who now man the political institutions of the U. S., do or do not represent the Providential intent which he seeks? How are we to know if they do or do not, or to what extent which of these do?

Insofar as the conservative consistently defends the irrationality of tradition against the powers of human reason, insofar as he denies the legitimacy of man's attempt collectively to build his own world and individually to control his own fate, then he cannot bring in reason again as a means of choosing among traditions, of deciding which changes are providential and which are evil forces. He cannot provide any rational guide in our choice of which leaders grasp Providence and act it out and which are reformers and levelers. In the end, the conservative is left with one single principle: the principle of gratefully accepting the leadership of some set of men whom he considers a received and sanctified elite. If such men were there for all to recognize, the conservative could at least be socially clear. But as it is, there is no guide-line within this view to help us decide which contenders for the natural distinction are genuine and which are not.

III

Conservatism, as Karl Mannheim makes clear, translates the unreflecting reactions of traditionalism into the sphere of conscious reflection. Conservatism is traditionalism become self-conscious and elaborated and forensic. A noble aristocracy, a peasantry, a petty-bourgeoisie with guild inheritance—that is what has been needed for a conservative ideology and that is what Prussia in the early nineteenth century had. It was to the spell of tradition among these surviving elements of a pre-industrial society that conservatism could appeal. The Prussian upper classes lacked the elasticity of the English, and their country lacked an important middle class. Accordingly, they could avoid the English gradualism and the blurring of clear-cut ideologies in parliamentary compromises. In addition, caught between military neighbors, their military set could become a key element in Prussian society. Burke was the stimulus, but it was the German elaboration of his response to the French Revolution that resulted in a fully developed conservatism, sharply polarized against liberalism.[1]

If England already softened conservative thought with liberal elements, in America, liberalism—and the middle classes that bore it as a deep-seated style of thought—has been so paramount as to preclude any flowering of genuinely conservative ideology.

Here, from their beginnings the middle classes have been predominant—in class and in status and in power.[2] There is one consequence of this simple fact that goes far to explain why there can be no genuinely conservative ideology in the United States:

There is simply no stratum or group in the population that is of any political consequence to whose traditions conservatism could appeal. All major sections and strata have taken on, in various degrees and ways, the coloration of a middle-class liberal ethos.

IV

The greatest problem of those American writers who would think out a conservative ideology of any political relevance is simply the need to locate the set of people and to make clear the interests that their ideology would serve. There are those, of course, who deny that politics has to do with a struggle for power, but they are of no direct concern to politics as we know it or can imagine it. There are also those who deny that political philosophies are most readily understood as symbols of legitimation, that they have to do with the defense and the attack of powers-that-be or of would-be powers; but by this denial a writer makes himself rather irrelevant to the intellectual features of the public decisions and debates that confront us.

The yearning for conservative tradition, when taken seriously, is bound to be a yearning for the authority of an aristocracy. For without such a more or less fixed and visible social anchor for tradition and for hierarchy, for models of conduct in private and in public life, that are tangible to the senses, there can be no conservatism worthy of the name. And it is just here—at the central demand of conservatism—that most American publicists of the conservative yen become embarrassed. This embarrassment is in part due to a fear of confronting and going against the all-pervading liberal rhetoric; but it is also due to four facts about the American upper class:

First, American writers have no pre-capitalist elite to draw upon, even in fond remembrance. Mr. Kirk, for example, cannot, as European writers have been able to do, contrast such hold-overs from feudalism, however modified, with the vulgarity of capitalist upper elements. The South, when it displayed an "aristocracy" was a region not a nation, and its "aristocrats," however rural, were as much a part of capitalist society as were the New England upper strata.

Second, the very rich in America are culturally among the very poor, and are probably growing even more so. The only dimension of experience for which they have been models to which serious conservatives might point is the material one of money-making and money-keeping. Material success is their sole basis of authority.

Third, alongside the very rich, and supplanting them as popular models, are the synthetic celebrities of national glamor who often make a virtue out of cultural poverty and political illiteracy. By their very nature they are transient figures of the mass means of distraction rather than sources of authority and anchors of traditional continuity.

Fourth, it is virtually a condition of coming to the top in the American political economy that one learns to use and use frequently a liberal rhetoric, for that is the common denominator of all proper and successful spokesmen.

There are, accordingly, no social strata which serious minds with a conservative yen might celebrate as models of excellence and which stand in contrast to the American confusion the conservatives would deplore.

V

The American alternative for those interested in a conservative ideology seems to be (1) to go ahead—as Mallock, for example, in his 1898 argument with Spencer did—and defend the capitalist upper classes, or (2) to become socially vague and speak generally of a "natural aristocracy" or a "self-selected elite" which has nothing to do with existing social orders, classes and powers.

The first is no longer so popular among free writers, although every little tendency or chance to do it is promptly seized upon by conservative publicists and translated into such pages as those of *Fortune* magazine. But, more importantly, if it is useful ideologically it must be a dynamic notion and hence no fit anchor for tradition. On the contrary, the capitalist elite is always, in the folklore and sometimes in the reality of capitalism, composed of self-making men who smash tradition to rise to the top by strictly personal accomplishments.

The second alternative is now the more popular. In their need for an aristocracy, the conservative thinkers become grandly vague and very general. They are slippery about the aristocrat; generalizing the idea, they make it moral rather than socially firm and specific. In the name of "genuine democracy" or "liberal conservatism" they stretch the idea of aristocracy in a quite meaningless way, and so, in the end, all truly democratic citizens become aristocrats. Aristocracy becomes a scatter of morally superior persons rather than a strategically located class. So it is with Ortega y Gasset and so it is with Peter Viereck, who writes that it is not "the Aristocratic class" that is valuable but "the aristocratic spirit"—which, with its decorum and noblesse oblige, is "open to all, regardless of class."

This is not satisfactory because it provides no widely accepted criteria for judging who is elite and who is not. Moreover, it does not have to do with the existing facts of power and hence is politically irrelevant. And it involves a mobile situation; the self-selecting elite can be no fixed anchor. Some have tried to find a way to hold onto such a view, as it were secretly, not stating it directly, but holding it as a latest assumption while talking about, not the elite, but "the mass." That, however, is dangerous, for again, it goes so squarely against the liberal rhetoric which requires a continual flattery of the citizens.

Both these alternatives, in fact, end up not with an elite that is anchored in a tradition and hierarchy but with dynamic and ever-changing elite continually struggling to the top in an expanding society. There is simply no socially, much less politically, recognized traditional elite and there is no tradition. Moreover, whatever else it may be, tradition is something you cannot create. You can only uphold it when it exists. And now there is no spell of unbroken tradition upon which modern society is or can be steadily based. Accordingly, the conservative cannot confuse greatness with mere duration, cannot decide the competition of values by a mere endurance contest.

VI

In one of its two major forms, as instanced by Mr. Kirk, the defense of irrationality rests upon pre-capitalist, in fact pre-industrial, bases: it is simply the image of a society in which authority is legitimated by traditionalism and interpreted by a recognized aristocracy.

In its other major form the defense rests upon what is perhaps the key point in classic liberal capitalism: it is the image of a society in which authority is at a minimum because it is guided by the autonomous forces of the magic market. In this view, providence becomes the unseen hand of the market; for in secular guise Providence refers to a faith that the unintended consequences of many wills form a pattern, and that this pattern ought to be allowed to work itself out.

In contrast to classic conservatism, this conservative liberalism, as a call to relax the urge to rational planning, is very deep in the American grain. Not wishing to be disturbed over moral issues of the political economy, Americans cling all the more to the idea that the government is an automatic machine, regulated by a balancing out of competing interests. This image of government is simply carried over from the image of the economy: in both we arrive at equilibrium by the pulling and hauling of each individual or group for their own interests, restrained only by legalistic and amoral interpretation of what the law allows.

George Graham has noted that although Americans think representative government a wonderful thing, they hold that representatives are merely "politicians" who as a class are of a fairly low order; that although they willingly honor the dead statesmen of the past, they dishonor the politicians of the present. Professor Graham infers from this, as well as other facts, that "perhaps what Americans yearn for is a complete mechanization of politics. Not a dictator but a political automat is the subconscious ideal," something that will measure up "to the modern standards of being fully automatic and completely impersonal."[3]

In the United States the economic order has been predominant among institutions, and therefore the types of men and their characteristic traits are best interpreted in terms of the evolving economic system. In turn, the top men, almost regardless of how top is defined, have always included in one way or another those who are at the top of the economic system.

Insofar as one can find a clue to the basic impulse of the Eisenhower administration, it is the attempt to carry out this sacrifice of politics to the free dominance of economic institutions and their key personnel. It is a difficult task, perhaps even one that only crackpot realists would attempt, for now depression and wars, as well as other perils and complications of modern life, have greatly enlarged the federal government and made it an unwieldy instrument.

At the center of their ideology, the capitalist upper circles and their outlying publicists have had and do have only one political idea: it is the idea of an automatic political economy. This is best known to us as simply the practical conservatism of the anti-New Dealers during the Thirties of which the late Senator Robert Taft was perhaps the prime exemplar. It has been given new life by the frightening spectacle of the enlarged, totalitarian states of Germany yesterday and Russia today. And now it has become the only socially anchored conservative rhetoric in the American managerial elite, who now blend with the formal political directorate.

VII

And yet on the practical political level the conservative groping has not been much more than a set of negative reactions to any signs of "liberal" or "progressive" policies or men. Conservatives have protested their individual rights rather than any common duties. Such duties as they have set forth—the trusteeship of big corporations, for example—have been all too transparently cloaks for harder and narrower interests. For a dozen years, the New and Fair Deals carried forth a series of specific personalities and policies and agencies that have been the shifting targets of conservative bile. Yet, for electoral purposes, that bile had to be ejected into the "progressive" atmosphere carried forth and sustained by the New Deal.

American conservatives have not set forth any conservative ideology. They are conservative in mood and conservative in practice but they have no conservative ideology. They have no connection with the fountainheads of modern conservative thought. In becoming aware of their power they have not elaborated that awareness into a conscious ideology. Perhaps it is easiest for people to be conservative when they have no sense of what conservatism means, no sense of the conservative present as being only one alternative to what the future might be. For if one cannot say that conservatism is un-consciousness, certainly conservatives are often happily unconscious.

VIII

The poverty of mind in U.S. politics is evidenced in practice by the fact that the campaign liberals have no aim other than to hold to the general course of the New and Fair Deals, and no real ideas about extending these adminis-trative programs. The campaign conservatives, holding firmly to utopian capitalism (with its small, passive government and its automatic economy), have come up against the same facts as the liberals and in facing them have behaved very similarly. They have no real ideas about how to jettison the welfare state and the managed war economy.

In the meantime both use the same liberal rhetoric, largely completed before Lincoln's death, to hold matters in stalemate. Neither party has a political vocabulary—much less political policies—that are up-to-date with the events, problems and structure of modern life. Neither party challenges the other in the realm of ideas, nor offers clear-cut alternatives to the electorate. Neither can learn nor will learn anything from classic conservatism of Mr. Kirk's variety. They are both liberal in rhetoric, traditional in intention, expedient in practice.

You can no more build a coherent conservative outlook and policy on a coalition of big, medium and small business, higher white collar employees and professional people, farmers and a divided South than you could build a radical outlook and policy on a coalition of big city machines, small business men, lower white collar people, a split and timid labor world, farmers and a divided South.

Within each party and between them there is political stalemate. Out of two such melanges, you cannot even sort out consistent sets of interests and issues, much less develop coherent policies, much less organize ideological guidelines for public debate and private reflection.

This means, for one thing, that "politics" goes on only within and between a sort of administrative fumbling. The fumbles are expedient. And the drift that they add up to leads practically all sensitive observers to construct images of the future that are images of horror.

IX

One thinks of the attempt to create a conservative ideology in the United States as a little playful luxury a few writers will toy with for a while, rather than a serious effort to work out a coherent view of the world they live in and the demands they would make of it as political men.

More interesting than the ideas of these would-be conservative writers is the very high ratio of publicity to ideas. This is of course a characteristic of fashions and fads, and there is no doubt that the conservative moods are now fashionable. But I do not think we can explain intellectual fashions, in particular this one, by the dialectic that runs through intellectual discourse, nor by the ready seizure by vested interests of ideas and moods that promise to justify their power and their policies.

For one thing, policy makers often do not usually feel the need for even reading, much less using in public, much less thinking about, the conservative philosophies. When Robert Taft, before his death, was asked if he had read Russell Kirk's book, he replied that he did not have much time for books. Like the radical writers of the previous decade, conservative writers of the 40's and 50's are not in firm touch with power elites or policy makers.

Another reason America has no conservative ideology is that it has no radical opposition. Since there is no radical party, those who benefit most from such goods and powers of life as are available have felt no need to elaborate a conservative defense of their positions. For conservatism is not the mere carrying on of traditions or defense of existing interests: it is a becoming aware of tradition and interests and elaborating them into an outlook, tall with principle. And this happens usually only when the tradition and the top position which benefit from it are really attacked.

Neither a radical ideology nor a conservative ideology but a liberal rhetoric has provided the terms of all issues and conflicts. In its generic ambiguities and generality of term this rhetoric has obfuscated hard issues and made possible a historical development without benefit of hard conflict of idea. The prevalence of this liberal rhetoric has also meant that thought in any wide meaning of the term has been largely irrelevant to such politics as have been visible.

Underneath the immediate groping for conservatism there is, of course, the prosperity that has dulled any deeper political appetite in America's post-war period. It is true that this prosperity does not rest upon an economy solidly on its own feet, and that for many citizens it is not so pleasant as they had probably imagined. For it is a prosperity that is underpinned politically by a seemingly permanent war economy, and socially by combined incomes. Still, no matter how partial or how phoney, by old fashioned standards, the atmosphere is one of prosperity.

It is true, of course, that the radicalism of western humanism did not and does not depend for its nerve or its muscle upon fluctuations of material well-being. For those who are of this persuasion are as interested in the level of public sensibility and the quality of everyday life as in the material volume and distribution of commodities. Still, for many, this prosperity, no matter how vulgar, has been an obstacle to any cultural, much less political, protest.

More specific than this general climate of prosperity has been the tiredness of the liberal, living off the worn-out rubble of his rhetoric; and, along with this, the disappointment of the radical, from the turns of Soviet institutions away from their early promise to all the defeats that have followed in the thirty years of crisis and the deflation of radicalism.

The tiredness of the liberal and the deflation of radicalism are in themselves causes of the search for some kind of a more conservative point of view. It is good, many seem to feel, to relax and to accept. To undo the bow and to fondle the bowstring. It is good also, perhaps, because of the generally flush state of the writers and thinkers, for we should not forget that American intellectuals, however we may define them, are also personally involved in the general level of prosperity. To this we must also add the plain and fancy fright of many who once spoke boldly; the attacks upon civil liberties have touched deeply their anxieties and have prodded them to search for new modes of acceptance.

These are sources of the conservative impulse from the standpoint of the old left and liberal centers—to which most of the intellectuals have felt themselves to belong. From the right of center, there have also been impulses—impulses that were always there, perhaps, but which have come out into large print and ample publicity only in the post-war epoch. First of all there are interests which no matter what their prosperity require defending, primarily large business interests, and along with this, there is the need, which is felt by many spokesmen and scholars as great, for cultural prestige abroad. One prime result of the increased travel abroad by scholars, stemming from the anti-American rebuffs they have experienced, is the need to defend in some terms the goodness of American life. And these little episodes have occurred in a larger context of power: a context in which the economic and military and political power of the U. S. greatly exceeds her cultural prestige, and is so felt by the more acute politicians and statesmen at home and abroad.

The campaign conservatives will continue to go in for public relations more than for ideology. Just now they do not really feel the need for any ideology; later a conservative ideology of the kinds we have been discussing will appeal to no one. The radical humanist will continue to believe that men collectively can and ought to be their own history-makers and that men individually can to some extent and should try fully to create their own biographies. For those who still retain this minimum definition, the current attempts to create a conservative ideology do not constitute any real problem.

In the meantime, political decisions are occurring, as it were, without benefit of political ideas; mind and reality are two separate realms; America— a conservative country without any conservative ideology—appears before the world a naked and arbitrary power.

Notes

1. Cf. Mannheim, "Conservative Thought," in *Essays in Sociology and Social Psychology,* ed. and trans. by Paul Kecskemeti (New York: Oxford, 1953).

2. For an elaboration of the factors in the triumph of liberalism in the U.S., see Gerth and Mills, *Character and Social Structure* (New York: Harcourt Brace, 1953), pp. 464–472.

3. *Morals in American Politics* (New York: Random House, 1953), p. 4.

TEN ❦ Mass Society and Liberal Education

MILLS GAVE THIS ADDRESS to the National Conference on Methods for the Study of the Urban Community in New Orleans in April 1954. The conference was sponsored by the Center for the Study of Liberal Education for Adults, which published the address as a pamphlet that June.

———∞———

The transformation of a community of publics into a mass society is one of the keys to the meaning of modern life. It is a structural trend that leads directly to many of the psychological and political problems that Americans, especially those concerned with liberal education, now confront. In every industrial society, these problems are of national relevance, and in each of them the trend is rooted in the nation as a set of metropolitan areas. For it is from such metropolitan centers that there has spread those forces that are destroying or minimizing the classic liberal public and making for the ascendancy of the mass society.

ONE: The "Community of Publics" and "The Mass Society"

The United States today is not altogether a mass society, and it has never been altogether a community of publics. These phrases are names for extreme types. Although they point to certain features of reality, they are themselves constructions. Social reality is always, or so it seems to me, some sort of mixture. But the point is that one can most readily understand just how much of what is mixed into it, if one first states, in terms of explicit dimensions, the clear-cut and extreme types.

At least four dimensions must be attended to if we are to understand the differences between public and mass: (I.) There is first, the ratio of the givers of opinion to its receivers, which is, I think, the simplest way to state the key meaning of the formal media of communication. More than anything else, it is the shift in this ratio which is central to the problems of the public and of public opinion in latter-day phases of democracy.[1] (II.) There is second, the organization of communication, of which the most decisive aspect is the possibility of answering back an opinion without internal or external reprisals being taken.[2] (III.) Third, there is the ease with which opinion is effective in the shaping of decisions of powerful consequence. This opportunity for people to act out their opinions collectively is of course limited by their positions in the structure of power.[3] (IV.) Fourth, there is the degree to which instituted authorities, with their sanctions and controls, infiltrate the public. Here, the key problem becomes the degree of genuine autonomy from instituted authority which the public has.[4]

By combining these dimensions, it is possible to construct models of publics and diagrams of the societies with which they seem congruent. Since "the problem of public opinion" is now set by the eclipse of the classic "bourgeois public," we are here concerned with only two types:[5]

In a *public* as I understand the term, virtually as many people express opinions as receive them; public communications are so organized that there is a chance immediately and effectively to answer back to any opinion expressed in public. Opinion formed by such discussion readily finds an outlet in effective action against, if necessary, prevailing systems and agents of authority, and authoritative institutions do not interpenetrate the public, which is thus more or less autonomous in its operations. When these conditions prevail, we have the working model of a community of publics, and this model, as we shall presently see, fits pretty closely the several assumptions of classic democratic theory.

At the opposite extreme, in a *mass*, far fewer people express opinions than receive them; for the community of publics becomes an abstracted collectivity of individuals who receive impressions from the mass media. The communications that prevail are so organized that it is difficult or impossible for the individual to answer back immediately or with any effect. The realization of opinion in action is controlled by authorities who organize channels for such action. The mass has no autonomy from institutions; on the contrary, agents of authorized institutions interpenetrate this mass, reducing any autonomy it may have in the formation of opinion by discussion.

The public and the mass may be most readily distinguished by their dominant modes of communications: in a community of publics, discussion is the ascendant mode of communication, and the mass media, if they exist, simply enlarge and animate discussion, linking one *primary public* with the discussions of another. In a mass society, the dominant type of communication is by the formal media and the publics become *media markets,* by which I mean all those exposed to the contents of given mass media.

TWO: *The Classic Public*

Let us pause for a moment and consider generously the classic public of democratic theory, in the spirit in which Rousseau once cried: "Opinion, Queen of the World, is not subject to the power of kings; they are themselves its first slaves."

The key feature of public opinion which the rise of the democratic middle classes initiates is the free ebb and flow of discussion. In this community of publics anyone who would speak, can and anyone who is interested, does. The possibilities of answering back, of organizing autonomous organs of public opinion, of realizing opinion in action, are automatically established by democratic institutions. For the public opinion that results from discussion is understood to be a resolution that is to be carried out by public action; it is, in one version, the "general will" of the people, which parliament or Congress enacts into law, thus lending to it institutional force. Parliament, as an institution, crowns all the primary publics; it is the archetype for each of the scattered little circles of face-to-face citizens discussing their public business.

This 18th-century idea of public opinion parallels the economic idea of the free market economy. Here is the public composed of discussing circles of opinion peers crowned by parliament; there is the market composed of freely competing entrepreneurs. As price is the result of anonymous, equally-weighted, bargaining individuals, so is the public of public opinion the result of each man having thought things out for himself and contributing his weight to the great formation. To be sure, some might have more influence on the state of opinion than others, but no one man or group monopolizes the discussion, or by himself determines the state of opinion that prevails.

Innumerable discussion circles are knit together by mobile people who carry opinions, and struggle for the power of larger command. The public is thus organized into associations and parties, each representing a viewpoint, each trying to acquire a place in parliament or Congress, where the discussion continues. The autonomy of these discussion circles is a key element in the idea of "public opinion" as a democratic legitimation. The opinions formed are actively realized within the prevailing institutions of power; and all authoritative agents are made or broken by the prevailing opinions of primary publics.

Insofar as the public is frustrated in realizing its demands upon its agents, it may come to question the symbols of authority to which it has been devoted. Such questioning is of course of a deeper order than criticism of specific policies, but new political parties, of left or right, may attempt in their agitation to use the discussion of specific policies in order to bring the legitimations themselves into question. So, out of the little circles of people talking with one another, the large forces of social movements and political parties develop; and the discussion of opinion is the phase in a total act by which public affairs are conducted.

So conceived, the public is the loom of classic, 18th-century democracy; discussion is at once the thread and the shuttle tying the discussion circles together. It lies at the basis of the conception of authority by discussion, based on the hope that truth and justice will somehow carve out of society a great apparatus of free discussion. The people are presented with problems. They discuss them. They decide on them. They formulate viewpoints. These viewpoints are organized, and they compete. One viewpoint "wins out." Then the people act out this view, or their representatives are instructed to act it out, and this they promptly do.

Such are the images of classic democracy which are still used as the working legitimations of power in American society. You will recognize this description as a set of images out of a fairy tale; they are not adequate even as an approximate model of how this society works.

In our situation of half-mass and half-public, the term public, in fact, has come to have a specialized meaning, which dramatically reveals its eclipse. From the standpoint of the public actor—the democratic politician, for example—some people who clamor publicly can be identified as "Labor" and others as "Business," and still others as "Farm." Those who cannot readily be so identified make up the "Public." In this usage, "the public" is composed of the unidentified and non-partisan in the world of defined and partisan interests. It is socially composed of well-educated salaried professionals, especially college professors; of non-unionized employees, especially white-collar people, along with non-employing, self-employed professionals and small businessmen.

In this faint echo of the classic notion, the public consists of those remnants of the middle classes, old and new, whose interests are not explicitly defined, organized, or clamorous. In a curious adaptation, "the public" often becomes, in fact, "the unattached expert," who, although well informed, has never taken a clear-cut, public stand on those controversial issues which are brought to a focus by organized interests. What the public stands for, accordingly, is often a vagueness of policy (called open-mindedness), a lack of involvement in public affairs (known as reasonableness), and a professional disinterest (often known as tolerance).

Some members of such official publics, as in the field of labor-management mediation, start out very young and make a career out of being careful to be informed but never to take a strong position; and there are many others, quite unofficial, who take such professionals as a sort of model. The only trouble is that they are acting as if they were disinterested judges but they do not have the power of judges. Hence their reasonableness, tolerance and open-mindedness do not often count for much in the shaping of human affairs.

From almost any angle of vision that we might assume, when we look upon the community of publics, we realize that we have moved a considerable distance along the road to the mass society. At the end of that road there is totalitarianism, as in Nazi Germany or in Communist Russia. We are not yet at that end; in the United States today, media markets are not entirely ascendant over primary publics. But surely we can see that the success of the demagogue in exploiting these media, and the decreased chance to answer back, is certainly more a feature of a mass society than of a community of publics. And there are many other signs.

What is happening might again be stated in terms of the historical parallel between the commodity market in the economic order and in the public of public opinion. In brief, there is a movement from widely scattered little powers to concentrated powers and the attempt at monopoly control from powerful centers. And in the centers of economics, of politics, and of opinion, power is partially hidden; they are centers of manipulation as well as of authority. The small shop serving a small neighborhood is replaced by the anonymity of the national corporation; mass advertisement replaces the personal influence of opinion between merchant and customer. The political leader hooks up his speech to a national network and speaks, with appropriate personal touches, to a million people he never saw and never will see.

Entire brackets of professions and industries are in the "opinion business," impersonally manipulating the public for hire. *In the primary public*, the competition of opinions goes on between people holding views in the service of their interests and their reasoning. *But in the mass society* of media markets, competition, if any, goes on between the crowd of manipulators with their mass media on the one hand, and the people receiving their propaganda on the other.

Under such conditions, it is not surprising that a conception of public opinion as a mere impressment or as a reaction—we cannot say "response"—to the content of the mass media should arise. In this view, the public is merely the collectivity of individuals each rather passively exposed to the mass media and rather helplessly opened up to the suggestions and manipulations that flow from these media. The fact of manipulation from centralized points of control constitutes, as it were, an expropriation of the information and change of opinion participated in by the old multitude of little opinion producers and consumers operating in a free and balanced market.

The Drift Towards Mass

In attempting to explain the ascendancy of mass over public, there are four major trends to which we should pay attention; for if we do not we shall not be able to speculate fruitfully about the task of the college for adults in the metropolitan society of masses. These four structural trends of our epoch seem to me to coincide in their effects; they transform public into mass.

I. The rise of bureaucratic structures of executive power, in the economic, the military, and the political orders, has lowered the effective use of all these smaller voluntary associations operating between the state and the economy on the one hand, and the family on the other. It is not only that the institutions of power have become large-scale and inaccessibly centralized; they have at the same time become less political and more administrative. It is within this great change of framework that the organized public has waned.

In terms of *scale*, the transformation of public into mass has been underpinned by the shift from a political public decisively restricted in size (by property and education, as well as by sex and age) to a greatly enlarged mass having only the qualifications of citizenship and age. In terms of *organization*, the transformation has been underpinned by the shift from the individual and his primary community to the voluntary association and the mass party as the major units of organized power.

Voluntary associations have become larger to the extent that they have become effective; and to the extent that they have become effective, they have become inaccessible to the individual who would participate by discussion in their policies. Accordingly, along with older institutions, these voluntary associations have lost their grip on the individual. As greater numbers of people are drawn into the political arena, these associations become mass in scale, and because of the increased scale of the power structure, the power of the individual becomes more dependent upon these mass associations, and yet these are less accessible to his influence.[6]

Elections become first (1) contests between two giant and unwieldy parties, neither of which the individual can truly feel that he influences, and neither of which is capable of winning psychologically impressive majorities. Second (2), more and more, elections are decided in the irrational terms of silly appeals; less and less on clear and simple statements of genuine issue. Certainly the techniques of advertisement, and their use in the mass persuasion of an electorate, becomes more important than rational argument over real issues in public. And, in all this, the parties are of the same general form as other mass associations.[7]

What is not available is the association which has three characteristics: the association that is at once (1) a context in which reasonable opinions may be reached, (2) an agency by which reasonable activities may be undertaken; and (3) a powerful enough unit, in comparison with other organizations of power, to make a difference. Now the primary publics are either so small as to be swamped, and hence give up; or so large as to be merely another unit of the generally distant structure of power, and hence inaccessible. And in either case they are the more readily subjected to distorted images of the world by the mass media.

II. As the scale of institutions has become larger and more centralized, so have the range and intensity of the opinion makers' efforts. For the means of opinion-making—and this is the second master trend—have paralleled in range and efficiency the other institutions of greater scale that make up the modern society of masses. There is universal compulsory education—the seed-bed of nationalist propaganda and white-collar skills—and there are the media of mass communication. These mass media have apparently great variety and competition, but each of them often seems to be competing in terms of variations of a few standardized themes; and freedom of effective opinion seems more and more to operate within and between vested interests, organized and unorganized, that have ready and continual access to the media.

Early observers such as Charles Horton Cooley believe that the increase of the range and volume of the mass media would, as I have said, enlarge and animate the public,[8] but what it has done has helped kill it off. I do not refer merely to the higher ratio of deliverers of opinion to receivers and to the decreased chance to answer back. Nor do I mean merely the violent banalization and stereotyping of our very sense organs which these media make almost necessary. I have in mind a sort of technological illiteracy, which is expressed in three ways:

First, these media, especially television, have encroached upon the small-scale discussion, upon the leisurely human interchange of opinion.

Second, these media do not connect the information on issues that they do provide with the troubles felt by the individual. They do not increase rational insight into tensions, neither those in the individual nor those of the society which are reflected in the individual. On the contrary, they distract attention from such tension. They carry a general tone of animated distraction, a suspended agitation, but it is going nowhere and has nowhere to go: the chief distracting tension of the media is between the wanting and the not having of commodities or of women held to be good looking. As they now generally prevail, the media not only fail as an educational force; they are a malign force—in that they do not reveal to the viewer the sources of his tension and anxiety, his inarticulate resentments and half-formed hopes.

Third, these media do not enable the individual to transcend the narrow milieux in which he lives, or truly connect them with the larger realities of what is happening in the world. On the contrary, they obscure these connections by distracting his attention and fastening it upon artificial frenzies that are resolved within the program framework, usually by violent action, or by what is called humor. In short, for the viewer, not really resolved at all. I shall later return to this point.

III. A third explanation for the ascendancy of masses has to do with the class, status and occupational structure of modern society, of which the most important shift in the twentieth century has been the numerical decline of the old middle class of independent entrepreneurs and practitioners, and the rise of the new middle class of dependent white-collar workers.[9] This change in the economic and social make-up of the middle classes carries two meanings for the transformation of public into mass:

(1) Up until the later nineteenth century, in fact into the Progressive Era, the old middle class acted as an independent base of power, for the individual and for the class. Political freedom and economic security were both anchored in the fact of small-scale independent properties, and these scattered properties, and their holders, were integrated economically by free and autonomous markets, and politically by the process of representative democracy. The white-collar groups are not such an independent base of power: economically, they are in the same situation as propertyless wage workers; politically they are in a worse condition, for they are not organized.

(2) The second meaning of this shift has to do with what is called civic spirit as well as what is called nationalism. Civic spirit is nationalism on a local basis; nationalism is civic spirit written large. At least, the psychological scheme for each is much the same:

People in the top levels of the nation or the city voluntarily run various enterprises and push various interests. The underlying population, identifying themselves with these top people, believe these enterprises to be in their interest also, and indeed accept the *identification of these interests with the welfare of the nation or the city as a whole.* Sometimes they are right; sometimes they are wrong; but in either case energetic management by the leaders and cheerful acquiescence of the population are indispensable requirements for the kind of morale known as civic spirit or nationalism.

In any well-run American city, the men and women of the independent middle class have been the traditional chieftains of civic drives and enterprise. For one thing, they usually have the time and money that is needed; at least some of them are fairly well educated. Their work in conducting a small business is said to train them for initiative and responsibility, and does put them in touch with the administrative and political figures of the city, who, in fact, are usually drawn from their circles. In addition, the small businessman often stands to benefit personally as a result of civic improvement: better roads and streets, for example, lead to greater sales for the retail merchant. Mere self-interest often dictates that the businessman should be someone civically. By participating actively in civic affairs, he widens his circle of contacts and customers.

There is no need to stress the point that as the old public rested upon such entrepreneurs, so the decline of the public rests upon the transformation of the middle class into salaried employees, often employees of a local branch of a national corporation.[10] In fact, one thing that is happening in America today is that the structure of such loyalty as was once centered in the city is shifting to the massive corporation.[11] In terms of power, this is realistic; in terms of notions of the classic public, it is disastrous.

IV. A fourth master trend making for a mass society is the rise of the metropolis, and the only point I want to make about it is that the growth of this metropolitan society has segregated men and women into narrowed routines and milieux, and it has done so with the consequent loss of community structure.

The members of a community of publics know each other more or less fully, because they meet in the several aspects of the total life routine. The members of a metropolitan society of masses know one another only fractionally: as the man who fixes the car, or as that girl who serves your lunch, or as the woman who takes care of your child at school during the day. Pre-judgment and stereotype flourish when people meet people only in this segmental manner. The humanist reality of others does not, cannot, come through.

There are two implications of this I would mention: (1) Just as people tend to select those mass media that confirm what they already believe and enjoy, so do they tend, by the mere fact of segregated milieux and routines, to come into touch with those whose opinions are similar to theirs. Others they tend to treat unseriously. In such a situation as the metropolitan society, they develop, in their defense, a blasé manner that reaches deeper than a manner. They do not, accordingly, experience genuine clash of viewpoint or issue. And when they do, they tend to consider it an unpleasantry. (2) They are so sunk in the routines of their milieux that they do not transcend, even in discussion, much less by action, these more or less narrow milieux. They do not gain a view of the structure of their society and of their role within it. The city is a structure composed of milieux; the people in the milieux tend to be rather detached from one another; being more or less confined to their own rather narrow ranges, they do not understand the structure of their society. As they reach for each other, they do so by stereotype and through prejudiced images of the creatures of other milieux. Each is trapped by his confining circle; each is split from easily identifiable groups. It is for people in such narrow milieux that the mass media can create a pseudo-world beyond, and a pseudo-world within, themselves as well.

Publics live in milieux, but they can transcend them—individually, by intellect and education; socially, by discussion and by public action. By reflection and debate, and by organized action, a community of publics comes to feel itself, and comes in fact to be, active at points of structural relevance. But members of a mass exist in milieux and they cannot get out of them, either by mind or by activity, except—in the extreme case—under "the organized spontaneity" of the bureaucrat on a motorcycle. We have not yet reached the extreme case, but observing metropolitan man in the mass we can surely see the psychological preparations for it.

The man in the mass is sunk into stereotyped experience, or even sunk by it; he cannot detach himself in order to observe it, much less to evaluate it. Rather than the internal discussion of reflection, he is often accompanied through his life with only a half conscious monologue. He has no projects of his own; he fulfills the routines that exist. He does not transcend whatever he is at any moment, he does not, he cannot, transcend even his daily milieux.

He takes things for granted and makes the best of them. He tries to look ahead, a year or two perhaps, or even longer if he has children or a mortgage, but he does not seriously ask, What do I want? How can I get it? A vague optimism sustains him, broken occasionally by little miseries and disappointments that are soon buried. He is smug, from the standpoint of those who think something might be the matter with the mass style of life in the metropolitan frenzy where self-making is an externally busy branch of industry. By what standards does he judge himself and his efforts? Where are the models of excellence for this man? In the mass, he tends to lose such self-confidence as he ever had, for life in such a society of masses both implants and implements insecurity and impotence.

The political structure of a democratic state assumes the public, and in its rhetoric asserts that this public is the very seat of sovereignty. But given (1) all those forces that have centralized and enlarged and made less political and more administrative the American political life; (2) given all the metropolitan segregation that is no community; (3) given the transformation of the old middle class into something which perhaps should not even be called middle class; and (4) given all the mass communications that do not truly communicate—what is happening is the decline of a set of publics that is sovereign, except in the most formal and in the most rhetorical sense. And moreover the remnants of such publics as remain in the interstices of the mass society are now being frightened out of existence. They lose their strength; they lose their will for rationality, and for rationally considered decision and action. They are alone and they are afraid.

FOUR: Tasks of the College for Adults

If even half of what I have said is true, you may well ask: what is the task of the liberal college for adults? Insofar as it is—in ideal at least—truly liberal, the first answer is: *to keep us from being overwhelmed.* Its first and continuing task is to help produce the disciplined and informed *mind* that cannot be overwhelmed. Its first and continuing task is to help develop the bold and sensible individual who cannot be overwhelmed by the burdens of modern life. The aim is nothing more and can be nothing less. And in this, the aim of the liberal school for adults is no different from that of any liberal education; but there are other answers, more specific answers.

The school for adults, after all, does start from a different juncture in the biography of the person and accordingly must deal with a different set of expectations. Knowledge and intellectual practice must be made directly relevant to the human need of the troubled person of the twentieth century, and to the social practices of the citizen. For he must see the roots of his own biases and frustrations if he is to think clearly about himself, or about anything else. And he must see the frustration of idea, of intellect, by the present organization of society, if he is to meet the tasks now confronting the intelligent citizen.

Given our interest in liberal, that is to say in liberating, education, there are two things that the college for adults can do and ought to do: (1) What the college ought to do for the individual is to turn personal troubles and concerns into social issues and rationally open problems. The aim of the college, for the individual student, is to eliminate the need in his life for the college; the task is to help him to become a self-educating man. For only that will set him free. (2) What the evening college ought to do for the community is to fight all those forces which are destroying genuine publics and creating an urban mass; or stated positively: to help build and to strengthen the self-cultivating liberal public. For only that will set them free.

These two concerns, if we take them seriously, come together in the three areas which are the focal concerns of the Center for the Study of Liberal Education for Adults: I. the content and methods of teaching; II. the development of leadership; and III. the coordination of the school with other organizations, which I shall discuss in terms of the political relevance of the college for adults.[12]

I

The college of the metropolitan area is usually concerned with the training of skills that are of more or less direct use in the vocational life. This is an important task to perform, but I shall not discuss it here, for (1) it is a matter that hinges in great part for each school upon the local labor market and upon the vocational interests of students; moreover (2) job advancement is not the same as self-development although the two are systematically confused.[13]

Very broadly speaking the function of education as it was first set up in this country was political: to make citizens more knowledgeable and better thinkers. In time, the function of education shifted from the political to the economic; to train people for better paying jobs. This was especially so with reference to the high school movement, which met the demands of the business economy for white-collar skills, at public expense. So far as the political task is concerned, in many schools, that has been reduced to the firm inculcation of nationalist loyalties and the trivialization of life known as "life-adjustment."

A liberal education, especially for adults, cannot be merely vocational,[14] but among "skills," some are more, and some are less, relevant to the liberal arts aim. I do not believe that skills and values can so easily be separated as in our search for the supposed neutrality of skills we sometimes assume. And especially not when we speak seriously of liberal education. Of course, there is a scale, with skills at one end and values at the other, but it is the middle range of this scale, which I would call *sensibilities,* that should interest us most.

To train someone to operate a lathe or to read and write is pretty much an education of skill; to evoke from someone an understanding of what they really want out of their life or to debate with them stoic, Christian and humanist ways of living, is pretty much a clear-cut education of values. But to assist in the birth among a group of people of those cultural and social and political and technical sensibilities which would make them genuine members of a genuinely liberal public—this is at once a training in skills and an education of values.

Alongside skill and value we ought to put sensibility, which includes them both and more besides: it includes a sort of therapy in the ancient sense of clarifying one's knowledge of one's self; it includes the imparting of all those skills of controversy, with oneself which we call thinking, and with others which we call debate.

We must begin with what concerns the student most deeply. We must proceed in such a way and with such materials as to enable him to gain increasingly rational insight into these concerns. We must try to end, with a man or a woman who can and will by themselves continue what we have begun: the end product of the liberal education, as I have said, is simply the self-cultivating man and woman.

Not the epistemology of, but the therapy resulting from, the Socratic maxim is perfectly sound, and especially so for the liberal education in the adult school. There should be much small group discussion, and at least some of the skills of the group therapist ought to be part of the equipment of the teacher.[15]

Whether he knows it or not, the man in the mass is gripped by personal troubles, and he is not able to turn them into social issues, or to see their relevance for his community nor his community's relevance for them.

The knowledgeable man in the genuine public is able to do just that; he understands that what he thinks and feels to be personal troubles are very often not only that but problems shared by others and indeed not subject to solution by anyone individual but only by modifications of the structure of the groups in which he lives and sometimes the structure of the entire society.

Men in masses have troubles although they are not always aware of their true meaning and source. Men in publics confront issues, and they are aware of their terms. It is the task of the liberal institution, as of the liberally educated man, continually to translate troubles into issues and issues into the terms of their human meaning for the individual.

In the absence of deep and wide political debate that is really open and free within the framework of a metropolitan community, the adult school could and should become a hospitable framework for just such debate. Only if such procedures are built into the college for adults will that college be liberal, that is liberating, and at the same time real; encouraging people to get in touch with the realities of themselves and of their world.

As for the Center's aim concerning leadership I would say this:

II

The network of informal communication in the primary public may select and refract, it may debunk or it may sanction what is said in the formal media, or by the authorities. Everyone who talks with others is part of this network, and the ideal public is composed of people who are opinion peers in a community of such publics. But there are gradations of social and intellectual skills: it is reasonable to suppose that certain types of people may be more important than others in channeling the flow of talk and in mediating the impact of the formal media, the authoritarian assertion, the demagogic shout. Some people will be more readily and more frequently articulate. Some will carry greater weight than others. I will not call these "opinion leaders" for that term has been used in a quite different sense than I intend here.[16] I shall call them simply informal leaders. They are the people who are willing to stand up and be counted, and who, while standing up, can say something that is listened to.

The existence of these informal leaders is one major reason why opinion is not subject to the overweening dominance of the structure of power and its mass media. For they rally those who by their informal discussions manufacture opinion. They are the radiant points, the foci of the primary public. This primary public is at times a resister of media and of their pressure upon the individual. If there is any socially organized intelligence that is free to answer back, and to give support to those who might answer back, it must somehow be this primary public. Now insofar as such circles exist, the effective strength of any formal medium lies in its acceptance by these informal circles and their unofficial leaders. And the same is true of liberal education.

The job of the college for adults, I should think, would be to try to get into touch with such informal leaders. For it is around them that real publics could develop. If they could be encouraged to look upon the adult college as a place in which to experience an expansion of their own social skills and public sensibilities they would, I am sure, become prime referral agencies; they could become your liaison with the various publics of your community. With them and through them you could strengthen and help animate such publics, and then you could set free in many of its members the process of self-education.

To bring such people out, to help develop them into a community, you must surround your students with models of straightforward conduct, clarified character, and open reasonableness, for I believe it is in the hope of seeing such models that many serious people go to lectures rather than more conveniently reading books. If there are not such men and women on your faculties, you will not attract those who are potential rallying points for the genuine liberal public. In the end, all talk of liberal education, of personnel and curriculum and programming and the rest of it, is nonsense if you do not have such men and women on your faculties. For in the end, liberal education is the result of the liberating and self-sustaining touch of such people.

And their existence in a community as a creative minority is, in the end, the only force that might prevail against the ascendancy of the mass society, and all the men and apparatus that make for it. For in the end, it is around them and through them that liberated and liberating publics come to articulate form and democratic action.

III

I have not yet discussed the relation of the school with other organizations in the metropolitan community, the third point of importance to the Center. It is a complicated issue that I cannot adequately cover in the time available. Let me say only that I doubt that education, for adults or for adolescents, is the strategic factor in the building of a democratic polity. I think it is in the picture and must be, but given its present personnel and administration, and its generally powerless position among other politically relevant organizations, it cannot and will not get the job done. Only if it were to become the framework within which more general movements that were under way— movements with more direct political relevance—were going on, only then would it have the chance to take the place in American political life that it ought to. Only then could it in fact do fully what I have suggested it ought nevertheless to try now to do. For men and women cannot develop and use their highest potentiality in and through educational institutions: they can do that only within and through all of their institutions. And educational work cannot be the sole preparation for such a humane and political life; it can only be part of it, helping it, to be sure, once it is part of the general movement of American civilization.

In the meantime, in the absence of such movements, we cannot dodge the fact that to the extent that the adult college is effective, it is going to be political; its students are going to try to influence decisions of power.

If there were parties or movements that were related to ideas and within which ideas of social life were truly debated and connected with real personal troubles; and if these movements had a chance to win or to influence power— then there might be less public need of colleges for adults. Or if they did exist, it would be within these movements.

But in the absence of such moving publics, these schools ought to become the framework within which such publics exist, at least in their inchoate beginnings, and by which their discussions are fed and sustained. But to do so, they are going to have to get into trouble. For publics that really want to know the realities of their community and nation and world are, by that determining fact, politically radical. Politics as we know it today often rests upon myths and lies and crackpot notions; and many policies, debated and undebated, assume inadequate and misleading definitions of reality. When such myth and hokum prevail, those who are out to find the truth are bound to be upsetting. This is the role of mind, of intellect, of reason, of ideas: to define reality adequately and in a publicly relevant way. The role of education, especially of education for adults, is to build and sustain publics that will "go for," and develop, and live with, and act upon, adequate definitions of reality.

Notes

1. At one extreme on the scale of communication two people talk personally with one another; at the other extreme, one spokesman talks impersonally through a communications net to millions of hearers and viewers. In between these two extremes, there are assemblages and political rallies, parliamentary sessions, law court debates, small discussion circles dominated by one man, open discussion circles with talk moving freely back and forth among fifty people, and so on.

2. Three conditions set the organization of communication: first, technical conditions of the means of communication, in imposing a lower ratio of speakers to listeners, may obviate the possibility of freely answering back. Second, informal rules, resting upon conventional sanction and upon the informal structure of opinion leadership, may govern who can speak, when, and for how long. Such rules may or may not be in congruence with, third, formal rules, with

institutional sanction, which govern the communication process. In the extreme case, we may conceive of an absolute monopoly of communication to pacified media groups whose members cannot answer back even "in private." At the opposite extreme, the conditions may allow and the rules may uphold the wide and symmetrical formation of opinion.

3. This structure may be such as to limit decisively this capacity, or it may allow or even invite it. The structure may confine it to local areas or enlarge its area of opportunity; may make it intermittent or more or less continuous.

4. At one extreme, no agent of the formal system of authority moves among the autonomous public. At the other extreme, the public becomes a mass terrorized into uniformity by the infiltration of informers and the universalization of suspicion. One thinks of the late Nazi street and block system, the 18th century Japanese kumi, the Soviet cell structure. In the end, the formal structure of power coincides, as it were, with the informal ebb and flow of influence by discussion, which is thus killed off.

5. I shall not here consider a type of "public" which might be called *conventional consensus,* and which is a feature of traditional societies in which there is no idea of public opinion as it has arisen in the modern, western world.

6. At the same time—and also because of the metropolitan segregation and distraction, which I shall discuss in a moment—the individual becomes more dependent upon the means of mass communication for his view of the structure as a whole.

7. Well might E. H. Carr conclude: "To speak today of the defense of democracy as if we were defending something which we knew and had possessed for many decades or many centuries is self-deception and sham–mass democracy is a new phenomenon—a creation of the last half-century—which it is inappropriate and misleading to consider in terms of the philosophy of Locke or of the liberal democracy of the nineteenth century. We should be nearer the mark, and should have a far more convincing slogan, if we spoke of the need, not to defend democracy, but to create it." *The New Society,* pp. 75–76.

8. In Cooley's optimistic view, written before radio and movies, the formal media are understood as simply multiplying the scope and pace of popular discussion. Modern conditions, he writes, "enlarge indefinitely the competition of ideas, and whatever has owed its persistence merely to lack of comparison is likely to go, for that which is really congenial to the choosing mind will be all the more cherished and increased." Still excited by the breakup of local, conventional consensus, he sees the means of communication as furthering the conversational dynamic of classic democracy and with it the growth of rational and free individuality. *Social Organization,* p. 93; see Chapter IX.

9. Cf. Mills, *White Collar* (New York: Oxford University Press, 1951). Roughly, in the last two generations, as proportions of the middle classes as a whole, the old middle class has declined from 85 to 44 per cent; the new middle class has risen from 15 to 56 per cent. See pp. 63 ff.

10. C. Wright Mills, "Small Business and Civic Welfare," Senate Document No. 135, 79th Congress, 2nd Session, Washington, 1946.

11. See, e.g., W. H. Whyte, Jr., *Is Anybody Listening?* (New York: Simon & Schuster, 1952).

12. Brochure, from the Center, undated.

13. *Cf.* C. Wright Mills, "Work Milieu and Social Structure," *Proceedings,* 1954, of Mental Health Society of Northern California.

14. I agree with A. E. Bestor, who writes that "if the schools are doing their job, we should expect educators to point to the significant and indisputable achievement in raising the intellectual level of the nation—measured perhaps by larger per capita circulation of books and serious magazines, by definitely improved taste in movies and radio programs, by higher standards of political debate, by increased respect for freedom of speech and of thought, by marked decline in such evidences of mental retardation as the incessant reading of comic books by adults." *Educational Wastelands* (Univ. of Ill., 1953), p. 7.

15. I do not believe in discussion for its own sake, or for its therapeutic effect alone, at least not in school. If people have not yet earned the intellectual right to an opinion they ought in a school to be made to shut up long enough to start earning the right.

16. Paul Lazarsfeld et al., *The People's Choice.*

ELEVEN ⦙ On Knowledge and Power

B EFORE "ON KNOWLEDGE AND POWER" was published in *Dissent,*
it was a speech on Dean's Day, part of a series of lectures organized by the
Alumni Association of Columbia College and the Faculty of Columbia
College, on March 20, 1954. Mills's lecture attracted 250 people, winning
special notice in a *New York Times* report. He presented a modified version in
February 1955 to a joint meeting of the William A. White and Harry S.
Sullivan Societies, in New York.

<hr>

I

During the last few years I have often thought that American intellectuals are
now rather deeply involved in what Freud once called "the miscarriage of
American civilization." I do not know exactly what he meant by the phrase,
although I suppose he intended to contrast the eighteenth-century ideals with
which this nation was so hopefully proclaimed with their sorry condition in
twentieth-century America.

Among these values none has been held higher than the grand role of
reason in civilization and in the lives of its civilized members. And none has
been more sullied and distorted by men of power in the mindless years we
have been enduring. Given the caliber of the American elite, and the immorality of accomplishment in terms of which they are selected, perhaps
we should have expected this. But political intellectuals too have been giving up the old ideal of the public relevance of knowledge. Among them

a conservative mood—a mood that is quite appropriate for men living in a political vacuum—has come to prevail.

Perhaps nothing is of more immediate importance, both as cause and as effect of this model, than the rhetorical ascendancy and the intellectual collapse of liberalism: As a proclamation of ideals, classic liberalism, like classical socialism, remains part of the secular tradition of the West. As a *theory* of society, liberalism has become irrelevant, and, in its optative way, misleading, for no revision of liberalism as a theory of the mechanics of modern social change has overcome the trade mark of the nineteenth century that is stamped upon its basic assumptions. As a political *rhetoric*, liberalism's key terms have become the common denominators of the political vocabulary, and hence have been stretched beyond any usefulness as a way of defining issues and stating positions.[1]

As the administrative liberalism of the Thirties has been swallowed up by economic boom and military fright, the noisier political initiative has been seized by a small group of petty conservatives, which on the middle levels of power, has managed to set the tone of public life. Exploiting the American fright of the new international situation for their own purposes, these political primitives have attacked not only the ideas of the New and Fair Deals; they have attacked the history of those administrations, and the biographies of those who took part in them. And they have done so in a manner that reveals clearly the basis upon which their attractive power rests: they have attacked the symbols of status and the figures of established prestige. By their attack upon men and institutions of established status, the noisy right has appealed not at all to the economically discontented, but to the status frustrated.[2] Their push has come from the *nouveau riche*, of small city as well as larger region, and, above all, from the fact of the rankling status resentment felt by these newly prosperous classes who, having achieved considerable wealth during and after World War II, have not received the prestige nor gained the power that they have felt to be their due.

They have brought into dramatic focus the higher immorality as well as the mindlessness of the upper circles of America. On the one hand, we have seen a decayed and frightened liberalism, and on the other hand, the insecure and ruthless fury of political gangsters. A Secretary of the Army, also a man of older family wealth, is told off by upstarts, and in public brawl disgraced by unestablished nihilists. They have brought into focus a new conception of national loyalty, which we came to understand as loyalty to individual gangs who placed themselves above the established legitimations of the state, and invited officers of the U. S. Army to do likewise. They have made plain the central place now achieved in the governmental process by secret police and secret "investigations," to the point where we must now speak of a shadow cabinet based in considerable part upon new ways of power which include the wire tap, the private eye, the widespread use and threat of blackmail. And they have dramatized one political result of the hollowing out and the banalizing of sensibility among a population which for a generation now has been steadily and increasingly subjected to the shrill trivialization of the mass means of entertainment and distraction.

As liberalism sat in these "hearings," liberals became aware, from time to time, of how close they were to the edge of the mindless abyss. The status edifice of bourgeois society was under attack, but since in America there is nothing from the past above that established edifice, and since those of once liberal and left persuasions see nothing in the future below it, they have become terribly frightened by the viciousness of the attack, and their political lives have been narrowed to the sharp edge of defense anxiety.

Post-war liberalism has been organizationally impoverished: the pre-war years of liberalism-in-power devitalized independent liberal groups, drying up their grass roots, making older leaders dependent upon the federal center and not training new leaders round the country. The New Deal left no liberal organization to carry on any liberal programs; rather than a new party, its instrument was a loose coalition inside an old one, which quickly fell apart so far as liberal ideas are concerned. Moreover, in using up, in one way or another, the heritage of liberal ideas, banalizing them as it put them into law, the New Deal turned liberalism into a set of administrative routines to defend rather than a program to fight for.

In their moral fright, post-war liberals have not defended any left-wing or even any militantly liberal position: their defensive posture has, first of all, concerned the civil liberties.

Many of the political intelligentsia have been so busy celebrating formal civil liberties in America, by contrast with their absence from Soviet Communism, that they have often failed to defend them. But more importantly, most have been so busy defending civil liberties that they have had neither the time nor the inclination to use them. "In the old days," Archibald MacLeish has remarked, freedom "was something you used ... [it] has now become something you save—something you put away and protect like your other possessions—like a deed or a bond in a bank."[3]

It is much safer to celebrate civil liberties than to defend them, and it is much safer to defend them as a formal right than to use them in a politically effective way: Even those who would most willingly subvert these liberties, usually do so in their very name. It is easier still to defend someone else's right to have used them years ago than to have something yourself to say *now* and to say it now forcibly. The defense of civil liberties—even of their practice a decade ago—has become the major concern of many liberal and once leftward scholars. All of which is a safe way of diverting intellectual effort from the sphere of political reflection and demand.

The defense posture, secondly, has concerned American Values in general, which, quite rightly it has been feared, the petty right seeks to destroy. Quite unwittingly, I am sure, the U. S. intelligentsia has found itself in the middle of the very nervous center of elite and plebian anxieties about the position of America in the world today. What is at the root of these anxieties is not simply international tension and the terrible, helpless feeling of many that another war is surely in the works. There is also involved in them a specific worry with which many serious-minded Americans are seriously concerned.

The United States is now engaged with other nations, particularly Russia, in a full-scale competition for cultural prestige based on nationality. In this competition, what is at issue is American music and American literature and American art, and, in the somewhat higher meaning than is usually given to that term, the American Way of Life. For what America has got abroad is power; what it has *not* got at home or abroad is cultural prestige. This simple fact has involved those of the new gentility in the curious American celebration, into which much scholarly and intellectual energy now goes. The celebration rests upon the felt need to defend themselves in nationalist terms against the petty right; and it rests upon the need, shared by many spokesmen and statesmen as urgent, to create and to uphold the cultural prestige of America abroad.[4]

The noisy conservatives, of course, have no more won political power than administrative liberals have retained it. While those two camps have been engaged in wordy battle, and while the intellectuals have been embraced by the new conservative gentility, the silent conservatives have assumed political power. Accordingly, in their imbroglio with the noisy right, liberal and once-left forces have, in effect, defended these established conservatives, if only because they have lost any initiative of attack, in fact, lost even any point of effective criticism. The silent conservatives of corporation, army and state have benefited politically and economically and militarily by the antics of the petty right, who have become, often unwittingly, their political shocktroops. And they have ridden into power on all those structural trends set into motion and accelerated by the organization of the nation for seemingly permanent war.

So, in this context of material prosperity, with the noisy little men of the petty right successfully determining the tone and level of public sensibility;

the silent conservatives achieving established power in a mindless victory; with the liberal rhetoric made official, then banalized by widespread and perhaps illicit use; with liberal hope carefully adjusted to mere rhetoric by thirty years of rhetorical victory; with radicalism deflated and radical hope stoned to death by thirty years of defeat—the political intellectuals have been embraced by the conservative mood. Among them there is no demand and no dissent, and no opposition to the monstrous decisions that are being made without deep or widespread debate, in fact with no debate at all. There is no opposition to the undemocratically impudent manner in which policies of high military and civilian authority are simply turned out as facts accomplished. There is no opposition to public mindlessness in all its forms nor to all those forces and men that would further it. But above all—among men of knowledge, there is little or no opposition to the divorce of knowledge from power, of sensibilities from men of power, no opposition to the divorce of mind from reality.

II

Once upon a time, at the beginning of the United States, men of affairs were also men of culture: to a considerable extent the elite of power and the elite of culture coincided, and where they did not coincide as persons they often overlapped as circles. Within the compass of a knowledgeable and effective public, knowledge and power were in effective touch; and, more than that, this classic public also decided much that was decided.

"Nothing is more revealing," James Reston has written, "than to read the debate in the House of Representatives in the Eighteen Thirties on Greece's fight with Turkey for independence and the Greek-Turkish debate in the Congress in 1947. The first is dignified and eloquent, the argument marching from principle through illustration to conclusion; the second is a dreary garble of debating points, full of irrelevancies and bad history."[5] George Washington in 1783 read Voltaire's "Letters" and Locke's "On Human Understanding"; Eisenhower, two hundred years later, read cowboy tales and detective stories.[6] For such men as now typically arrive in the higher political, economic and military circles, the briefing and the memorandum seem to have pretty well replaced not only the serious books, but the newspapers as well. This is, perhaps, as it must be, given the immorality of accomplishment, but what is somewhat disconcerting about it is that these men are below the level on which they might feel a little bit ashamed of the uncultivated level of their relaxation and of their mental fare, and that no intellectual public, by its reactions, tries to educate them to such uneasiness.

By the middle of the twentieth century, the American elite have become an entirely different breed of men from those who could on any reasonable grounds be considered a cultural elite, or even for that matter, cultivated men of sensibility. Knowledge and power are not truly united inside the ruling circles; and when men of knowledge do come to a point of contact with the circles of powerful men, they come not as peers but as hired men. The elite of power, wealth and celebrity are not of the elite of culture, knowledge and sensibility. Moreover, they are not in contact with it, although the banalized and ostentatious fringes of the two worlds do overlap in the world of the celebrity.

Most men are encouraged to assume that, in general, the most powerful and the wealthiest are also the most knowledgeable or, as they might say, the smartest. Such ideas are propped up by many little slogans about those who "teach because they can't *do*," and about "if you're so smart, why aren't you rich?" But all that such wisecracks mean is that those who use them assume that power and wealth are sovereign values for all men and especially for men "who are smart." They assume also that knowledge always pays off in such ways, or surely ought to, and that the test of genuine knowledge is just such pay-offs. The powerful and the wealthy *must* be the men of most knowledge; otherwise how could they be where they are? But to say that those who succeed to power must be "smart," is to say that power *is* knowledge. To say that those who succeed to wealth must be smart, is to say that wealth *is* knowledge.

These assumptions do reveal something that is true: that ordinary men, even today, are prone to explain and to justify power and wealth in terms of knowledge or ability. Such assumptions also reveal something of what has happened to the kind of experience that knowledge has come to be. Knowledge is no longer widely felt as an ideal; it is seen as an instrument of power and wealth, and also, of course, as an ornament in conversation, a tid-bit in a quiz program.

What knowledge does to a man (in clarifying what he is, and setting it free)—that is the personal ideal of knowledge. What knowledge does to a civilization (in revealing its human meaning, and setting it free)—that is the social ideal of knowledge. But today, the personal *and* the social ideals of knowledge have coincided in what knowledge does *for* the smart guy: it gets him ahead; and for the wise nation: it lends cultural prestige, haloing power with authority.

Knowledge seldom lends power to the man of knowledge. But the supposed, and secret, knowledge of some men-on-the-powerful-make, and their very free use thereof, has consequence for other men who have not the power of defense. Knowledge, of course, is neither good nor bad, nor is its use good or bad. "Bad men increase in knowledge as fast as good men," John Adams wrote, "and science, arts, taste, sense and letters, are employed for the purpose of injustice as well as for virtue." That was in 1790; today we have good reason to know that it is so.

The problem of knowledge and power is, and always has been, the problem of the relation of men of knowledge with men of power. Suppose we were to select the one hundred most powerful men, from all fields of power, in America today and line them up. And then, suppose we selected the one hundred most knowledgeable men, from all fields of social knowledge, and lined them up. How many men would be in *both* our line-ups? Of course our selection would depend upon what we mean by power and what we mean by knowledge—especially what we mean by knowledge. But, if we mean what the words seem to mean, surely we would find few if any men in America today who were in both groups, and surely we could find many more at the time this nation was founded than we could find today. For, in the eighteenth century, even in this colonial outpost, men of power pursued learning, and men of learning were often in positions of power. In these respects we have, I believe, suffered grievous decline.[7]

There is little union in the same persons of knowledge and power; but persons of power do surround themselves with men of some knowledge, or at least with men who are experienced in shrewd dealings. The man of knowledge has not become a philosopher king; but he has often become a consultant, and moreover a consultant to a man who is neither king-like nor philosophical. It is not natural in the course of their careers for men of knowledge to meet with those of power. The links between university and government are weak, and when they do occur, the man of knowledge appears as an "expert" which usually means as a hired technician. Like most others in this society, the man of knowledge is himself dependent for his livelihood upon the job, which nowadays is a prime sanction of thought control. Where getting ahead requires the good opinions of more powerful others, their judgments become prime objects of concern. Accordingly, in so far as intellectuals serve power directly—in a job hierarchy—they often do so unfreely.

The characteristic member of the higher circles today is an intellectual mediocrity, sometimes a conscientious one, but still a mediocrity. His intelligence is revealed only by his occasional realization that he is not up to the decisions he sometimes feels called upon to confront. But usually he keeps such feelings private, his public utterances being pious and sentimental, grim and brave, cheerful and empty in their universal generality. He is open only to abbreviated and vulgarized, pre-digested and slanted ideas. He is a commander of the age of the memo and the briefing. He is briefed, but not for longer than one page; he talks on the phone, rather than writes letters or holds conversations.

By the mindlessness and mediocrity of men of affairs, I do not, of course, mean that these men are not sometimes intelligent men, although that is by no means automatically the case. It is not, however, primarily a matter of the distribution of "intelligence"—as if intelligence were a homogeneous something of which there may be more or less. It is rather a matter of the quality of mind, a quality which requires the evaluation of substantive rationality as the key value in a man's life and character and conduct. That evaluation is what is lacking from the American power elite. In its place there is "weight" and "judgment" which count for much more in their celebrated success than any subtlety of mind or force of intellect.

All around, just below the weighty man of affairs, are his technical lieutenants of power who have been assigned the role of knowledge and even of speech: his public relations man, his ghost, his administrative assistants, his secretaries. And do not forget The Committee. With the increased means of decision, there is a crisis of understanding among the political directorate of the United States, and accordingly, there is often a commanding indecision.

The lack of knowledge as an experience and as a criterion among the elite ties in with the malign ascendancy of the expert, not only as fact but as a defense against public discourse and debate. When questioned recently about a criticism of defense policies made by the leader of the opposition party, the Secretary of Defense replied, "Do you think he is an expert in the matter?" When pressed further by reporters he asserted that the "military chiefs think it is sound, and I think it is sound," and later, when asked about specific cases, added: "In some cases, all you can do is ask the Lord."[8] With such a large role so arrogantly given to God, to experts, and to Mr. Wilson, what room is there for political leadership? Much less for public debate of what is after all every bit as much a political and a moral as a military issue?

Beyond the lack of intellectual cultivation by political personnel and advisory circles, the absence of publicly relevant minds has come to mean that powerful decisions and important policies are not made in such a way as to be justified and attacked, in short, debated in any intellectual form. Moreover, the attempt to so justify them is often not even made. Public relations displace reasoned argument; manipulation and undebated decisions of power replace democratic authority. More and more, as administration has replaced politics, decisions of importance do not carry even the panoply of reasonable discussion in public, but are made by God, by experts, and by men like Mr. Wilson.

And more and more the area of the official secret expands, as well as the area of the secret listening in on those who might divulge in public what the public, not being composed of experts with Q clearance, is not to know. The entire series of decisions concerning the production and the use of atomic weaponry has been made without any genuine public debate, and the facts needed to engage in that debate intelligently have been officially hidden, distorted, and lied about. As the decisions become more fateful, not only for Americans but literally for mankind, the sources of information are closed up, and the relevant facts needed for decision, and even of the decisions made, are, as politically convenient "official secrets," withheld from the heavily laden channels of information.

In the meantime, in those channels, political rhetoric continues to slide lower and lower down the scale of cultivation and sensibility. The height of such mindless communications to masses, or what are thought to be masses, is the commercial propaganda for toothpaste and soap and cigarettes and automobiles. It is to such things, or rather to Their Names, that this society sings its loudest praises most frequently. What is important about this is that by implication and omission, by emphasis and sometimes by flat statement, this astounding volume of propaganda for commodities is often untruthful and misleading; and is addressed more often to the belly or to the groin than to the head or to the heart. And the point to be made about this is that public communications from those who make powerful decisions or who would have us vote them into such decision-making places, competes with it, and more and more takes on those qualities of mindlessness and myth which commercial propaganda or advertising have come to exemplify.

In America today, men of affairs are not so much dogmatic as they are mindless. For dogma has usually meant some more or less elaborated justification of ideas and values, and thus has had some features (however inflexible and closed) of mind, of intellect, of reason. Nowadays what we are up against is precisely the absence of mind of any sort as a public force; what we are up against is a lack of interest in and a fear of knowledge that might have liberating public relevance. And what this makes possible is the prevalence of the kindergarten chatter, as well as decisions having no rational justification which the intellect could confront and engage in debate.

It is not the barbarous irrationality of uncouth, dour Senators that is the American danger; it is the respected judgments of Secretaries of State, the earnest platitudes of Presidents, the fearful self-righteousness of sincere young American politicians from sunny California, that is the main danger. For these men have replaced mind by the platitude, and the dogmas by which they are legitimated are so widely accepted that no counter-balance of mind prevails against them. Such men as these are crackpot realists, who, in the name of realism have constructed a paranoid reality all their own and in the name of practicality have projected a utopian image of capitalism. They have replaced the responsible interpretation of events by the disguise of meaning in a maze of public relations, respect for public debate by unshrewd notions of psychological warfare, intellectual ability by the agility of the sound and mediocre judgment, and the capacity to elaborate alternatives and to gauge their consequences by the executive stance.

III

In our time, all forms of public mindlessness must expropriate the individual mind, and we now know that this is an entirely possible procedure.[9] We also know that ideas, beliefs, images—symbols in short—stand between men and the wider realities of their time, and that accordingly those who professionally create, destroy, elaborate these symbols are very much involved in all literate men's very images of reality. For now, of course, the live experience of men falls far short of the objects of their belief and action, and the maintenance of adequate definitions of reality is by no means an automatic process, if indeed it ever was. Today that maintenance requires intellectuals of quite some skill and persistence, for much reality is now officially defined by those who hold power.

As a type of social man, the intellectual does not have any one political direction, but the work of any man of knowledge, if he is the genuine article, does have a distinct kind of political relevance: his politics, in the first instance, are the politics of truth, for his job is the maintenance of an adequate definition of reality. In so far as he is politically adroit, the main tenet of his politics is to find out as much of the truth as he can, and to tell it to the right people, at the right time, and in the right way. Or, stated negatively: to deny publicly what he knows to be false, whenever it appears in the assertions of no matter whom; and whether it be a direct lie or a lie by omission, whether it be by virtue of official secret or an honest error. The intellectual ought to be the moral conscience of his society, at least with reference to the value of truth, for in the defining instance, that is his politics. And he ought also to be a man absorbed in the attempt to know what is real and what is unreal.

Power and authority involve the actual making of *decisions*. They also involve the *legitimation* of the power and of the decisions by means of doctrine, and they usually involve the pomp and the halo, the *representations* of the powerful.[10] It is connection with the legitimations and the representations of power and decision that the intellectual—as well as the artist—becomes politically relevant.

Intellectual work is related to power in numerous ways, among them these: with ideas one can uphold or justify power, attempting to transform it into legitimate authority; with ideas one can also debunk authority, attempting to reduce it to mere power, to discredit it as arbitrary or as unjust. With ideas one can conceal or expose the holders of power. And with ideas of more hypnotic though frivolous shape, one can divert attention from problems of power and authority and social reality in general.

So the Romantic poets symbolize the French Revolution to an English public and elaborate one strain of its doctrinal legitimation; so Virgil as a member of the Roman ruling class writes his *Georgics*; so John Reed reports to America the early phase of Bolshevism; so Rousseau legitimates the French Revolution, Milton the regime of Cromwell, Marx—in vulgarized form—the Russian revolution.

And so, in an intellectually petty way, do the U. S. intellectuals now embraced by the conservative mood—whether they know it or not—serve to legitimate the mindless image of the American ascendancy abroad, and the victory of the silent conservatives at home. And more important than that: by the work they do not do they uphold the official definitions of reality, and, by the work they do, even elaborate it.

Whatever else the intellectual may be, surely he is among those who ask serious questions, and, if he is a political intellectual, he asks his questions of those with power. If you ask to what the intellectual belongs, you must answer that he belongs first of all to that minority which has carried on the big discourse of the rational mind, the big discourse that has been going on—or off and on—since western society began some two thousand years ago in the small communities of Athens and Jerusalem.[11] This big discourse is not a vague thing to which to belong—even if as lesser participants—and it is the beginning of any sense of belonging that is worthwhile, and it is the key to the only kind of belonging that free men in our time might have. But if we would belong to it, we ought to try to live up to what it demands of us. What it demand of us, first of all, is that we maintain our sense of it. And, just now, at this point in human history, that is quite difficult.

IV

The democratic man assumes the existence of a public, and in his rhetoric asserts that this public is the very seat of sovereignty. We object to Mr. Wilson, with his God and his Experts, because in his assertion he explicitly denies two things needed in a democracy: articulate and knowledgeable publics, and political leaders who if not men of reason are at least reasonably responsible to such knowledgeable publics as exist. Only where publics and leaders are responsive and responsible, are human affairs in democratic order, and only when knowledge has public relevance is this order possible. Only when mind has an autonomous basis, independent of power, but powerfully related to it, can it exert its force in the shaping of human affairs. Such a position is democratically possible only when there exists a free and knowledgeable public, to which men of knowledge may address themselves, and to which men of power are truly responsible. Such a public and such men— either of power or of knowledge, do not now prevail, and accordingly, knowledge does not now have democratic relevance in America.

Notes

1. See Mills, "Liberal Values in the Modern World," *Anvil and Student Partisan*, Winter 1952.
2. Although this interpretation is now widely published, Paul Sweezy's and Leo Huberman's original article remains the most forthright account of it: "The Roots and Prospects of McCarthyism," *Monthly Review*, January 1954.
3. *Atlantic Monthly*, August 1949.
4. Examples of The American Celebration are embarrassingly available. Unfortunately no one of them is really worth examining in detail: In order that the sort of thing I have in mind may be clear, by all means see Jacques Barzun, *God's Country and Mine* (Boston: Little Brown, 1954). Mr. Barzun believes that "the way to see America is from a lower berth about two in the morning," and so far as I can tell from his book, he really means it. For a less flamboyant example, done in at least dim daylight, see Daniel J. Boorstin, *The Genius of American Politics* (Chicago: University of Chicago Press, 1953); for a scatter of celebrants, see *America and The Intellectuals* (New York: PR series, Number Four, 1953).
5. *The New York Times*, January 31, 1954, editorial page.
6. *The New York Times Book Review*, August 23, 1953.
7. In *Perspectives, USA*, No. 3, Mr. Lionel Trilling has written optimistically of "new intellectual classes," and has even referred to the Luce publications as samples of high "intellectual talent." What lends his view its optimistic tone, I believe, is less the rise of any new intellectual classes than (1) old intellectual

groups becoming a little prosperous, even successful, in a minor way, on American terms, and, (2) of course, the confusion of knowledge as a goal with knowledge as a mere technique and instrument. For an informed account of new cultural strata by a brilliantly self-conscious insider, see Louis Kronenberger, *Company Manners* (Indianapolis: Bobbs-Merrill, 1954).

8. Charles E. Wilson. Cf. *The New York Times*, March 10, 1954, p. 1.

9. See Czeslaw Milosz, *The Captive Mind* (New York: Knopf, 1953), which is surely one of the great documents of our time.

10. Cf. Gerth and Mills, *Character and Social Structure* (New York: Harcourt Brace, 1953), pp. 413 ff. for a further discussion of these three aspects of authority.

11. Joseph Wood Krutch, *The Measure of Man* (Indianapolis: Bobbs-Merrill, 1954).

The Power Elite
Comment on Criticism

I DO NOT MIND telling you (altho I hope you will not mention it to anyone) that 'criticisms' of *The Power Elite* hit me very hard indeed," Mills wrote to his friend Bill Miller on February 5, 1957. "I suppose the whole thing coincided with a lot of self-criticism I've been giving myself and for a while I damn near lost my nerve for writing. It is hard to carry a load as big as Luther's when damn near all the world tells you it's only a bag of peanuts."

This reply to critics was published in the Winter 1957 issue of *Dissent*.

———

Dear Friends,

I hope you will forgive me if—being more interested in criticism than in critics—I don't mention names but rather bring up points. I want briefly to comment on some of the criticism of *The Power Elite* not because I believe the book invulnerable to criticism nor because I want to take a crack at people who have taken one at me, but because I think the angry character of many of the reviews suggests political and moral questions that are of intellectual interest.

This anger, I believe, is due to the fact that whether it is generally right or generally wrong, the book is taken as a blow at the smooth certainties and agreeable formulas that now make up the content of liberalism. This liberalism now determines the standard view of American civilization; most reviewers are liberals of one sort or another, or at least think of themselves as such. But since they are often intelligent as well, their liberalism is rather insecure. Therefore they are easily upset. Therefore they become very angry.

Therefore, they want to wiggle out of any arguments about the liberal platitudes and qualifications to which they cling.

What is interesting is the way they wiggle.

I

One journal of liberal opinion, rather than review the book, runs a piece containing one thought: professors who read *White Collar* "liked every part of it except the one about professors." They thought this part "only half true, a kind of caricature." So, concludes the reviewer, perhaps the pictures in *The Power Elite* of all the other groups—bureaucrats and politicians and millionaires—are also caricatures.

Of course they are. *All* concepts are "caricatures." They invite attention to selected features of some object. The question is to what extent they specify important features and to what extent they obfuscate them. This critic suggests that the test of social conceptions is whether or not those to whom they refer find them pleasantly in line with their own self-image. He suggests further that *they* should know best since it is "one kind of life that they [know] about." It is difficult to think of a more misleading test. I've never studied any group that had an adequate view of its own social position. But whether that is always true or not, merely to assume the contrary, is to assume a degree of rational self-consciousness and self-knowledge that not even eighteenth-century psychologists would allow.

II

There's one question most liberal reviewers find quite unanswerable: If the American elite is all this bad, "how come it hangs together—and, despite defects, provides people with the highest content of economic, esthetic and intellectual opportunity yet offered a population block of 165 million?"

I can't really conceive, as the question assumes, that the American elite is the *author* of all the happy values of American civilization. Such an assumption makes them much more omnipotent than I've ever thought them to be. But many reviewers seem really to believe, and their question certainly implies, that American prosperity may be taken as proof of the virtues of the contemporary elite.

In the same vein one might ask: If the Soviet elite are such villains as all good Americans know them to be, how come in a mere thirty years they've raised an illiterate, backward, starving peasant mass into the biggest nation in the world, created one of the world's two foremost industrial plants, demonstrated for the first time in human history that classic capitalism is only one of the ways to industrialize, etc.?

In brief: such critics have swallowed the vulgar notion that the "success" of a nation, however defined, is the basis on which to judge that nation's elite. I think to state the assumption is to indicate its inadequacy.

III

To blunt the edge of an argument, contemporary critics often try to assimilate it to old stereotypes—the common coin of the lazier reviewer's mint.

To say "old stuff" or "new stuff" is equally irrelevant—unless you get very specific, as my critics in this line have not done. The argument ("It's all old stuff") equates "old" with "untrue." I don't of course accept that fashionable and easy equation. But apart from that, if this is all old stuff, where is the new stuff? If *The Power Elite* is about some world that's now long past, where is the image of the 1950's that stands in such irrefutable contrast? There isn't any documented image; what such reviewers are doing is wallowing in that intellectual climate, now so fashionable, which is based solely upon the fact of material prosperity. Given that, they can't conceive of *any* critical statement of a modern society being credible. That my book isn't primarily about prosperity and poverty but about power and status makes no difference to them. Having come of age in a time when poverty was the key problem, they can't really recognize any other.

The more interesting question underneath the charge of "old stuff" is how best to study trends. Quite deliberately, of course, I have stated in *The Power Elite* an "extreme position"—which means that in order to make matters clear I try to focus on each trend just a little ahead of where it now is, and more importantly, that I try to see all the trend at once, as part of a total structure. It is much easier for the liberal to acknowledge one trend at a time, keeping them scattered as it were, than to make the effort to see them altogether. To the literary empiricist, writing his balanced little essay, first on this and then on that, any attempt to see the whole is "extremism." Yet there is truth in one reviewer's assertion that I tend to confuse prediction with description. These two, however, are not to be sharply separated, and they are not the only ways of looking at trends. One can examine trends in an effort to answer the question: "Where are we going?"—which is of course what I have tried to do. In doing so I have tried to study history rather than to retreat into it; to pay attention to present trends without being merely journalistic; to gauge the future of these trends without being prophetic. All this is very hard to do. You've got to remember that you are dealing with historic materials; that they do change very fast; that there are counter-trends. And you've always got to balance the precision of knife-edge description with the generality needed to bring out their meaning for your time. But above all, you've got to see the several major trends together—structurally, rather than as a mere scatter of happenings adding up to nothing new, in fact not adding up at all.

IV

"The judgment to be made of Mills," one scientific reviewer writes "is never that what he says is true but unimportant, as can be said for much of the reporting in the social sciences; rather what he says is clearly important but not unquestionably valid."

Of course the argument of *The Power Elite* is not "unquestionably valid." In the language of the social studies, it's an elaborated hypothesis, anchored, I believe, at key points to acknowledged fact. There is no other way to write now, as a social student, about such large topics.

In the social studies today there are as many know-nothings who refuse to say anything, or at least really to believe anything, about modern society unless it has been through the fine little mill of The Statistical Ritual. It's usual to say that what they produce is true but unimportant. I don't think I agree with that: more and more I wonder how true it is. If you have ever seriously studied, as I have, for a year or two some thousand hour-long interviews, carefully coded and punched, you'll have begun to see how very malleable these thousands of bits of fact really are. Moreover, increasingly I come to feel that it is very important when some of the best minds among us spend their lives studying trivialities because the methods to which they are dogmatically committed don't allow them to study anything else. Much of this work, I am convinced, has become the mere following of a ritual—which happens to have gained commercial and foundation value—rather than, in the words of The Social Scientist, any "commitment to the hard [why hard?] demands of scientific social analysis."

On the other hand, there are many literary and journalistic people who distribute larger images of the social structure in which we live. By refusing to comment on these images, much less to take them in hand, the pseudo-scientific know-nothings allow, as it were, these literary types to create and to sustain all the images that guide and all the myths that obfuscate—as the case may be—our view of social reality.

That's one feature of the intellectual situation in which I think I—along of course with others—have been trying to write. We've tried to use what we found useful of newer research techniques, but we've refused to give up the larger problems because of any initial dogma about method. Above all, we've refused to become silly about transferring the models of physical and mathematical proof into the social studies. We've kept the *problem*, whatever it is, foremost in mind and we've felt, I suppose, as working researchers rather than self-appointed Statesmen of Research, that we'd just have to work out the best methods we could as we went along trying to solve the problem. The social studies, I am convinced, will not be advanced by pontifical dogma about method or pretentious cowardice about Social Science. It will go forward out of highly self-conscious work on real problems.

V

But, then, half a dozen reviewers exclaim: "In this book, you take it upon yourself to *judge*; now really, should a sociologist judge?"

The answer is: "Does he have any choice?" If he spends his intellectual force on the petty details of elections or boy gangs or what not, he is of course as a man of intellect making himself irrelevant to the political conflicts and forces of his time. But he is also, in a tacit way and in effect, "accepting" the whole framework of the society. Only he who accepts the basic structure of his society—and is not aware of his acceptance—can turn his back on the problem of moral judgment. Now I do *not* merely assume that structure. In fact, it is my job to make it explicit and to study it as a whole. *That* is my major judgment. Because there are so many myths about American society, merely to describe it neutrally is considered, in the words of one reviewer, a "savage naturalism." Of course, I have elected to do more than that. Such judgments as I wish to make I try to make explicitly. It would not, as you know, be difficult to hide them; there's a very pretty apparatus at hand for that: the jargon of modern social science, especially sociology. (You don't write "authority," for example, which has a clean, hard edge; you write "imperative coordination," which is neutral—and Scientific too.)

Whether he wants it or not, anyone today who spends his life studying society and publishing the results is acting politically. The question is whether you face that and make up your own mind or whether you conceal it from yourself and drift morally. Most social scientists are today uneasily liberal. They conform to the prevailing tone of liberal American politics and the accompanying fear of any passionate commitment. *This*, and not "scientific objectivity" is what is really wanted by those who complain about "value judgments."

VI

Teaching, by the way, I do not regard as altogether in the same case as writing. When you publish a book it becomes a public property; your only responsibility to your reading public is to make it as good a book as you can, and you are the sole judge of that. But you have further responsibilities when you are teaching. To some extent your students are a captive audience, and to some extent they are dependent upon you. If you are worth a damn as a teacher, you are something of a model to them. Your job—and it is your prime job—is to reveal to them just how a supposedly self-disciplined mind works. The art of teaching is the art of thinking out loud. In a book you are trying to persuade others of the result of your thinking; in a classroom you are trying to show others how one man thinks—and at the same time reveal what a fine feeling you get when you do it well. You ought then, it seems to me, to make very, very explicit the assumptions, the facts, the methods, the judgments. You ought not to hold back anything, but you ought to take it very slowly and at all times and repeatedly make clear what the full range of moral alternatives [is] before you give your own choice. To write that way would be enormously dull, and impossibly self-conscious. That's one reason why very successful lectures don't usually print well.

VII

What I suppose has to be called "highbrow" criticism tends to pay less attention to the content of a book than to its publication as an event and a stratagem. As for content, I must say such "highbrow" reviews of *The Power Elite* as I've seen seem in rather complete agreement with it. They don't question the general idea I've constructed; they restate and accept my view of the newer relations of property and the state; they see quite clearly that the intellectual target of my attack is the classic liberal image of modern American society.

Basic agreement, however, is often hidden by the surface tone of the "highbrow" review. Considering the book as an event, one such reviewer makes the point that (like all other products) radical criticism in America can become a "saleable commodity." Of course. And so can reviewers' criticism of radical criticism. The only sure-fire way to avoid this situation is silence or suicide. Considering the book as political strategy, they make the point that it is negative in that it offers no "saving myth." Quite true. But then they call this "posturing." I don't quite see why, especially since they seem to agree with my judgment of the intellectual and moral character of the power elite as well as my statement of the mass society. The "highbrow" style, it seems to me, often consists merely of telling the revolutionaries they are not revolutionary enough, the theologians they aren't theologically pure, the Freudians that they disregard The Founder's biases. Perhaps the Craving for Authenticity stands in place of, or at least in the way of, a passion to know what's what. Writing for me has always been, first of all, an effort to state what is so, as I see it. When there's no other public that might accept the ideas *and* act upon them with consequence, one still has to go ahead and try to say what's so. That's all one can usefully say of the weary complaint about possible misuse of radical criticism.

VIII

But the salient point about so much "highbrow" reviewing is that in it presentation simply runs away with belief. Such reviewers ignore their own agreement or disagreement with the book at hand and adopt a tone. It is a tone which assumes superior accomplishment without ever revealing it; it is any attempt to turn all questions, in particular the question of truth, into matters of taste. In such magazines as *Partisan Review* one finds writers who have made a real thing out of such pretension; in fact, it has become the very token of what is sometimes called "brilliant." In the post-war period it has gone very well with the ostentatious boredom with political questions of larger scope—which is to say, with conservatism.

In "highbrow" reviews of *The Power Elite* this posture doesn't come off because—for one thing—the "highbrows" try to stand outside or above the book, but in fact they have no place to stand. The tone they imitate from one another is therefore obviously a mere surface manner rather than intrinsic to some point of view that is truly their own. The key to this posture is simply a lack of moral confidence. The way to overcome it is also clear: to take on a substantive job of work, one that forces you to deal imaginatively with a mass of facts. Were they to do that, such critics might come to see more of the world they live in, as well as in the work of writers they read, than "strategies of presentation." In the meantime, in striving to be intellectually fastidious, they only succeed in displaying moral weakness.

IX

Contemporary reviewers make wide use of the *ad hominem* argument: anyway, it's all resentment, these shrewd psychologists conclude—the implication being that therefore it's all a little personal show and nothing else.

Now, I take "resentment" to mean that I want to be like somebody else but can't be, so I dislike them. This is of course the expected imputation to make of any critical book about the higher circles. It is also cheap and easy in that it merely *assumes* that the book's author shares the values of those about whom he writes and therefore wants them for himself.

So far as the social fact of their existence and its consequence goes, my liking or disliking the power elite, whether it shows in the book or not, is altogether irrelevant. That's the foremost point. For it means that were I just dying to become a millionaire, this would not in itself effect the truth or falsity of what I've written about the millionaires in American society.

But I certainly am not aware of any desire to be more like the rich in the sense that I *am* sometimes aware of wanting to be more like some of the crack mechanics I know. Of course, although it means something to me, the comparison is a little unreal. I'm a third type of man—and on the whole glad to be such.

X

One type of reasonable liberal broadly accepts my "account of who holds the power in American society" but complains that I really don't say "*what* the elite does with its power..." This, of course, is to ask for a full-scale American history of our times, military, economic and political. And this I clearly have not done nor attempted to do in *The Power Elite*. An account of the power elite, in one volume at least, must work from examples. Seemingly realizing this, such reviewers then object to the examples I use as "...the most obvious ones conceivable." They are of course the big events of our time which have involved major decisions: Hiroshima, Korea, etc. And of course they are obvious. Should I seek out esoteric ones? But I think such reviewers have the notion—although they certainly didn't get it from my book—that, if there's anything to the idea, the power elite *must* be all the time secretly at work doing secret things that nobody knows about. Then they complain that I don't tell what these things are. Of course, my idea of the power elite is not of that order. It is an interpretation of well-known historical events, not a notion of a secret cabal making decisions. Such decisions do enter into it, but they are by no means its defining characteristic. Naturally I sought examples that were not questionable; it is their interpretation that we are arguing about.

This line of reflection permits reasonable liberals to accept much of my account with a little moral shrug which helps bury the consequences of accepting it. They do so by reiterating a few of my points with the comment that "most modern governments" are of this sort. This of course is merely to accept the facts as if they were inevitable and obvious while refusing to confront the democratic problem of responsibility, in fact any problems of democracy, to which they lead.

A second objection along the same line is that I don't really say "what are the interests on the basis of which the power elite decides policy." This again is either to ask for a detailed history—this time in large part a psychological one—or it is to assume that there must be some one all-embracing, unifying interest, in short, that the unity of the elite must be based on conscious interests, or even ideology. This, I believe, is too rationalistic a means of interpretation. It is possible to say, as I do, that socially their decisions run to a maintenance of the status quo and personally, to a consolidation of their personal state, both materially and ideally, in it. But this, of course, is a quite formal assertion which holds of other groups as well as of those on top.

One key to such elite unity as exists lies in the "coincidence" of several structural trends I've traced; another is the psychological and status facts on which I've spent so many pages. Only third and last have I brought into the picture the explicit following of explicitly known interests. The whole idea of the power elite is set up and presented in this way in order to avoid the kind of "conspiracy" theory into which some reviewers, with a rather crude lack of theoretical acuteness, try to force a much more complicated and quite different view.

Yet one reviewer, for example, believes that I am "hinting at" an idea needed by my argument but which I can't really accept—the idea of an elite interest in "a permanent war economy." The fact is I don't hint at all. I think it obvious that war and the preparation for war as we know it is a perfectly marvelous way of solving and of ditching all sorts of problems confronted by the several members of the power elite, as well as by many other people.

XI

Some of the most interesting reviews I've seen are given over to consideration of the several pivotal decisions which I've used to illustrate the nature of decision-making in our time: Hiroshima, Dienbienphu, etc. Such reviewers typically acknowledge the only points I felt the need to make in connection with these examples: that they are pivotal and that very few persons indeed had any real say-so about them. "In any case," one acknowledges, "the first atomic bomb was dropped on the responsibility of one man who was the beneficiary of very sketchy advice from a handful of other men." Exactly. And on Korea: "This decision was made in the course of a few hours by a few men." Just so.

But such reviewers seem to think that this refutes my idea of the power elite because (1) not a little crowd, but often only a few men, are in on such decisions; (2) these men don't always agree but are divided in their counsel; (3) in their decisions, they sometimes take into account the state of public opinion or the policy of other countries; (4) sometimes the decision made is "taken against the better judgment of the power elite." Each of these points I readily accept, indeed I've stated them myself, and nothing in my conception of the power elite, or in the nature of the big decisions of our time, is upset by them.

The power elite is not a homogeneous circle of a specified number of men whose solidified will continuously prevails against all obstacles. Accordingly, I take such discussion of these pivotal events as an interesting and informed carrying on of the kind of social history I've urged, in which the idea of the power elite is refined and elaborated.

XII

The most important problem for political reflection in our time has to do with the problem of responsibility. I'm really sorry that only one reviewer takes up what is of course the chief moral theme of *The Power Elite*. He puts his point this way:

Mills sees himself standing outside society. Even though he's "generally humanistic in his outlook," he makes a rigid distinction between life and history. "The tragic view of life is barred to them [people like Mills] . . . Feeling no personal responsibility—I do not mean accountability in the social and political sense but rather involvement in the tragic and comic sense—their view is almost certain to be irresponsible."

Here is my answer to this:

Yes, I do feel that I stand, with most other people, outside the major history-making forces of my epoch, but at the same time I feel that I am among those who take the consequences of these forces. That is why I do not make a rigid distinction between "life and history," and that is one major reason why I am a political man. No one is outside society; the question is where you stand within it.

The "tragic view of life," at least as it seems to be meant in this review, is not "barred" to me. Having examined it carefully, I have rejected it as a political blind alley, as sociologically unreal, and as morally irresponsible. It is a romanticism which in his social and personal loneliness the American adolescent finds very attractive, but it is not a mood that will stand up to even a little reflection. It is a way of saying to oneself: "We're all in this together, the butcher and the general and the ditch digger and the Secretary of the Treasury and the cook and the President of the United States. So let's all feel sad about one another, or if we're up to it, let's just see it all as one great comedy." But "we" are *not* all in this together—so far as such decisions as are made and can be made are concerned. "We" are not all in this together—so far as bearing the consequences of these decisions is concerned. To deny either statement is to deny the facts of power, in particular the fact that different men hold very different portions of such power as is now available. Only if all men everywhere were actors of equal power in an absolute democracy of power could we seriously hold the "tragic view" of responsibility.

The difference between this "tragic view" and the romantic pluralism of ordinary balance-of-power theories is that, being more politically sophisticated, the tragedians generalize the "we" to the generically human and in so doing try to shove it beyond the political sphere. But I'm afraid the distinction between "political accountability" and "tragic responsibility" which they make will not hold up. Certainly not today, certainly not in the United States today. If it did hold up it would offer a convenient escape from the frustrations of politics, and at the same time provide a grand view of one's own role in human affairs. But, in fact, it is nothing more than a shallow form of fatalism, which, adorned with a little liberal rhetoric, leads to political irresponsibility.

XIII

I've seen only two reviews in which the reviewer tries to pigeon-hole the book from the left of it. One of them borders on an obstinate silliness over words like "capitalism" and "class"—words that have become cliches by which True Radicals try to retain the insurgency of their political adolescence yet avoid thinking freshly about what might be going on in the world today. Such a reviewer is likely to ask: "If the contemporary trends in corporate business power and its influence in government are as here suggested, why pretend that government and business are any longer importantly apart?" Why indeed? Since the war, neither business nor government can be understood as a separate realm of power. That is not enough for the True Radicals. They want to believe that the corporations and the state are identical, that they have become one big structure. Well, if not that, what do they mean? If they want me merely to evoke the good old party emotions that flood up in some people when they are told that the state is "a committee of the ruling class," I am sorry, I can't oblige. I don't believe it is quite that simple.

A second question occurs to the True Radicals. "Well," they ask (as if they'd just thought of it and all alone), are you implying "that big business is increasingly in the position to dominate political democracy?" Of course. And I not only imply it; I spell it out in detail. Nevertheless, they continue, "Mills' failure to deal with the meanings for democracy of the impressive power trends he analyzes is the colossal loose-end of *The Power Elite*." In fact, one of the major themes of the book is that many key decisions are made outside the parliamentary mechanism which thus drops to a secondary position, to the middle levels of power. On this level, there is very often a semi-organized stalemate. That is the key meaning of the power elite for democracy. But that's no answer for the True Radicals, for, you see, I've not used the old romantic words loosely enough to make them feel happy.

XIV

Several reviewers assert that I don't "really know what power is," but one radical critic spells this out: I put too much emphasis on force. Well, I do believe that in the last resort, coercion is the "final" form of power, but I also believe—despite Hungary and Suez—that we are not constantly at the last resort. *Authority* (or power that is made legitimate by the beliefs of the obedient) and *manipulation* (power that is wielded unbeknown to the powerless)—along with coercion—make up the major and well-known types of power which must constantly be sorted out when we think about the elite. The point that is relevant to this criticism, I believe, is that authority is no longer so explicit as it was, say in the medieval epoch, and that along with this, the ideology (justification or legitimations of power) of ruling groups is no longer so relevant to understanding phenomena of modern power. For many of the great decision of our time, mass "persuasion" has not been "necessary"; the fact is simply accomplished. Further, more often than not such ideologies as are available for the power elite are neither taken up nor used by them. In modern times, ideology, and hence legitimate authority, arises as a response to effective debunking, to thorough-going criticism; in the United States such opposition has not been recently available, has not been effective enough to create the felt need for ideologies of rule. As a result, there has come about neither acceptance nor rejection of the old symbols of authority, but simply political indifference. This—and I use the word with care—spiritual condition seems to me the key to much modern malaise, as well as the key to many political features of the power elite in the United States. What we've recognized as conviction is not necessary, in either the ruling or the ruled, for the structure of power as well as its elite formations to persist and even flourish. So far as ideologies are concerned, that is one of the interpretative guides I've found most helpful in trying to understand the nature of contemporary types of power.

XV

Another complaint from the left is that all this business of the elite does not jibe with true "radical values." Such criticism is more likely to be buttressed by general statements about "the latent political bias" of "elite theory" than by concrete reference to *The Power Elite*. But what are "radical values?" "For radical criticism to have any meaning it must utter its judgments from some moral norm that transcends the system, or from some standard that recognizes an immanent, unfulfilled, potential in the existing state of things." I want to make very clear that in so far as this is the meaning, I am *not* a Radical Critic and never have been. I have never found either a transcendent or an immanent ground for moral judgment. The only moral values I hold I've gotten from right inside history; in fact they are always proclaimed by many and, within the possibilities of various life-ways, practiced in small circles in western history whose members I've taken as models of character. Moral judgment, I suppose, is a matter of wanting to generalize and to make available for others those values you've come to choose. Foremost among them is the chance of truth. Simple descriptions of elite persons and groups can be politically neutral, but I don't think they usually are. When little is known, or only trivial items publicized, or when myths prevail, then plain description becomes a radical fact—or at least is taken to be radically upsetting.

The study of elite groups, at least as I have carried it on, does not blind one "to the real potential for fundamental social change..." After all, the only "potential" mentioned by critics who make this charge ends up merely as the commonplace thought that "prosperity" and "contemporary trends" will not last forever. Surely. But no writer about such topics as these is writing "forever"; one writes for now. I don't of course believe that the contemporary power elite is here "forever." War and the preparation for war, is one of its major conditions, although not its only one. I don't suppose it could survive a really disastrous slump, but I don't see the conditions of such a slump in the immediately foreseeable future. Let us not be so urgent for hope of fundamental change that we slip over into the falsely wise mood of This Too Shall Pass, as many "radical" philosophers border on doing. The fundamental political error of so much "radicalism" is its tendency, borrowed directly from the optimistic bourgeois notion of progress, to confuse the cry for hope with the metaphysics of history.

XVI

But the "radical" criticism goes deeper: it holds that there is some "latent ideological bias" in "the elite theory" and that it's this bias that's against "radical values," whatever they are. My trouble here is that I don't really understand what is meant by "the elite theory." There is no one such thing. Merely to study elite groups is not automatically to accept some one definite theory of elites. Do the critics mean Pareto's theory of the circulation of the elite? I don't accept that. Michels' iron law of oligarchy? I think it's a fairly good description of what has in fact happened in most mass organization. But what is "the hidden ideological bias" in "the elite theory" or in empirical work on elite groups? Do they mean only that "elite theory" reduces power to "a conquest theory of politics?" If so, then certainly I do not hold "the elite theory." I don't think history is merely a succession of elites which, one after the other, conquer the institutional means of power. That is an omnipotent theory of the elite and an elite theory of history from which I have been very careful to dissociate my view. The structural mechanics of institutions must indeed be given due weight. My point, in this connection, is simply that the shape of these institutions—for example, their extreme centralization— makes the action and the policies of those who exercise such human control over them and through them as nowadays exists, more consequential, more relevant to an understanding of the history of our times—than, let us say, in the model society of the Jeffersonian scatter.

The study of elites does not rule out an acceptance of the kind of structural view one finds, for example, in Marx. In fact, one must pay attention to both. The historical structure of opportunity is more important, I hold, than "the seizure of power" by elites of which some critics talk so much. The relation of institutional structure and elite formations is of course a two-sided play. Institutions, as I've repeatedly documented, select and form those who come to their top. In fact, sometimes the norms of selection and the shaping influences of institutional structures are more important to understanding human affairs and even the affairs of the powerful than the actual circles of men on top at any given time. I believe that is true just now, for example, in many corporations. But it's also true, given the shape of major institutions in the United States today, that those at the top are more than privileged persons: to a varying extent, in different historical situations, they are also powerful with all the means of power now at their disposal.

XVII

Many reviewers of *The Power Elite*—liberal, radical and highbrow—complain that the book is "too pessimistic" or "too negative." Only one of them it seems to me, has been self-conscious enough to be altogether honest about this: he writes that he does not "respond more readily" to the book "in part, no doubt, because [its] conclusions are gloomy . . . " What many reviewers really want, I think, is less of a program than a lyric upsurge—at least at the end. They want a big thump on the intellectual and political back. They want a sturdy little mood of earnest optimism, out of which we step forward all nice and fresh and shining. But the world I'm trying to understand does not make me politically hopeful and morally complacent, which is to say, I find it difficult to play the cheerful idiot. Many people tend, often without knowing it, to judge a position in terms of optimism-pessimism, the pessimistic being not nearly so good as the optimistic. Personally, as you know, I'm a very cheerful type, but I must say that I've never been able to make up my mind whether something is so or not in terms of whether or not it leads to good cheer. First you try to get it straight, to make an adequate statement. If it's gloomy, too bad; if it's cheerful, well fine. Anyway, just now isn't it obvious that it's not at all a question of what "we're" going to do; the question is what are a lot of other people doing? In the meantime, the charges of irresponsibility, the pseudo-crying for a program, are really signs of fear, of an incapacity to face facts as they are, even if these facts are decidedly unpleasant—and so irrelevant to the truth or falsity of my views.

Svanemollevej 64
Copenhagen, Denmark

Yours truly,
C. Wright Mills

THIRTEEN | Science and Scientists

"SCIENCE AND SCIENTISTS" was published as chapter 22 of Mills's pamphlet *The Causes of World War Three* (1958). An earlier version was titled "The American Scientist" and delivered to the Seventh Annual Forum of Democracy, Columbia College, on the theme of "Science and Democracy," February 24, 1955.

———————

Within the internationalism of science, the nations of Western Europe have occupied a more central place than has the United States or the Soviet Union. In part, this has been due to their historical lead and in part to the fact that in Europe science has been an integral part of the broader European cultural traditions. Historically, America and Russia have stood as provincials to Western Europe in matters of theoretical innovation in basic science.

U.S. science has not developed a firm scientific tradition in the European manner. Here science has been virtually identified with its technological products, its engineering developments, its techniques; and it has recently become subjected to the corporate technique of the assembly line. It is in the use of science, in the know-how of development projects, in the mass-production exploitation of its legacy, that the U.S. has excelled. This kind of industrial and military science stands in contrast to the classic, academic tradition in which individual scientific investigators or small groups are part of an un-coordinated cultural tradition. In brief, the U.S. has built a Science Machine: a corporate organization and rationalization of the process of technological development and to some extent—I believe unknown—of scientific discovery itself.

It is to the engineering "crash program," made possible by the Science Machine, that the U.S. science has been increasingly geared. And it is in just this respect that the Soviet Union has at first imitated and now, it would seem, overtaken the United States.

In both superstates, the incentive and the climax of such a development are making of science a firm and managed part of the machinery of war. It is true that Russia is unhampered by the wasteful character of a Science Machine subjected to private capitalist profit. More easily than the U.S. elite, the Soviet elite can probably focus her science upon basic or upon immediately technological purposes. But under the cold-war pressure, the overriding aim of both is a Science Machine geared to the war machine. In Russia as well as in America, accordingly, scientists are viewed as a vital national resource; tight secrecy is demanded of scientists; many who would be scientists are converted into engineering types. The scientist, in short, is to be a unit of the Science Machine; the Science Machine, in turn, is to be managed by nonscientific personnel or by new types of managerial scientists. The ethos of basic science and the role of the creative individual—as they have been known in Western civilization—are violated by the construction and the maintenance of military Science Machines, in the U.S. version of which over one third of creative scientists are now deeply and directly involved.

It should not be supposed that American scientists have not reacted to all this, or to the uses to which the fearful products of the Science Machine have been put and the uses now officially planned. On the issue of the bomb, scientists have probably been more politically conscious than any other professional group. It is true that their initial reactions and influence following World War II were greatly blunted by official action in the case of J. Robert Oppenheimer and by the dissolution of the wartime Office of Scientific Research and Development. Still, a significant number of scientists quietly refuse to do weapons work; many more are active enough in "the campaign to stop the testing of bombs" to circulate and to sign petitions. Many scientists, moreover, have fought hard against the excess of the "security program"; they have demanded that materials be declassified, and that "top secret" restrictions upon human knowledge be removed.

The power of science to change the world has increased; but the influence of scientists over the Science Machine has become a public issue. For scientists, that issue is not merely the position they will take on the cold war or even whether as individuals they will work on the new weaponry. It is not merely a question of basic versus applied science. Behind these issues and others like them is the contradiction of the classic scientific ethos by the Science Machine. The issue is basic science as part of a cultural tradition of international scope versus the nationalistic, secret Science Machine.

Especially among younger scientists in the United States (I do not know about the Soviet Union in this respect) scientists are becoming more fully aware of what it means to work in the one or in the other; of the fact that as scientists they are part of a broader tradition which includes the humanities and the liberal arts; of the difference between scientists who are necessarily in and of this broader tradition and technologists and engineers who are not necessarily a part of it at all; of the fact that within the Science Machine certain types of scientists are rising who know nothing of the classic ethos of science. Within the scientific community, in brief, there has come about a split which scientists increasingly feel called upon to confront.

I

The first thing scientists should do is join the intellectual community more fully than they have and, as members, take up with other cultural workmen the tasks I have been outlining. They should develop and work to fulfill a program for peace. More specifically: They should attempt to deepen the split among themselves and to debate it.

II

Scientists of all nations ought to honor publicly those of their colleagues who have already made their declarations for peace and against the war of the Science Machine. As scientists and as cultural workmen they ought to be gladdened by the courage displayed by such men as the eighteen German physicists who have made their declarations against working on the new weaponry. A West German spokesman recently said, "The possibility of a veto by the Eighteen still hangs like a sword of Damocles over all government decisions concerning defense policy." And Robert Jungk has written: "It even seems that the fear of the uproar that might be roused by a second declaration by the atomic scientists has again and again forced the Bonn Government to camouflage and even revise its armament and foreign policy programs."

III

Scientists of all nations ought to declare against those among them who, as scientists, make their calling, in the words of Norman Cousins, "seem more mysterious than it is, and who allow this mystery to interfere with public participation in decisions involving science or the products of science." They ought, as Harrison Brown has recently done, to declare against those individual scientists who lend their prestige and their official names to the program for war undertaken by governments. They should point out the position and the prestige which, inside the iron wall of secrecy, enable some scientists to make pronouncements which cannot be checked or refuted by critics. Scientists should not lend their authority to the propaganda output of the A.E.C. or to Presidential assertion. More of them ought, on appropriate occasion, to make such statements as this one by Harrison Brown: "I believe that Dr. Teller is willfully distorting the realities of the situation, I believe that it is possible for us to secure agreements with the Soviet Union to stop tests, and I believe further that the agreements could be of such a nature that the Soviet Union would adhere to them because it would be very much to her advantage to do so."

IV

Scientists should establish their own private forums and public outlets. For the time is overripe for an intensified and responsible communication between scientists and other cultural workmen, and between scientists and larger publics. When scientific answers are needed to clarify questions of public policy but are not known, after consultation with one another scientists should admit this. When answers are known, they should publicize them responsibly as scientists. In short, they ought to informally but professionally to constitute themselves a politically neutral but politically relevant "higher civil service." Only in some such way can they avoid irresponsible controversies among themselves and avoid being used by officials and warlords who would lie and bluff for their own ends. Only in some such way can they avoid establishing themselves before publics as hired men of ruling circles, and come to be seen as members of the cultural community, and so responsible to mankind.

V

The scientists' debate ought to result in the development of a code of ethics for scientists. Just as lawyers and doctors become aware of their deep social involvement, set up a code of professional ethics, so now should scientists. The purpose of such a code among any professional group is to protect the practitioners from each other and from other groups; often the code is no more than that. But it ought also to protect society from unethical practices of the practitioners, and of course to define such practices. Philip Siekovitz—a biochemist and medical researcher—has recently proposed such a code for scientists. Its purpose, he suggests, is not "to govern society, but only to assist in the self-regulation of individuals; it would serve not for the control of research, but for the maintenance of standards. Psychologists have no business helping some groups fashion keys for opening, surreptitiously, the pocketbooks of others. Medical scientists, chemists, and bacteriologists have no business working for the special interests of some against the interests of the many. These men are no longer scientists; they are technicians in the employ of men with exclusive interests. What we need is a kind of guild system in science which would exclude such technicians from the practice of research. . . ."

One of the great yields of any attempt by scientists to formulate such a code and to enforce it among themselves would be the furthering of moral and political debate within the scientific community.

VI

Out of such debate one might also hope that the demand would arise for the establishment of a civilian "Department of Science and Technology." All scientific agencies of the government should be placed in this department, which should become the focal point of the scientists' effort as scientists and as cultural workmen aware of their political role. To replace the present labyrinth and confusion of committees and consultants by such a centralized organization would increase the chance for a responsible public role of science and scientists. It would constitute a forum within which debates about science and policy debates by scientists could be made democratically open and responsible. And it would increase the chance that scientific endeavor would be removed from military authority and Pentagon decision.

VII

Scientists as scientists and as members of the cultural community ought not, I believe, to encourage or aid the U.S. elite to straighten out its Science Machine in order to catch up with and overtake the U.S.S.R.'s. They ought not to worry about the United State's science lag as such. They ought to use that worry to spur reflection about the uses of scientific rationality in both the U.S. and the U.S.S.R. The scientific community ought to debate, and to encourage among wide publics the debate, as to whether, given the human community and the world's resources, scientific work and technological development are being responsibly focused.

They ought, for example, publicly to ask and to ask themselves: Who wants to go to the moon anyway? Do you? Really? Aren't there other things you'd much rather do? And however you feel, do you realize that an increasing part of your life effort is being spent on just this kind of little trip—at an increasing risk to your life?

I am less concerned that any one point of view on this prevail than that the decisions involved be made public issues and, as such, debated by publics and by cultural workmen before publics. I am concerned that the human exploration of space be placed in the context of a properly developing society, rather than in that of the military metaphysic.

My own view, however, is that only those who make a fetish of Scientific Progress, irrespective of its direction and result, would today think the emphasis on space travel a reasonable and proper use of man's rationality, effort, and resources. Given its military bearing and the military perils on which it rests and which it increases, it is an irrational focus for such total scientific effort. And given the human condition today, it is an immoral expenditure of economic energy. But as a climactic step in an irresponsible series of decisions and defaults, it fits very well the military metaphysic which possess the crackpot elites of Russia, the United States, and points in between.

VIII

Scientists should demand that all security and loyalty restrictions be removed from all scientific work, and that qualified scientists anywhere on the globe—specifically and immediately including J. Robert Oppenheimer—be invited to participate in it. They should make it clear that there is no security in "scientific secrecy," that such secrecy leads to anxiety and fear, to nervous officials and to official nervousness; that secrecy leads only to insecurity.

To those who accuse them of "defeatism" or of "favoring Soviet armament" they ought to reply in the words of the German physicist, Max von Lau: "Suppose I live in a big apartment house and burglars attack me; I am allowed to defend myself and, if need be, I may even shoot, but under no circumstances may I blow up the house. It is true that to do so would be an effective defense against burglars, but the resulting evil would be much greater than any I could suffer. But what if the burglars have explosives to destroy the whole house? Then I would leave them with the responsibility for the evil, and would not contribute anything to it."

IX

As conscious members of the cultural community, scientists ought to work within their scientific tradition and refuse to become members of a Science Machine under military authority. Within the civilian Department of Science, within their profession, and before larger publics, they should publicly defend and practice science in terms of its classic, creative ethos, rather than in terms of the gadgets of the overdeveloped society or the monstrous weapons of the war machines. They should demand that a free interchange of information and theory be focused upon the industrial problems of the world. For reasons I have already given, they ought, with other cultural workmen, to seek to remove scientific research and development directly or indirectly relevant to the military from the private economy. They should contend that Washington let no contracts of a scientific character to any private business corporation. As a profession they should debate the refusal to work under such contracts and consider the professional boycotting of given projects. In passive and in active ways, they ought unilaterally to withdraw from, and so abolish, the Science Machine as it now exists.

"But if I don't do it," some scientists feel, "others will. So what's the difference?" This is less an argument than the mannerism of the irresponsible. It is based upon a conception of yourself as an altogether private man, upon the acceptance of your own impotence, upon the idea that the act in question, whatever it be, is part of fate and so not subject to your decision.

My answers to this mannerism are: If you do not do it, you at least are not responsible for its being done. If you refuse to do it out loud, others may quietly refrain from doing it, and those who still do it may then do it only with hesitation and guilt. To refuse to do it is to begin the practice of a professional code, and perhaps the creation of that code as a historical force.

To refuse to do it is an act affirming yourself as a moral center of responsible decision; it is an act which recognizes that you as a scientist are now a public man—whether you want to be or not; it is the act of a man who rejects "fate," for it reveals the resolution of one human being to take at least his own fate into his own hands.

FOURTEEN | # A Pagan Sermon to the Christian Clergy

MILLS DELIVERED THIS ADDRESS in Toronto on Thursday, February 27, 1958, before the annual meeting of the Board of Evangelical and Social Service, United Church of Canada. The next morning, the *Toronto Daily Star* reported that a "pagan professor" had delivered a "blistering address."

All through the spring of 1958, with fear of total war aroused by Sputnik, clergymen read Mills's sermon aloud from their pulpits while magazines such as *The Christian Century, The Catholic World, The Catholic Worker* and *The Christian Evangelist* reprinted or excerpted it. No essay by Mills elicited a greater response. "I feel that I simply must take time out to write," said a typical letter to *The Nation*, which published the sermon on March 8. "I have read and reread (and will probably read some more) Mr. C. Wright Mills's 'A Pagan Sermon to the Christian Clergy.' Offhand, I can't recall ever reading anything better in your pages—or anywhere else for that matter. It was simply wonderful; a powerful, powerful piece, a ringing indictment."

To say that war has become total is to say that the reach of modern weaponry now makes every soul on earth a quite possible victim of sudden hell. It is to say that weapons have become absolute, and that every calculation from on high now includes a military calculation. It is to say that the decision-makers of every nation, in particular those of the United States, are now possessed by the crackpot metaphysics of militarism. But more than that: it is to say that the morality of war now dominates the curious spiritual life of the fortunate peoples of Christendom.

World War III is already so total that most of its causes are accepted as "necessity"; most of its meaning as "realism." In our world "necessity" and "realism" have become ways to hide lack of moral imagination. In the cold war of the politicians and journalists, intellectuals and generals, businessmen and preachers, it is above all else moral imagination that is most obviously lacking. One reason for this lack, I am going to argue, is what surely must be called the moral default of the Christians.

The ethos of war is now the ethos of virtually all public thought and sensibility. But I must limit this article to the fact of moral insensibility in the Western world and to the religious failure that supports it.

By moral insensibility I refer to the mute acceptance—or even the unawareness—of moral atrocity. I mean the lack of indignation when confronted with moral horror. I mean the turning of this atrocity and this horror into morally approved conventions of feeling. I mean, in short, the incapacity for *moral* reaction to event and character, to high decision and the drift of human circumstance.

Such moral insensibility has its roots in World War I; it became full-blown during World War II. The "saturation bombing" of that war was an indiscriminate bombing of civilians on a mass scale; the atomic bombing of the peoples of Hiroshima and Nagasaki was an act committed without warning and without ultimatum. By the time of Korea, the strategy of obliteration had become totally accepted as part of our moral universe.

The pivotal decision, made by the United States and by the Soviet Union, is the monstrous one, as Lewis Mumford has put it, of trying "to solve the problem of absolute power, presented by nuclear weapons, by concentrating their national resources upon instruments of genocide." The spokesmen of each side say they know that war is obsolete as a means of any policy save mutual annihilation, yet they search for peace by military means and in doing so, they succeed in accumulating ever new perils. Moreover, they have obscured this fact by their dogmatic adherence to violence as the only way of doing away with violence. There has not before been an arms race of this sort—a scientific arms race dominated by the strategy of obliteration. And at every turn of this hideous competition, each side becomes more edgy, and the chance becomes greater that accidents of character or of technology will trigger the sudden hell.

The key moral fact about this situation is the virtual absence within ourselves of absolute opposition to these assumptions of our ruling elites, to their strategy, and to the policies by which they are carrying it out. And the key public result is the absence of any truly debated alternatives. In some part the absence both of opposition and of alternatives rests upon, or at least is supported by, the fact of moral insensibility.

Between catastrophic event and everyday interest there is a vast moral gulf. Who in North America experienced, as human beings, World War II? Men fought; women waited; both worked. About the war they all said the same kinds of things. Nobody rebelled, nobody knew public grief. In the emotional economy, there was efficiency without purpose. It was a curiously unreal business. A sort of numbness seemed to prohibit any real awareness of what was happening. It was without dream and so without nightmare, and if there were anger and fear and hatred—and there were—still no mainsprings of feeling and conviction and compassion were let loose in despair or furor; no human complaint was focused rebelliously upon the political and moral meanings of the universal brutality. People sat in the movies between production shifts watching with aloofness and even visible indifference, as children were "saturation bombed" in the narrow cellars of European cities. Man had become an object; and in so far as those for whom he was an object felt about the spectacle at all, they felt powerless, in the grip of larger forces, having no part in those affairs that lay beyond their immediate areas of daily demand and gratification. It was a time of moral somnambulance. And worst of all, from the religious point of view, the people of this continent were often brightly hopeful—while what used to be called the deepest convictions were as fluid as water.

It is as if the ear had become a sensitive soundtrack, the eye a precision camera, experience and exactly-timed collaboration between microphone and lens. And in this expanded world of mechanically vivified communications, the capacity for experience is alienated, and the individual becomes the spectator of everything but the human witness of nothing.

In all the emotional and spiritual realms of life, facts now outrun sensibility, and these facts, emptied of their human meanings, are readily gotten used to. There is no more human shock in official man; there is no more sense of moral issue in his unofficial follower. There is only the unopposed supremacy of technique for impersonal, calculated, wholesale murder. This lack of response I am trying to sum up by the altogether inadequate phrase "moral insensibility," and I am suggesting that the level of moral sensibility, as part of public and private life, has in our time sunk below human sight.

Religion today is part of this sorry moral condition; to understand the crucial decisions of our pivotal times, it is not necessary to consider religious institutions or personnel or doctrine. Neither preachers nor laity matter; what they do and what they say can be readily agreed with, and safely ignored. I am aware that there are exceptions, but the average output is correctly heard as a parade of worn-out phrases. In the West, religion has become a subordinate part of the overdeveloped society.

If there is one safe prediction about religion in this society, it would seem to be that if tomorrow official spokesmen were to proclaim XYZ-ism, next week 90 percent of religious declaration would be XYZ-ist. At least in their conforming rhetoric, religious spokesmen would reveal that the new doctrine did not violate those of the church. As a social and as a personal force, religion has become a dependent variable. It does not originate; it reacts. It does not denounce; it adapts. It does not set forth new models of conduct and sensibility; it imitates. Its rhetoric is without deep appeal; the worship it organizes is without piety. It has become less a revitalization of the spirit in permanent tension with the world than a respectable distraction from the sourness of life. In a quite direct sense, religion has generally become part of the false consciousness of the world and of the self.

Among the cheerful robots of the mass society, not human virtue but human shortcomings, attractively packaged, lead to popularity and success. They are men and women without publicly relevant consciousness, without awareness of shocking human evil, and their religion is the religion of good cheer and glad tidings. That it is a religion without dreary religious content is less important than that it is socially brisk and that it is not spiritually unsettling. It is a getting chummy with God, as a means to quite secular good feelings.

With such religion, ours is indeed a world in which the idea of God is dead. But what is important is that this fact itself is of no felt consequence. Men and women, in brief, are religiously indifferent; they find no religious meanings in their lives and in their world.

The verbal Christian belief in the sanctity of human life has not of course been affected by the impersonal barbarism of twentieth-century war. But this belief does not itself enter decisively into the plans now being readied for World War III. A savage politician once asked how many divisions the Pope had—and it was a relevant question. No one need ask how many chaplains any army that wants them has. The answer is: as many as the generals and their other satraps feel the need of. Religion has become a willing spiritual means and a psychiatric aide of the nation-state.

Total war must indeed be difficult for the Christian conscience to confront, but the current Christian way out makes it easy; war is defended morally and Christians easily fall into line—as they are led to justify it—in each nation in terms of "Christian faith" itself. Men of religious congregations do evil; ministers of God make them feel good about doing it. Rather than guide them in the moral cultivation of their conscience, ministers, with moral nimbleness, blunt that conscience, covering it up with peace of mind.

The moral death of religion in North America is inherent neither in religion nor specifically in Christianity. At times this religion has been insurgent; at other times, complacent; and it has been characterized by repeated revivals. Just now it is neither revolutionary nor reactionary, and it makes no real effort to revive itself in order to examine great public issues and the troubles of individuals from a fresh religious perspective. It does not count in the big political balance of life and death.

This is not surprising. In their struggle for success, religious institutions have come into competition with two great contemporary forces: amusement and politics. Each of these has been winning over religion; and when religion has seemingly won over them, it has failed as religion.

The most obvious competition is with the world of industrialized entertainment. Competing with these mass means of distraction, churches have themselves become minor institutions among the mass media of communications. They have imitated and borrowed the strident techniques of the insistent publicity machines, and in terms of the pitch-man (with both the hard and the soft sell), they have quite thoroughly banalized the teachings, and indeed the very image, of Christ.

I do not believe that anything recognizably Christian can be put over in this way. I suggest that this religious malarkey *diseducates* congregations; that it kills off any real influence religious leaders might have. Even if the crowds come, they come only for the show, and if it is the nature of crowds to come, it is also their nature soon to go away. And in all truth, are not all the television Christians in reality armchair atheists? In value and in reality they live without the God they profess; despite ten million Bibles sold each year in the United States alone, they are religiously illiterate. "If Christ had been put on television to preach the Sermon on the Mount," Malcolm Muggeridge has recently remarked, "viewers would either have switched on to another channel, or contented themselves with remarking that the speaker had an interesting face. Christ might have become a television personality, but there would have been no Christianity."

If you, as Christian ministers, accept the entertainment terms of success, you cannot succeed. The very means of your "success" make for your failure as witnesses, for you must appeal to such diverse moral appetites that your message will necessarily be generalized to the point of moral emptiness. If you do not specify and confront real issues, what you say will surely obscure them.

If you do not alarm anyone morally, you will yourself remain morally asleep. If you do not *embody* controversy, what you say will inevitably be an acceptance of the drift to the coming hell. And in all this you will continue well the characteristic history of Christianity, for the Christian record is rather clear: from the time of Constantine to the time of global radiation and the uninterceptible missile, Christians have killed Christians and been blessed for doing so by other Christians.

Politics, like religion, has of course also come into competition with and been deeply influenced by the world of entertainment and its means of attraction and distraction. But the realities of politics and of economics are nowadays very difficult to ignore; they just won't down, for they are part of the insistent military lie that now dominates official civilized endeavor.

Religion cannot compete with this political peril. What vision of hell compares with the realities we have and do now confront? And the point is that ministers of God are not foremost among those few men who would define and expose the morality of the political decisions and lack of decisions that lie back of these morally atrocious events and preparations. For a church whose congregation contains all political views and which is out for statistical success feels it must prosperously balance "above" politics—which means that it serves whatever moral default the affairs of mankind reveal.

As a mass medium, religion has become a religiously ineffective part of the show that fills up certain time slots in the weekly routine of cheerful robots. The minister goes his curious way, bringing glad tiding into each and every home.

Believe me, I do not wish to be rude, but I am among those pagans who take declarations seriously, and so I must ask you, as declared Christians, certain questions:

What does it mean to preach? Does it not mean, first of all, to be religiously conscious? I do not see how you can preach unless as a man you are the opposite to the religiously indifferent. To be religiously conscious, I suppose, is to find some sort of religious meaning in one's own insecurities and desires, to know oneself as a creature in some kind of relation with God which increases your hope that your expectations and prayers and actions will come off. I must ask: for you, today, what is that religious meaning?

To preach, secondly, means to serve as a moral conscience, and to articulate that conscience. I do not see how you can do that by joining the publicity fraternity and the weekend crusaders. You cannot do it by "staying out of politics." I think there is only one way in which you can compete as religious men with religious effect: you must be yourself in such a way that your views emanate unmistakably from you as a moral center. From that center of yourself, you must speak. So I must ask: why do you not make of yourself the pivot, and of your congregation the forum, of a public that is morally led and that is morally standing up? The Christian ethic cannot be incorporated without compromise; it can live only in a series of individuals who are capable of morally incorporating themselves.

Do not these times demand a little Puritan defiance? Do not they demand the realization of how close hell is to being a sudden and violent reality of man's world today? Should not those who still have access to the peoples of Christendom stand up and denounce with all the righteousness and pity and anger and charity and love and humility their faith may place at their command the political and the militarist assumptions now followed by the leaders of the nations of Christendom? Should they not denounce the pseudo-religiosity of men of high office who would steal religious phrases to declare crackpot policies and immoral lack of policies? Should they not refuse to allow immorality to find support in religion? Should they not refuse to repeat the official, un-Christian slogans of dull diplomats who do not believe in negotiation, who mouth slogans which are at most ineffective masks for lack of policy? Should they not realize that the positive moral meaning of what is called "neutralism" lies in the resolve that the fate of mankind shall not be determined by the idiotically-conducted rivalry of the United States and the Soviet Union?

I do not wish to be politically dogmatic, but merely brief and, as you gentlemen surely have recognized, I am religiously illiterate and unfeeling. But truly I do not see how you can claim to be Christians and yet not speak out totally and dogmatically against the preparations and testing now under way for World War III. As I read it, Christian doctrine in contact with the realities of today cannot lead to any other position. It cannot condone the murder of millions of people by clean-cut young men flying intricate machinery over Euro-Asia, zeroed in on cities full of human beings—young men who two years before were begging the fathers of your congregations for the use of the family car for a Saturday night date.

There is no necessity for more military emphasis on missiles. There is no need for more "science" in education; it is not "realism" to spend more money on arms. Necessity and need and realism are the desperate slogans of the morally crippled. The necessity is for moral imagination. The need is for political new beginnings. Realism means to stop at once and if need be unilaterally all preparations for World War III. There is no other realism, no other necessity, no other need.

You will not find in moral principles the solution to the problems of war, but without moral principles men are neither motivated nor directed to solve them. But nowadays we pagans see that Christian morals are more often used as moral cloaks of expedient interests than ways of morally uncloaking such interests.

War is not today inevitable; it is, immediately, the result of nationalist definitions of world reality, of dogmatic reliance upon the military as the major or even the only means of solving the explosive problems of this epoch of despair and of terror. And because this is now so, to lift up and to make knowledgeable the level of moral sensibility is the strategic task of those who would be at peace. Your role in the making of peace is less the debating of short-run and immediate policies than the confrontation of the whole attitude toward war and the teaching of new views of it by using them in criticism of current policies and decisions. And in the end, I believe the decisive test of Christianity lies in your witness of the refusal by individuals and by groups to engage in war. Pacifism, I believe, is the test of your Christianity—and of you. At the very least, it ought to be *the* debate within Christendom.

The brotherhood of man is now less a goal than an obvious condition of biological survival. Before the world is made safe again for American capitalism or Soviet communism or anything else, it had better be made safe for human life.

But you may say; "Don't let's get the church into politics." If you do say that, you are saying, "Don't let's get the church into the world; let's be another distraction from reality." This world is political. Politics, understood for what it really is today, has to do with the decisions men make which determine how they shall live and how they shall die. They are not living very well, and they are not going to die very well, either. Politics is now the locale of morality; it is the locale both of evil and of good. If you do not get the church into the moral issues of politics, you cannot confront evil and you cannot work for good. You will be a subordinate amusement and a political satrap of whatever is going. You will be the great Christian joke.

Men and ideas, the will and the spirit, are now being tested, perhaps in all truth for the final time; and in this testing so far, you Christians are standing in default. The key sign of this is the fact of your general lack of effective opposition, of your participation in the fact of moral insensibility. That, of course, is a world fact about publics and masses and elites, but it is all the more grievous among Christians, if only because of the expectations that they have aroused about themselves. Yet who among you has come out clearly on the issues of internecine war and the real problems of peace? Who among you is considering what it means for Christians to kill men and women and children in ever more efficient and impersonal ways? Who among you uses his own religious imagination to envision another kind of basis for policies governing how men should treat with one another? Who among you, claiming even vague contact with what Christians call "The Holy Spirit," is calling upon it to redeem the day because you know the times are evil?

If you are not today concerned with this—the moral condition of those in your spiritual care—then, gentlemen, what is your concern? As a pagan who is waiting for your answer, I merely say: you claim to be Christians. And I ask: what does that mean as a biographical and a public fact?

In moral affairs you are supposed to be among the first of men. No moral affair today compares with the morality of warfare and the preparation for it, for in these preparations men usurp—as you might say—the prerogatives of God. By sitting down and by keeping quiet, by all too often echoing the claptrap of all the higher immorality that now passes for political leadership— you are helping to enfeeble further in this time of cruel troubles the ideals of your Founder. Christianity is part of the moral defeat of man today. Perhaps it is no longer important enough to be considered a cause of it; perhaps it is only among the passive doctrines of the spectators of man's moral defeat.

I hope you do not demand of me gospels and answers and doctrines and programs. According to your belief, my kind of man—secular, prideful, agnostic and all the rest of it—is among the damned. I'm on my own; you've got your God. It is up to you to proclaim gospel, to declare justice, to apply your love of man—the sons of God, all of them, you say—meaningfully, each and every day, to the affairs and troubles of men. It is up to you to find answers that are rooted in ultimate moral decision and to say them out so that they are compelling.

I hope your Christian conscience is neither at ease nor at attention, because if it is I must conclude that it is a curiously expedient and ineffective apparatus. I hope you do not believe that in what you do and in how you live, you are denouncing evil, because if you do, then I must conclude that you know nothing of evil and so nothing of good. I hope you do not imagine yourselves to be the bearers of compassion, because if you do, you cannot yet know that today compassion without bitterness and terror is mere girlish sentiment, not worthy of any full-grown man. I hope you do not speak from the moral center of yourself, because if you do, then in the dark nights of your soul, in fear and in trembling, you must be cruelly aware of your moral peril in this time of total war, and—given what you, a Christian, say and believe—I, a pagan, pity you.

FIFTEEN § The Man in the Middle

THIS WAS AN ADDRESS before the International Design Conference in Aspen, Colorado, on June 28, 1958. "Social Forces and the Frustrations of the Designer" was the theme. Afterward, in a letter to Richard Hofstadter, Mills reported that he "had a fine time with designers, architects, city planners, artists, and other disgruntled types. I still think I ought to have been an architect. But since it's too late I am going to theorize for them! God they are a confused but good willing lot. They now confront all the problems the political intellectuals grappled with in the thirties; amazing really."

"The Man in the Middle" was published in *Industrial Design* in November 1958.

—∞∞∞—

The American designer is at once a central figure in what I am going to call the cultural apparatus and an important adjunct of a very peculiar kind of economy. His art is a business, but his business is art and curious things have been happening both to the art and to the business—and so to him. He is caught up in two great developments of 20th-century America: One is the shift in economic emphasis from production to distribution, and along with it, the joining of the struggle for existence with the panic for status. The other is the bringing of art, science and learning into subordinate relation with the dominant institutions of the capitalist economy and the nationalist state.

Designers work at the intersection of these trends; their problems are among the key problems of the overdeveloped society. It is their dual involvement in them that explains the big split among designers and their frequent guilt; the enriched muddle of ideals they variously profess and the insecurity they often feel about the practice of their craft; their often great disgust and their crippling frustration. They cannot consider well their position or formulate their credo without considering both cultural and economic trends, and the shaping of the total society in which these are occurring.

I want briefly (1) to define certain meanings and functions of the cultural apparatus, and (2) to indicate the economic context in which the designer now does his work. It may then be useful (3) to invite you to reconsider certain ideals for which the designer might stand in the kind of world in which Americans are coming to live.

Our Worlds Are Second-Hand

Our images of this world and of ourselves are given to us by crowds of witnesses we have never met and never shall meet. Yet for each of us these images—provided by strangers and dead men—are the very basis of our life as a human being. None of us stands alone directly confronting a world of solid fact. No such world is available: the closest we come to it is when we are infants or when we become insane: then, in a terrifying scene of meaningless events and senseless confusion, we are often seized with the panic of near-total insecurity. But in our everyday life we experience not solid and immediate facts but stereotypes of meaning. We are aware of much more than what we have ourselves experienced, and our experience itself is always indirect and always guided. The first rule for understanding the human condition is that men live in a second-hand world.

The consciousness of men does not determine their existence; nor does their existence determine their consciousness. Between the human consciousness and material existence stand communications and designs, patterns and values which influence decisively such consciousness as they have.

The mass arts, the public arts, the design arts are major vehicles of this consciousness. Between these arts and the everyday life, between their symbols and the level of human sensibility, there is now continual and persistent interplay. So closely do they reflect one another that it is often impossible to distinguish the image from its source. Visions whispered long before the age of consent, images received in the relaxation of darkness, slogans reiterated in home and in classroom, determine the perspective in which we see and fail to see the worlds in which we live; meanings about which we have never thought explicitly determine our judgments of how well and of how badly we are living in these worlds. So decisive to experience itself are the results of these communications that often men do not really believe what they "see before their very eyes" until they have been "informed" about it by the official announcement, the radio, the camera, the hand-out. Communications not only limit experience; often they expropriate the chances to have experience that can rightly be called "our own." For our standards of credibility, and of reality itself, as well as our judgments and discernments, are determined much less by any pristine experience we may have than by our exposure to the output of the cultural apparatus.

For most of what we call solid fact, sound interpretation, suitable presentation, we are increasingly dependent upon the observation posts, the interpretation centers, the presentation depots of the cultural apparatus. In this apparatus, standing between men and events, the meanings and images, the values and slogans that define all the worlds men know are organized and compared, maintained and revised, lost and found, celebrated and debunked.

By the cultural apparatus I mean all those organizations and milieux in which artistic, intellectual and scientific work goes on. I also mean all the means by which such work is made available to small circles, wider publics, and to great masses.

The most embracive and the most specialized domain of modern society, the cultural apparatus of art, science and learning fulfills the most functions: it conquers nature and remakes the environment; it defines the changing nature of man, and grasps the drift of world affairs; it revivifies old aspirations and shapes new ones. It creates models of character and styles of feeling, nuances of mood and vocabularies of motive. It serves decision-makers, revealing and obscuring the consequences of their decisions. It turns power into authority and debunks authority as mere coercion. It modifies the work men do and provides the tools with which they do it; it fills up their leisure, with nonsense and with pleasure. It changes the nature of war; it amuses and persuades and manipulates; it orders and forbids; it frightens and reassures; it makes men weep and it makes men laugh, go numb all over, then become altogether alive. It prolongs the life-span and provides the violent means to end it suddenly. It predicts what is going to happen and it explains what has occurred; it helps to shape and to pace any epoch, and without it there would be no consciousness of any epoch.

The world men are going to believe they understand is now, in this cultural apparatus, being defined and built, made into a slogan, a story, a diagram, a release, a dream, a fact, a blue-print, a tune, a sketch, a formula; and presented to them. Such part as reason may have in human affairs, this apparatus, this put-together contraption, fulfills; such role as sensibility may play in the human drama, it enacts; such use as technique may have in history and in biography, it provides. It is the sect of civilization, which—in Matthew Arnold's phrase—is "the humanization of man in society." The only truths are the truths defined by the cultural apparatus. The only beauty is experiences and objects created and indicated by cultural workmen. The only goods are the cultural values with which men are made morally comfortable or morally uneasy.

From Production to Distribution to "Merchandising"

As an institutional fact, the cultural apparatus has assumed many forms. In some societies—notably that of Russia—it is established by an authority that post-dates capitalism: it is thus part of an official apparatus of psychic domination. In some—notably the nations of Western Europe—it is established out of a tradition that pre-dates capitalism; it is thus part of an Establishment in which social authority and cultural prestige overlap. Both cultural tradition and political authority are involved in any cultural Establishment, but in the USA the cultural apparatus is established commercially: it is part of an ascendant capitalist economy. This fact is the major key to understanding both the quality of everyday life and the situation of culture in America today.

The virtual dominance of commercial culture is the key to America's cultural scope, confusion, banalization, excitement, sterility. To understand the case of America today, one must understand the economic trends and the selling mechanics of a capitalist world in which the mass production and the mass sale of goods has become The Fetish of human life, the pivot both of work and of leisure. One must understand how the pervasive mechanisms of the market have penetrated every feature of life—including art, science and learning—and made them subject to the pecuniary evaluation. One must understand that what has happened to work in general in the last two centuries has in the 20th century been happening to the sphere of artistic and intellectual endeavor; these too have now become part of society as a salesroom. To understand the ambiguous position of the cultural workman in America one must see how he stands in the overlap of these two worlds: the world of such an overdeveloped society with its ethos of advertisement, and the world of culture as men have known it and as they might know it.

However harsh its effects upon the nature of work, the industrialization of underdeveloped countries must be seen as an enormous blessing: it is man conquering nature, and so freeing himself from dire want. But as the social and physical machineries of industrialization develop, new purposes and interests come into play. The economic emphasis moves from production to distribution and, in the overdeveloped society, to what is called "merchandising." The pivotal decade for this shift in the USA was the Twenties, but it is in the era since the ending of World War II that the new economy has flowered like a noxious weed. In this phase of capitalism, the distributor becomes ascendant over both the consumer and the producer.

As the capacity to produce goes far beyond existing demand, as monopoly replaces competition, as surpluses accumulate, the need is for the creation and maintenance of the national market and for its monopolistic closure. Then the salesman becomes paramount. Instead of cultivating and servicing a variety of publics, the distributor's aim is to create a mass volume of continuing sales. Continuous and expanding production requires continuous and expanding consumption, so consumption must be speeded up by all the techniques and frauds of marketing. Moreover, existing commodities must be worn out more quickly for as the market is saturated, the economy becomes increasingly dependent upon what is called replacement. It is then that obsolescence comes to be planned and its cycle deliberately shortened.

Silly Designs for Silly Needs

There are, I suppose, three kinds of obsolescence: (1) technological, as when something wears out or something better is produced; (2) artificial, as when something is deliberately designed so that it will wear out; and (3) status obsolescence, as when fashions are created in such ways that consumption brings disgrace or prestige in accordance with last year's or with this year's model, and alongside the old struggle for existence, there is added the panic for status.

It is in this economic situation that the designer gets his Main Chance. Whatever his esthetic pretension and his engineering ability, his economic task is to sell. In this he joins the advertising fraternity, the public relations counsel, and the market researcher. These types have developed their skills and pretensions in order to serve men whose God is the Big Sell. And now the designer joins them.

To the firm and to its products he adds the magical gloss and dazzle of prestige. He plans the appearance of things and their often fraudulent packaging. He lays out the interiors and decorates the exteriors of corporate businesses as monuments to advertising. And then, along with his colleagues, he takes the history of commercial fraud one step further. With him, advertising is not one specialized activity, however central; with his capitalist advent, the arts and skills and crafts of the cultural apparatus itself become not only adjuncts of advertising but in due course themselves advertisements. He designs the product itself as if it were an advertisement, for his aim and his task—acknowledged by the more forthright—is less to make better products than to make products sell better. By brand and trademark, by slogan and package, by color and form, he gives the commodity a fictitious individuality, turning a little lanolin and water into an emulsified way to become erotically blessed; concealing the weight and quality of what is for sale; confusing the consumer's choice and banalizing her sensibilities.

The silly needs of salesmanship are thus met by the silly designing and redesigning of things. The waste of human labor and material become irrationally central to the performance of the capitalist mechanism. Society itself becomes a great sales room, a network of public rackets, and a continuous fashion show. The gimmick of success becomes the yearly change of model as fashion is made universal. And in the mass society, the image of beauty itself becomes identified with the designer's speed-up and debasement of imagination, taste and sensibility.

The Growth of the Star System

The cultural workman himself, in particular the designer, tends to become part of the means of distribution, over which he tends to lose control. Having "established a market," and monopolized access to it, the distributor—along with his market researcher—claims to "know what they want." So his orders—even to the free-lance—become more explicit and detailed. The price he offers may be quite high; perhaps too high, he comes to think, and perhaps he is right. So he begins to hire and to manage in varying degree a stable of cultural workmen. Those who allow themselves to be managed by the mass distributor are selected and in time formed in such a way as to be altogether proficient, but perhaps not quite first-rate. So the search goes on for "fresh ideas," for exciting notions, for more alluring models; in brief, for the innovator. But in the meantime, back at the studio, the laboratory, the research bureau, the writers' factory—the distributor is ascendant over many producers who become the rank-and-file workmen of the commercially established cultural apparatus.

In this situation of increasing bureaucratization and yet of the continual need for innovation, the cultural workman tends to become a commercial hack or a commercial star. By a star, I mean a producer whose productions are so much in demand that he is able, to some extent at least, to make distributors serve as *his* adjuncts. This role has its own conditions and its own perils: The star tends to be trapped by his own success. He has painted this sort of thing and he gets $20,000 a throw for it. This man, however affluent, may become culturally bored by this style and wants to explore another. But often he cannot: he is used to $20,000 a throw and there is demand for it. As a leader of fashions, accordingly, he is himself subject to fashion. Moreover, his success as a star depends upon his playing the market: he is not in educative interplay with a public that supports him as he develops and which he in turn develops. He too, by virtue of his success, becomes a marketeer.

The star system of American culture—along with the commercial hacks—tend to kill off the chance of the cultural workman to be a worthy craftsman. One is a smash hit or one is among the failures who are not produced; one is a best seller or one is among the hacks and failures; one is either absolutely tops or one is just nothing at all.

As an entrepreneur, you may value as you wish these several developments; but as a member of the cultural apparatus, you surely must realize that whatever else you may be doing, you are also creating and shaping the cultural sensibilities of men and women, and indeed the very quality of their everyday lives.

The Big Lie: "We Only Give Them What They Want"

The mere prevalence of the advertiser's skills and the designer's craft makes evident the falseness of the major dogma of the distributor's culture. That dogma is that "we only give them what they want." This is the Big Lie of mass culture and of debased art, and also it is the weak excuse for the cultural default of many designers.

The determination of "consumer wants and tastes" is one characterizing mark of the current phase of capitalism in America—and as well as what is called mass culture. And it is precisely in the areas in which wants are determined and changed that designers tend to do their work.

The merchandising apparatus, of which many designers are now members, operates more to create wants than to satisfy wants that are already active. Consumers are trained to "want" that to which they are most continually exposed. Wants do not originate in some vague realms of the consumer's personality; they are formed by an elaborate apparatus of jingle and fashion, of persuasion and fraud. They are shaped by the cultural apparatus and the society of which it is a part. They do not grow and change as the consumer's sensibilities are enlarged; they are created and they are changed by the process by which they are satisfied and by which old satisfactions are made unsatis-factory. Moreover, the very canons of taste and judgment are also managed by status obsolescence and by contrived fashion. The formula is: to make people ashamed of last year's model; to hook up self-esteem itself with the purchasing of this year's; to create a panic for status, and hence a panic of self-evaluation, and to connect its relief with the consumption of specified commodities.

In this vast merchandising mechanism of advertisement and design, there is no inherent social purpose to balance its great social power; there is no built-in responsibility to anybody except to the man who makes the profit. Yet there is little doubt that this mechanism is now a leading fixer of the values and standards of American society, the foremost carrier of cultural sensibility, and quite comparable in influence to school, to church, to home.

This apparatus is now an adjunct of commercial establishments which use "culture" for their own noncultural—indeed anticultural—ends, and so de-base its very meaning. These uses of culture are being shaped by men who would turn all objects and qualities, indeed human sensibility itself, into a flow of transient commodities, and these types have now gotten the designer to help them; they have gotten him to turn himself into the ultimate ad-vertising man. When you think about it—if you do—it really is amazing: the old helpmate of the salesman, the Air Brush Boy, the corporal of retailing—has become the generalissimo of anxious obsolescence as the American way of life.

Craftsmanship as a Value

I have of course been describing the role of the designer at what I hope is its worst. And I am aware that it is not only in the field of design that the American ambiguity of cultural endeavor is revealed, that it is not only the designer who commits the cultural default. In varying degrees all cultural workmen are part of a world dominated by the pecuniary ethos of the crackpot business man and also of a world unified only vaguely by the ideals of cultural sensibility and human reason. The autonomy of all types of cultural workmen has in our time been declining. I also want to make it clear that I am aware of the great diversity among designers and the enormous difficulty any designer now faces in trying to escape the trap of the maniacs of production and distribution.

The problem of the designer can be solved only by radical consideration of fundamental values. But like most fundamental considerations his can begin very simply.

The idea of the cultural apparatus is an attempt to understand human affairs from the standpoint of the role within them of reason, technique and sensibility. As members of this cultural apparatus, it is important that designers realize fully what their membership means. It means, in brief, that you represent the sensibilities of man as a maker of material objects, of man as a creature related to nature itself and to changing it by a humanly considered plan. The designer is a creator and a critic of the physical frame of private and public life. He represents man as a maker of his own milieu. He stands for the kind of sensibility which enables men to contrive a world of objects before which they stand delighted and which they are delighted to use. The designer is part of the unity of art, science and learning. That, in turn, means that he shares one cardinal value, that is the common denominator of art, science and learning and also the very root of human development. That value, I believe, is craftsmanship.

From craftsmanship, as ideal and as practice, it is possible to derive all that the designer ought to represent as an individual and all that he ought to stand for socially and politically and economically. As ideal, craftsmanship stands for the creative nature of work, and for the central place of such work in human development as a whole. As practice, craftsmanship stands for the classic role of the independent artisan who does his work in close interplay with the public, which in turn participates in it.

The most fundamental splits in contemporary life occur because of the break-up of the old unity of design, production and enjoyment. Between the image and the object, between the design and the work, between production and consumption, between work and leisure, there is a great cultural vacuum, and it is this vacuum that the mass distributor, and his artistic and intellectual satraps, have filled up with frenzy and trash and fraud. In one sentence, what has been lost is the fact and the ethos of man as craftsman.

By craftsmanship I refer to a style of work and a way of life having the following characteristics:

(1) In craftsmanship there is no ulterior motive for work other than the product being made and the processes of its creation. The craftsman imagines the completed product, often even as he creates it; and even if he does not make it, he sees and understands the meaning of his own exertion in terms of the total process of its production. Accordingly, the details of the craftsman's daily work are meaningful because they are not detached in his mind from the product of the work. The satisfaction he has in the results infuses the means of achieving it. This is the root connection between work and art: as esthetic experiences, both involve the power "to catch the enjoyment that belongs to the consummation, the outcome, of an undertaking and to give to the im-

plements, the objects that are instrumental in the undertaking, and to the acts that compose it something of the joy and satisfaction that suffuse its successful accomplishment."[1]

To quite small circles the appeal of modern art—notably painting and sculpture, but also of the crafts—lies in the fact that in an impersonal, a scheduled, a machined world, they represent the personal and the spontaneous. They are the opposite of the stereotyped and the banalized.

(2) In craftsmanship, plan and performance are unified, and in both, the craftsman is master of the activity and of himself in the process. The craftsman is free to begin his working according to his own plan, and during the work he is free to modify its shape and the manner of its shaping. The continual joining of plan and performance brings even more firmly together the consummation of work and its instrumental activities, infusing the latter with the joy of the former. Work is a rational sphere of independent action.

(3) Since he works freely, the craftsman is able to learn from his work, to develop as well as use his capacities. His work is thus a means of developing himself as a man as well as developing his skill. This self-development is not an ulterior goal, but a cumulative result of devotion to and practice of his craft. As he gives to work the quality of his own mind and skill, he is also further developing his own nature; in this simple sense, he lives in and through his work, which confesses and reveals him to the world.

(4) The craftsman's way of livelihood determines and infuses his entire mode of living. For him there is no split of work and play, of work and culture. His work is the mainspring of his life; he does not flee from work into a separate sphere of leisure; he brings to his non-working hours the values and qualities developed and employed in his working time. He expresses himself in the very act of creating economic value; he is at work and at play in the same act; his work is a poem in action. In order to give his work the freshness of creativity, he must at times open himself to those influences that only affect us when our attentions are relaxed. Thus for the craftsman, apart from mere animal rest, leisure may occur in such intermittent periods as are necessary for individuality in his work.

(5) Such an independent stratum of craftsman cannot flourish unless there are publics who support individuals who may not turn out to be first-rate. Craftsmanship requires that such cultural workmen and such publics define what is first-rate. In the Communist bloc, because of official bureaucracies, and in the capitalist, because of the commercial ethos, standards are now not in the hands of such cultural producers and cultural publics. In both the mere distributor is the key to both consumption and production.

Some cultural workmen in America do of course remain independent. Perhaps three or four men actually earn a living here just by composing serious music; perhaps fifty or so by the writing of serious novels. But I am concerned now less with economic than with cultural requirements. The role of the serious craftsman requires that the cultural workman remain a cultural workman, and that he produce for other cultural producers and for circles and publics composed of people who have some grasp of what is involved in his production. For you cannot "possess" art merely by buying it; you cannot support art merely by feeding artists—although that does help. To possess it you must earn it by participating to some extent in what it takes to design it and to create it. To support it you must catch in your consumption of it something of what is involved in the production of it.

It is, I think, the absence of such a stratum of cultural workmen, in close interplay with such a participating public, that is the signal fault of the American cultural scene today. So long as it does not develop, the position of the designer will contain all the ambiguities and invite all the defaults I have indicated. Designers will tend to be commercial stars or commercial hacks. And human development will continue to be trivialized, human sensibilities blunted, and the quality of life distorted and impoverished.

As practice, craftsmanship in America has largely been trivialized into pitiful hobbies: it is part of leisure, not of work. As ethic, it is largely confined to small groups of privileged professionals and intellectuals. What I am suggesting to you is that designers ought to take the value of craftsmanship as the central value for which they stand; that in accordance with it they ought to do their work; and that they ought to use its norms in their social and economic and political visions of what society ought to become.

Craftsmanship cannot prevail without a properly developing society; such a society I believe would be one in which the fact and the ethos of crafts-manship would be pervasive. In terms of its norms, men and women ought to be formed and selected as ascendant models of character. In terms of its ethos, institutions ought to be constructed and judged. Human society, in brief, ought to be built around craftsmanship as the central experience of the unalienated human being and the very root of free human development. The most fruitful way to define the social problem is to ask how such a society can be built. For the highest human ideal is: to become a good craftsman.

Notes

1. G. H. Mead, *The Philosophy of the Act* (Chicago, 1938), p. 454.

M ILLS GAVE THIS ADDRESS in Toronto on February 7, 1959, before
"The Troubled Metropolis," a conference sponsored by the Candian
Institute on Public Affairs.

"The overdeveloped megalopolis" was a familiar target of his cultural
criticism, though the timing of this address held immediate, personal
meaning. He was building a home in West Nyack, a hamlet in Rockland
County.

No record remains of the Columbia students Mills conscripted into the
digging of dirt, but he worked on his home with the diligence of the
craftsman he supposed himself to be, fusing structure to foundation, de-
lighting in the intelligent application of force against matter. In this address,
he encouraged city planners, designers, and architects to join him in trans-
forming the built environment from an object of private capital into a social
art. "Our task—as professional people and as citizens—is to formulate
standards; to set forth as a conference ten or twelve propositions on which we
are willing to stand up. Let us begin this, here and now."

—◦◦◦—

Consider the metropolis—the horrible, beautiful, ugly, magnificent sprawl of
the great city. For many upper-class people, the personal solution to "the
problem of the city" is to have an apartment (with private garage under it)
in the heart of the city, and one hundred miles out, a house and garden
by notable architects, on a hundred acres of private land. In these two controlled environments—with a small staff at each end and a private helicopter
connection—most people could solve many of the personal problems caused

them by the facts of the city. But all this, however splendid, does not solve the public issues that the structural fact of the city poses. What should be done with this wonderful monstrosity? Break it all up into scattered units, combining residence and work? Refurbish it as it stands? Or, after evacuation, dynamite it and build new cities according to new plans in new places? What would those plans be? And who is to decide and to accomplish whatever choice is made? These are structural issues; to confront them and to solve them requires us to consider political, economic and esthetic issues that affect innumerable *milieux*.

I

Perhaps the most fruitful distinction with which the sociological imagination works is this distinction—between personal troubles and public issues.

Troubles have to do with an individual's character and with those limited areas of social life of which he is directly and personally aware. Accordingly, to state and to resolve troubles we must look at the individual as a biographical entity and examine the scope of his immediate *milieu*—the social setting that is directly open to his personal experience and to some extent to his willful activity. A trouble is a private matter: values cherished by an individual are felt by him to be threatened.

Issues have to do with matters that transcend these local environments of the individual and the limited range of his life. They have to do with the organization of many such *milieux* into the institutions of society as a whole, with the ways, for example, in which various neighborhoods overlap to form the larger structures of a great metropolitan area. An issue is a public matter: values cherished by publics are felt to be threatened. Often there is debate about what these values really are, and about what it is that really threatens them. It is the very nature of an issue, unlike even widespread trouble, that it cannot very well be defined in terms of the everyday environments of ordinary men. An issue, in fact, often involves a crisis in institutional arrangements.

Such a crisis now exists in connection with the big cities of the Western societies.

In terms of troubles and issues—to illustrate the distinction further—consider briefly unemployment. When, in a city of 100,000, only *one* man is unemployed, that is his personal trouble, and for its relief we properly look to the character of this man, his skills, and his immediate opportunities. But when in a nation of 50 million employees, 15 million are unemployed, that is an issue, and we may not hope to find its solution within the range of opportunities open to any one individual. The very structure of opportunities has collapsed.

Consider war. The personal problem of war, when it occurs, may be how to survive it or how to die in it with honor; how to make money out of it; or how to climb into the higher safety of the military apparatus. In short, according to one's values, to find a set of *milieux* and within it to survive the war or to make one's death in it effective. But the structural issues of war have to do with its causes; with what types of men it throws up into command; with its effects upon economic and political and religious institutions; with the unorganized irresponsibility of a world of nation-states.

Consider marriage. Inside a marriage a man and a woman may experience personal troubles, but when the divorce rate during the first four years of marriage is 250 out of every 1,000 attempts, that indicates a structural issue having to do with the institutions of marriage and the family and other institutions that bear upon these.

Insofar as the elements of an economy are so arranged that slumps occur, the problem of unemployment becomes incapable of personal solution. Insofar as war is inherent in the nation-state system and in the uneven industrialization of the world, the ordinary individual, in his restricted *milieu*, will be powerless—with or without psychiatric aid—to solve the troubles this lack of system imposes upon him. Insofar as the family as an institution turns women into darling little slaves and men into their chief providers and unweaned dependents, the problem of a satisfactory marriage remains incapable of purely private solution.

And insofar as the overdeveloped megalopolis and the overdeveloped automobile are built-in features of the overdeveloped society, the problems of urban living will not be solved by personal ingenuity and private wealth.

What we experience in the specific, everyday *milieux* of the city is often caused by structural changes in the society as a whole. Accordingly, to understand the changes of many personal *milieux*, we are required to look beyond them. And the number and variety of such structural changes increase as the institutions within which we live become more embracing and more intricately connected with one another.

II

The forces that are shaping the big city are structural forces.

But the awareness and the effective action of "the citizens" are limited to a scatter of local *milieux*.

That, I think, is a good definition of what is meant by a mass society, and of the city as its major locale. As we become more aware of our condition we come to feel that we are living in a world in which we are merely spectators. We are acted upon, but we do not act. We feel that our personal experience is civically irrelevant, and our political will a minor illusion. Although we do not panic, we are often distracted and we are usually slightly bewildered. The more we come to understand our condition as a mass, the more frustrated we are likely to become—for we feel that our very knowledge leads to power-lessness. We live in metropolitan areas that are not communities in any real sense of the word, but rather unplanned monstrosities in which we, as men and women, are segregated into narrowed routines and limited *milieux*. In this metropolitan society, we develop, in our defense, a blasé manner that reaches deeper than a manner. We do not, accordingly, experience genuine clash of viewpoint. And when we do, we tend to consider it merely rude. We are sunk in our routines, and by them. We do not gain a view of the structure of our society as a whole and of our role within it. Our cities are composed of narrow slots, and we, as the people in these slots, are more and more confined to our own rather narrow ranges. Each is trapped in his confining circle; each is split from easily identifiable groups.

Given all those forces that have made our cities less political and more administrative; all the mass communications that do not truly communicate; all the metropolitan segregation that is no community—what is happening is the decline of a set of *publics* that is sovereign, except in the most formal and in the most rhetorical sense.

III

All this—and more—is what we mean when we speak of a mass society. The big city, I believe, is the focus for the human problems of this kind of society, if only because it is a convenient way to present what I am afraid seem utopian solutions. I would call your attention to that fact: virtually all truly sensible plans to re-shape the big city into some kind of reasonably human environment do seem utopian. The great point is always to ask *why* this is so. For then we come upon those forces over which we seem to have little or no control, but which in fact are determining how we must try to live. Rea-sonable and human plans seem utopian, from the standpoint of the practical and irrational, the often stupid and selfish interests that are now shaping our big cities.

Historically, these cities have come about without design, indeed without any reasoning about their meaning for the way men live in them. They are the results of many small decisions of innumerable people; but also, increasingly, of the deliberate—although always partial—plans of larger interests. These larger and more powerful interests are now often quite explicit and quite wide in their consequence.

The main forces that *consciously* shape the structure of the city today are private commercial interests, along with the presumably public interests that are more or less beholden to them. What has happened to Toronto (and to St. Louis) first of all, is the private expropriation and the profitable misuse of the very landscape in which the men, the women, the children of these cities are now trying to live.

These conscious interests, however, are allowed to operate in their chaotic and often disastrous manner because of *the civic vacuum* into which the people of a mass society have now fallen. What has happened to Toronto (and to St. Louis) is planless drift, civic incompetence, and civic apathy.

Such cities as these are the focal points of a society full of private people in a state of public lethargy, alternating on occasion with a state of animated distraction. Many people live in ugly wastelands, but in the absence of imaginative standards, most of them do not even know it. Their cities and suburbs are filled with built-in inconvenience, with nagging frustrations of the everyday life; but being habituated to these, many people often take them to be part of some natural order.

(i) In part, I have noted, the city is the result of blind drift. Accordingly, the problem of the city is how to transcend local *milieux* in order to consider publicly, imaginatively, planfully the city as a structure: to see it, in brief, as a public issue, and to see ourselves as a public—rather than as men in a mass trapped by merely personal troubles. We must realize, in a word, that we *need* not drift blindly; that we can take matters into our own hands.

(ii) In part, I have noted the city is the result of the partial planning of deliberate interests. Accordingly, the problem of the city is the problem of political or civic irresponsibility. Intellectually, this means that we must locate the blame for decisions being made and lack of decisions being committed about our cities. How else can we speak of responsibility? Politically, it means that we must organize and agitate against these sources of decision and lack of decision that fail to consider properly the human landscape in which we must live.

(iii) The city is necessarily a collective product and one that is never finished. In this it is unlike the variety of paintings and sculptures which we possess; at the same time it is the major locale of man's art; the visual scene in which he lives. But increasingly it is an inhuman landscape. Accordingly, the city is *the* esthetic problem—but more than that, it is the problem of the politics of esthetics. And to solve this problem there must come about a truly wide and deep discussion of the esthetics of the urban area—which is to say, a discussion of the quality and meaning of human life itself in our time.

IV

I cannot answer for you the political and esthetic problems of your cities. You must answer them, first of all by confronting them boldly. In an effort to make more concrete what I have been trying to say here, I should like to address myself, in conclusion, to members of those rather inchoate professions that are directly concerned with the city.

Most city planners and designers work mainly on *milieux*; most architects beautify the *milieux* of the rich and polish up the face of the corporation. They patch up bits and pieces of already partial structures. But now at least the best among them have reached a point where they are uneasy about the work they do. They are coming up against structural problems, and up against those who by their decisions and defaults determine many *milieux*. Men are not equal in power. The private in an army has no chance to view the whole structure of the army, much less to direct it. But the general does. *His* means of information, of vision, of decision are much greater. In like manner with the owner of a development tract, as against an individual householder. In short, are we not coming to see that the chaos of our cities is first of all part of an irresponsible economic and political system? And second, that, after all, the city planners themselves are in something of an esthetic chaos?

Let me put all this in terms of some questions to the city planners, and to those interested in the city as a place for human living.

(i) Is the ugly, frustrating and irrational structure of the city *now* due so much to fate, to haphazard forces, or can you now identify circles of men who are responsible for decisions that affect the innumerable *milieux* that make up the city? Historically, the answer is obviously fate. But the bulldozer fleet and the real estate interests are now putting an end to fate of this kind. And city governments too—surely you will agree that often they seem most readily understandable as committees for a complex of real estate interests?

(ii) Is the architect merely to work on beautifying the isolated *milieux* of wealthy persons—or is he to be concerned with the planning of the human landscape for all people? Is he content to be the subordinate of the irrational and greedy powers that now shape the structure of our environment—or is he to be a member of an autonomous profession that demands a voice in decisions of structural consequence being debated by publics?

(iii) There has been much talk about the lack of any discernible *order* in our present environment. I think this largely nonsense. Is not the common denominator capital gain and material accumulation? Is not the pattern of our environment very largely that of real estate interests and advertising maniacs? To such types our cities are not at all disorderly; on the contrary, they are as orderly as the files to title deeds.

(iv) The sensibility of the designer, the architect, the artists, the city planner—is it not in conflict with this ethos of the capitalist? Are they content to be the subordinates of men who, seeing a forest, immediately think only of board feet? Of men who, seeing a new color, think immediately of how it might make obsolete last year's fashion in ladies' dresses, automobiles and soon, private houses? Are they in short willing to be part and parcel of the commercial frenzy, the banalization of sensibility and the deliberate planning of obsolescence?

(v) The people really concerned with the problems of the city are now confronting questions, I believe, that the intellectuals of the thirties confronted. For example, is there a contradiction between corporate capitalism and publicly responsible planning? What are the proper relations of reform and revolution? What *is* "practical" and what *is* "utopian?" Does not utopian mean merely: whatever acknowledges other values as relevant and possibly even as sovereign? But in truth, are not those who in the name of realism act like crackpots, are they not the utopians? Are we not now in a situation in which the only practical, realistic down-to-earth thinking and acting is just what these crackpot realists call "utopian?"

Our professions and crafts that have to do with the city are now in chaos, and without agreed-upon standards. Our task—as professional people and as citizens—is to formulate standards; to set forth as a conference ten or twelve propositions on which we are willing to stand up. Let us begin this, here and now.

SEVENTEEN

Culture and Politics

The Fourth Epoch

THIS WAS THE FIRST in a series of three University Lectures in Sociology at the London School of Economics (LSE) on the subject of
culture and politics. Mills drew the lecture-series from a manuscript entitled
The Cultural Apparatus, or the American Intellectual. These three LSE lectures,
reprinted here in the order he delivered them, best represent this unfinished
project, all the more so because he heartily approved of the editing. "Culture
and Politics: The Fourth Epoch" was given in London on January 12, 1959,
then broadcast on the BBC's Third Programme on March 6, then published in
the March 12 issue of its magazine, *The Listener.*

⸎

We are at the ending of what is called The Modem Age. Just as Antiquity was
followed by several centuries of Oriental ascendancy which Westerners pro-
vincially call The Dark Ages, so now The Modem Age is being succeeded by a
post-modern period. Perhaps we may call it: The Fourth Epoch.

The ending of one epoch and the beginning of another is, to be sure, a
matter of definition. But definitions, like everything social, are historically
specific. And now our basic definitions of society and of self are being overtaken by new realities. I do not mean merely that we *feel* we are in an epochal
kind of transition. I mean that too many of our explanations are derived from
the great historical transition from the Medieval to the Modern Age; and that
when they are generalized for use today, they become unwieldy, irrelevant,
not convincing. And I mean also that our major orientations—liberalism and

socialism—have virtually collapsed as adequate explanations of the world and of ourselves.

Two Ideologies from the Enlightenment

These two ideologies came out of The Enlightenment, and they have had in common many assumptions and two major values: in both, freedom and reason are supposed to coincide: increased rationality is held to be the prime condition of increased freedom. Those thinkers who have done the most to shape our ways of thinking have proceeded under this assumption; these values lie under every movement and nuance of the work of Freud: to be free, the individual must become more rationally aware; therapy is an aid to giving reason its chance to work freely in the course of an individual's life; these values underpin the main line of marxist work: men, caught in the irrational anarchy of production, must become rationally aware of their position in society; they must become "class conscious"—the marxian meaning of which is as rationalistic as any term set forth by Bentham.

Liberalism has been concerned with freedom and reason as supreme facts about the individual; marxism as supreme facts about man's role in the political making of history. But what has been happening in the world makes evident, I believe, why the ideas of freedom and of reason now so often seem so ambiguous in both the capitalist and the communist societies of our time: why marxism has so often become a dreary rhetoric of bureaucratic defense and political abuse; and liberalism, a trivial and irrelevant way of masking social reality. The major developments of our time can be adequately understood in terms of neither the liberal nor the marxian interpretation of politics and culture. These ways of thought, after all, arose as guide-lines to reflection about types of society which do not now exist. John Stuart Mill never examined the kinds of political economy now arising in the capitalist world. Karl Marx never analyzed the kinds of society now arising in the Communist bloc. And neither of them ever thought through the problems of the so-called underdeveloped countries in which seven out of ten men are trying to exist today.

The ideological mark of The Fourth Epoch—that which sets it off from The Modern Age—is that the ideas of freedom and of reason have become moot; that increased rationality may not be assumed to make for increased freedom.

The Individual and the Organization

The underlying trends are well known. Great and rational organizations—in brief, bureaucracies—have indeed increased, but the substantive reason of the individual at large has not. Caught in the limited milieux of their everyday lives, ordinary men often cannot reason about the great structures—rational and irrational—of which their milieux are subordinate parts. Accordingly, they often carry out series of apparently rational actions without any ideas of the ends they serve, and there is the increasing suspicion that those at the top as well—like Tolstoy's generals—only pretend they know. That the techniques and the rationality of Science are given a central place in a society does not mean that men live reasonably and without myth, fraud and superstition. Science, it turns out, is not a technological Second Coming. Universal education may lead to technological idiocy and nationalist provinciality, rather than to the informed and independent intelligence. Rationally organized social arrangements are not necessarily a means of increased freedom—for the individual or for the society. In fact, often they are a means of tyranny and manipulation, a means of expropriating the very chance to reason, the very capacity to act as a free man.

The atrocities of The Fourth Epoch are committed by men as "functions" of a rational social machinery—men possessed by an abstracted view that hides from them the humanity of their victims and as well their own humanity. The moral insensibility of our times was made dramatic by the Nazis, but is not the same lack of human morality revealed by the atomic bombing of the peoples of Hiroshima and Nagasaki? And did it not prevail, too, among fighter pilots in Korea, with their petroleum-jelly broiling of children and women and men? Auschwitz and Hiroshima—are they not equally features of the highly rational moral-insensibility of The Fourth Epoch? And is not this lack of moral sensibility raised to a higher and technically more adequate level among the brisk generals and gentle scientists who are now rationally—and absurdly—planning the weapons and the strategy of the third world war? These actions are not necessarily sadistic; they are merely businesslike; they are not emotional at all; they are efficient, rational, technically clean-cut. They are inhuman acts because they are impersonal.

Structure of a New World

In the meantime, ideology and sensibility quite apart, the compromises and exploitations by which the nineteenth-century world was balanced have collapsed. In this sixth decade of the twentieth century the structure of a new world is indeed coming into view.

The ascendancy of the U.S.A., along with that of the U.S.S.R., has relegated the scatter of European nations to subsidiary status. The world of The Fourth Epoch is divided. On either side, a super-power now spends its most massive and co-ordinated effort in the highly scientific preparation of a third world war.

Yet, for the first time in history, the very idea of victory in war has become idiotic. As war becomes total, it becomes absurd. Yet in both the super-states, virtually all policies and actions fall within the perspective of war; in both, élites and spokesmen—in particular, I must say, those of the United States— are possessed by the military metaphysic, according to which all world reality is defined in military terms. By both, the most decisive features of reality are held to be the state of violence and the balance of fright.

Back of this struggle there is the world-encounter of two types of political economy, and in this encounter capitalism is losing. Some higher capitalists of the U.S.A. are becoming aware of this, and they are very much frightened. They fear, with good justification, that they are going to become an isolated and a second-rate power. They represent utopian capitalism in a world largely composed of people whose experiences with real capitalism, if any, have been mostly brutal. They profess "democracy" in a nation where it is more a formal outline than an actuality, and in a world in which the great majority of people have never experienced the bourgeois revolutions, in a world in which the values deposited by the Renaissance and the Reformation do not restrain the often brutal thrust to industrialize.

United States foreign policy and lack of foreign policy is firmly a part of the absurdity of this world scene, and it is foremost among the many defaults of the Western societies. During the last few years, confronting the brinks, I have often suspected that the world is not at the third world war largely because of the calculation and the forbearance of the Soviet élite.

What Kind of a Society?

What kind of a society is the U.S.A. turning out to be in the middle of the twentieth century? Perhaps it is possible to characterize it as a prototype of at least "The West." To locate it within its world context in The Fourth Epoch, perhaps we may call it The Overdeveloped Society.

The *Underdeveloped Country* as you know, is one in which the focus of life is necessarily upon economic subsistence; its industrial equipment is not sufficient to meet Western standards of minimum comfort. Its style of life and its system of power are dominated by the struggle to accumulate the primary means of industrial production.

In a *Properly Developing Society*, one might suppose that deliberately cultivated styles of life would be central; decisions about standards of living would be made in terms of debated choices among such styles; the industrial equipment of such a society would be maintained as an instrument to increase the range of choice among styles of life.

But in *The Overdeveloped Nation*, the standard of living dominates the style of life; its inhabitants are possessed, as it were, by its industrial and commercial apparatus: collectively, by the maintenance of conspicuous production; individually, by the frenzied pursuit and maintenance of commodities. Around these fetishes, life, labor and leisure are increasingly organized. Focused upon these, the struggle for status supplements the struggle for survival; a panic for status replaces the proddings of poverty.

In underdeveloped countries, industrialization, however harsh, may be seen as man conquering nature and so freeing himself from want. But in the overdeveloped nation, as industrialization proceeds, the economic emphasis moves from production to merchandizing, and the economic system which makes a fetish of efficiency becomes highly inefficient and systematically wasteful. The pivotal decade for this shift in the United States was the 'twenties, but it is since the ending of the second world war that the overdeveloped economy has truly come to flourish.

Surely there is no need to elaborate this theme in detail; since Thorstein Veblen formulated it, it has been several times "affluently" rediscovered. Society in brief, has become a great sales-room—and a network of rackets: the gimmick of success becomes the yearly change of model, as in the mass-society fashion becomes universal. The marketing apparatus transforms the human being into the ultimately-saturated man—the cheerful robot-and makes "anxious obsolescence" the American way of life.

Beneath the Obvious Surface

But all this—although enormously important to the quality of life—is, I suppose, merely the obvious surface. Beneath it there are institutions which in the United States today are as far removed from the images of Tocqueville as is Russia today from the classic expectations of Marx.

The power structure of this society is based upon a privately incorporated economy that is also a permanent war economy. Its most important relations with the state now rest upon the coincidence of military and corporate interests—as defined by generals and businessmen, and accepted by politicians and publics. It is an economy dominated by a few hundred corporations, economically and politically interrelated, which together hold the keys to economic decision. These dominating corporation hierarchies probably represent the highest concentration of the greatest economic power in human history, including that of the Soviet Union. They are firmly knit to political and military institutions, but they are dogmatic—even maniacal—in their fetish of the "freedom" of their private and irresponsible power.

I should like to put this matter in terms of certain parallel developments in the U.S.A. and the U.S.S.R. The very terms of their world antagonism are furthering their similarities: Geographically and ethnically both are super-societies; unlike the nations of Europe, each has amalgamated on a continental domain great varieties of peoples and cultures. The power of both is based upon technological development. In both, this development is made into a cultural and a social fetish, rather than an instrument under continual public appraisal and control. In neither is there significant craftsmanship in work or significant leisure in the non-working life. In both, men at leisure and at work are subjected to impersonal bureaucracies. In neither do workers control the process of production or consumers truly shape the process of consumption. Workers' control s as far removed from both as is consumers' sovereignty.

In both the United States and the Soviet Union, as the political order is enlarged and centralized, it becomes less political and more bureaucratic; less the locale of a struggle than an object to be managed. In neither are there nationally responsible parties which debate openly and clearly the issues which these nations, and indeed the world, now so rigidly confront. Under some conditions, must we not recognize that the two-party state can be as irresponsible as is a one-party state?

In neither the U.S.A. nor the U.S.S.R. is there a senior civil service firmly linked to the world of knowledge and sensibility and composed of skilled men who, in their careers and in their aspirations, are truly independent—in the U.S.A. of corporation interests, in the U.S.S.R. of party dictation.

In neither of these super-powers are there, as central facts of power, voluntary associations linking individuals, smaller communities and publics, on the one hand, with the state, the military establishment, the economic apparatus on the other. Accordingly, in neither are there readily available vehicles for reasoned opinions and instruments for the national exertion of public will. Such voluntary associations are no longer a dominant feature of the political structure of the overdeveloped society.

The classic conditions of democracy, in summary, do not exactly flourish in the overdeveloped society; democratic formations are not now ascendant in the power structure of the United States or of the Soviet Union. Within both, history-making decisions and lack of decisions are virtually monopolized by élites who have access to the material and cultural means by which history is now powerfully being made.

An Emphasis on Differences

I stress these parallels, and perhaps exaggerate them, because of the great nationalist emphasis upon the differences between the two world antagonists. The parallels are, of course, due in each case to entirely different sources; and so are the great differences. In the capitalist societies the development of the means of power has occurred gradually, and many cultural traditions have restrained and shaped them. In most of the Communist societies they have happened rapidly and brutally and from the beginning under tightly centralized authority; and without the cultural revolutions which in the West so greatly strengthened and gave political focus to the idea of human freedom.

You may say that all this is an immoderate and biased view of America, that America also contains many good features. Indeed that is so. But you must not expect me to provide A Balanced View. I am not a sociological book-keeper. Moreover, "balanced views" are now usually surface views which rest upon the homogeneous absence of imagination and the passive avoidance of reflection. A balanced view is usually, in the phrase of Royden Harrison, merely a vague point of equilibrium between platitudes.

I feel no need for, and perhaps am incapable of arranging for you, a lyric upsurge, a cheerful little pat on the moral back. Yet perhaps, by returning to my point of beginning, I can remind you of the kinds of problems you might want to confront. I must make two points only: one about fate and the making of history; the other about the roles many intellectuals are now enacting.

Fate has to do with events in history that are the summary and unintended results of innumerable decisions of innumerable men. Each of their decisions is minute in consequence and subject to cancellation or reinforcement by other such decisions. There is no link between any one man's intention and the summary result of the innumerable decisions. Events are beyond human decisions: history is made behind men's backs.

So conceived, fate is not a universal fact; it is not inherent in the nature of history or in the nature of man. In a society in which the ultimate weapon is the rifle; in which the typical economic unit is the family farm and shop; in which the national-state does not yet exist or is merely a distant framework; and in which communication is by word of mouth, handbill, pulpit—in *such* a society, history is indeed fate.

But consider now the major clue to our condition, to the shape of the overdeveloped society in The Fourth Epoch. In modern industrial society the means of economic production are developed and centralized, as peasants and artisans are replaced by private corporations and government industries. In the modern nation-state the means of violence and of administration undergo similar developments, as kings control nobles and self-equipped knights are replaced by standing armies and now by fearful military machines. The *post-modern* climax of all three developments—in economics, in politics, and in violence—is now occurring most dramatically in the U.S.A. and the U.S.S.R. In the polarized world of our time, international as well as national means of history-making are being centralized. Is it not thus clear that the scope and the chance for conscious human agency in history-making are just now uniquely available? Élites of power in charge of these means do now make history—to be sure, "under circumstances not of their own choosing"—but compared to other men and other epochs, these circumstances themselves certainly do not appear to be overwhelming.

And surely here is the paradox of our immediate situation: the facts about the newer means of history-making are a signal that men are not necessarily in the grip of fate, that men can now make history. But this fact stands ironically alongside the further fact that just now those ideologies which offer men the hope of making history have declined and are collapsing in the overdeveloped nation of the United States. That collapse is also the collapse of the expectations of the Enlightenment, that reason and freedom would come to prevail as paramount forces in human history. It also involves the abdication of many Western intellectuals.

In the overdeveloped society, where is the intelligentsia that is carrying on the big discourse of the Western world *and* whose work as intellectuals is influential among parties and publics and relevant to the great decisions of our time? Where are the mass media open to such men? Who among those in charge of the two-party state and its ferocious military machines are alert to what goes on in the world of knowledge and reason and sensibility? Why is the free intellect so divorced from decisions of power? Why does there now prevail among men of power such a higher and irresponsible ignorance?

In The Fourth Epoch, must we not face the possibility that the human mind as a social fact might be deteriorating in quality and cultural level, and yet not many would notice it because of the overwhelming accumulation of technological gadgets? Is not that the meaning of rationality without reason? Of human alienation? Of the absence of any role for reason in human affairs? The accumulation of gadgets hides these meanings: those who use them do not understand them; those who invent and maintain them do not understand much else. That is why we may not, without great ambiguity, use technological abundance as the index of human quality and cultural progress.

To formulate any problem requires that we state the values involved and the threat to these values. For it is the felt threat to cherished values—such as those of freedom and reason—that is the necessary moral substance of all significant problems of social inquiry, and as well of all public issues and private troubles.

The values involved in the cultural problem of freedom and individuality are conveniently embodied in all that is suggested by the ideal of The Renaissance Man. The threat to that ideal is the ascendancy among us of The Cheerful Robot, of the man with rationality but without reason. The values involved in the political problem of history-making are embodied in the Promethean ideal of its human making. The threat to that ideal is twofold: On the one hand, history-making may well go by default, men may continue to abdicate its willful making, and so merely drift. On the other hand, history may indeed be made—but by narrow élite circles without effective responsibility to those who must try to survive the consequences of their decisions and of their defaults.

I do not know the answer to the question of political irresponsibility in our time or to the cultural and political question of The Cheerful Robot; but is it not clear that no answers will be found unless these problems are at least confronted? Is it not obvious that the ones to confront them, above all others, are the intellectuals, the scholars, the ministers, the scientists of the rich societies? That many of them do not now do so, with moral passion, with intellectual energy, is surely the greatest human default being committed by privileged men in our times.

EIGHTEEN | The Cultural Apparatus

THIS WAS THE SECOND in a series of three University Lectures in Sociology at the London School of Economics (LSE) on the subject of culture and politics. Mills drew the lecture-series from a manuscript entitled *The Cultural Apparatus, or the American Intellectual.* These three LSE lectures, reprinted here in the order he delivered them, best represent this unfinished project, all the more so because he heartily approved of the editing.

"The Cultural Apparatus" was given in London on January 13, 1959, then broadcast on the BBC's Third Programme on March 13, then published in the March 26 issue of its magazine, *The Listener.*

———— ∞ ————

The first rule for understanding the human condition is that men live in second-hand worlds: they are aware of much more than they have personally experienced; and their own experience is always indirect. No man stands alone directly confronting a world of solid facts. No such world is available. The closest men come to it is when they are infants or when they become insane: then, in a terrifying scene of meaningless events and senseless confusion, they are often seized with the panic of near-total insecurity. But in their everyday lives the experience of men is itself selected by stereotyped meanings and shaped by ready-made interpretations. Their images of the world, and of themselves, are given to them by crowds of witnesses they have never met and never will meet. Yet for every man these images—provided by strangers and dead men—are the very basis of his life as a human being.

Interpretation Centres

The consciousness of men does not determine their material existence; nor does their material existence determine their consciousness. Between consciousness and existence stand meanings and designs and communications which other men have passed on—first, in human speech itself, and, later, by the management of symbols. For most of what he calls solid fact, sound interpretation, suitable presentations, every man is increasingly dependent upon the observation posts, the interpretation centres, the presentation depots, which in contemporary society are established by means of what I am going to call the cultural apparatus.

This apparatus is composed of all the organizations and milieux in which artistic, intellectual, and scientific work goes on, and by which entertainment and information are produced and distributed. It contains an elaborate set of institutions: of schools and theaters, newspapers and census bureaux, studios, laboratories, museums, little magazines, radio networks. It contains truly fabulous agencies of exact information and of trivial distraction, exciting objects, lazy escape, and strident advice. Inside this apparatus, standing between men and events, the images, meanings, slogans that define the world in which men live are organized and compared, maintained and revised, lost and cherished, hidden, debunked, celebrated. It is the source of the Human Variety—of styles of living and of ways to die.

So decisive to experience itself are the results of these communications that often men do not really believe what "they see before their very eyes" until they have been "informed" about it by the national broadcast, the close-up photograph, the official announcement. With such means, each nation tends to offer a selected, closed-up, and official version of world reality. The cultural apparatus not only guides experience; often as well it expropriates the very chance to have experience that can rightly be called "our own." For our standards of credibility, our definitions of reality, our modes of sensibility— as well as our immediate opinions and images—are determined much less by any pristine experience than by our exposure to the output of the cultural apparatus.

This apparatus is the seat of civilization, which, in Matthew Arnold's phrase, is "the humanization of man in society." It is in terms of some such conception as this apparatus that the politics of culture may be understood.

Intellectuals, Active and Withdrawn

Around the world today some intellectuals play leading roles in the politics of their nation; others are altogether withdrawn from political concerns; seemingly without political orientation, they are political inactionaries.

But the politics of cultural work is not to be identified with the explicit political views or activities of cultural workmen. There is a great difference between enacting a political role and being, by virtue of one's work, politically relevant. The political choices of individuals must be distinguished from the political functions, uses and consequences of the cultural work they do.

That a scientist working in a laboratory may honestly conceive of himself as a disembodied spirit does not make any the less real the consequences of his discovery for the ultimate ends of bombing the population of a city of which he has never heard.

That an artist simply may not care about anything but the way a certain shade of blue explodes in the eye does not make any the less real the function of his picture when it is seized upon by men of nationalistic purpose. And nowadays any artistic product may well be seized upon in the building of cultural prestige for national authority.

That a sociologist cares only about the mathematical properties of "a new scaling device for attitude studies" does not detract from the objective function of his work in helping generals to prod farm boys to kill off more Japanese, or corporation executives to manipulate all the more brightly their sounds and images going out endlessly to 50,000,000 homes in order to increase the sales-volume of a new shade of lipstick—or a new presidential face.

Although not all cultural workmen are concerned with politics, their work is increasingly of central relevance to the great issues of history, and to the quality of everyday life. We cannot examine merely the individual workman and his choices; the cultural apparatus as a whole is established and used by dominant institutional orders. Growing up and working with it, educated by it, many cultural workmen today never feel the need to make political choices simply because they are in fact committed before the age of political consent.

The "Establishment"

As an institutional fact, the cultural apparatus assumes many forms, but everywhere today it tends to be part of some national establishment. This term, "establishments," is of course your English term. The ambiguity with which you use it is at once too lovely and too useful for a mere sociologist to avoid stealing it, although I promise that I shall try not to make of it A Concept. The essential feature of any establishment is a traffic between culture and authority, a tacit co-operation of cultural workmen and authorities of a ruling institution. This means of exchange between them includes money, career, privilege; but, above all, it includes *prestige*. To the powerful, cultural prestige lends "weight.". Ideologies may justify explicitly, but it is prestige that truly celebrates. The prestige of culture transforms power into spell-binding authority. That is why the cultural apparatus, no matter how in-ternally free, tends in every nation to become a close adjunct of national authority and a leading agency of nationalist propaganda.

To the cultural workman, the prestige borrowed from association with authority lends increased "dignity" to his work—and to himself. It makes of him a national point of reference for that rank-order of cultural work and of cultural workmen. What is so loosely called "the climate of opinion" refers to just such points of national reference for the producers, the consumers, and the products of cultural work. National establishments tend to set the rela-tions of culture and politics the important tasks, the suitable themes: the major uses of the cultural apparatus. In the end, what is "established" are definitions of reality, judgments of value, canons of taste and of beauty.

In any economy, without some continuing financial support, cultural activities cannot very well go on, must less be established. A set of publics is also required. These may consist of small circles of producers who form their own publics, or of 100,000,000 inexpert consumers of culture. The size of the cultural public—as well as the prestige, class, and power of its members—are major clues to cultural orientation. A John Stuart Mill writing with a re-ceptive parliament in mind clearly occupies a different position than a Soviet novelist oriented to party officials or an American professor writing for other professors.

A great deal of the modern history of culture, until well into the twentieth century, has to do with the transition from the patronage—which I shall call Stage One—to Stage Two—the emergence of bourgeois public. In fact, most of our inherited images of "the intellectual" and of "the artist" are based upon experience of this second stage. It has provided the models of the cultural creator that still prevail among us: the inherently and necessarily free man, and the cherished and heroic notion of the advanced-guard. This notion, one might say, is "the myth" of the intellectual, the artist, the lone inventor, and even of the scientist. It is still clung to mightily, being identified with freedom itself by those whose ideal is *not* to become established.

In the third stage of cultural development, which we now enter, several tendencies evident in the second are carried to their logical outcome: the cultural workman becomes a man who is qualified, politically or commercially. Both money and public are "provided," and in due course so are cultural products themselves: cultural work is not only guided: culture is produced and distributed—and even consumed—to order. Commercial agencies or political authorities support culture, but, unlike older patrons, they do not form its sole public.

In the extreme, as in modern totalitarianism, all "observation posts" are available only to the duly qualified; all "interpretation centres" are subject to doctrinal or pecuniary review; all "presentation depots" are carefully-guarded points of access to masses or to markets. The competition of ideas and of images is confined to the narrowed range, the exact limits of which are seldom known. By trial and error they must be found out, and the attempt to do so is judged officially, sometimes bloodily; or it is judged commercially, often ruthlessly.

Today, of course, all three stages of establishment exist side by side, in one nation or another, in one division of culture or another. Accordingly, around the world today, the politics of culture and the culture of politics are quite various.

In Underdeveloped Countries—

In underdeveloped countries, the cultural apparatus is usually confined to very small circles and to rudimentary middle classes. Often it consists of only a few distributors and consumers, linked by education to the cultural machineries of more developed nations. These unhappy few often form the only public available for cultural products and services. Their countries are often filled with masses of people whose lives are dominated by the historical round of subsistence in family, village and tribe; by mass illiteracy and the preindustrial grind of poverty. Such facts limit and often make impossible any larger public and any larger support for cultural activities.

What is characteristic of the cultural establishment of leading West-European nations is their historic duration as semi-official formations of prestige which are somewhat independent from national authority but which have great relevance to it. Although decisively modified, they often retain something of the flavour of patronage.

In France, it is said, Men of Letters have historically formed a sort of tribune that is in part a political, in part a literary, and altogether a nationalist matter. The writer is "the public conscience.". The centre of the French establishment is The Academy, and The Ministry of Education which embrace virtually all features of cultural endeavour. Even the most "radical" of Frenchmen tend somehow still to feel themselves inside representatives of French culture.

In Germany, the professoriate, historically seated in state universities, has been the bearer of German science and scholarship, its members the national insiders of the German establishment. Near the top of the general hierarchy for prestige, they have also been among the higher servants of the state, and yet once seated, rather autonomous within it.

In England, what is called "The Establishment" at any given time seems a vague formation and rather closed-up. Yet, viewed historically, it appears to have been generously assimilative. At its centre have been the older universities, the churches, the higher civil service, the monarchy; these have been firmly connected with county families and their gentry culture. Historically, from the points of this triangle of university, government, and social class, The Establishment has radiated wondrously in the attempted embrace of the politics and culture of nation, empire, and commonwealth.

In all these European countries, established cultural workmen have often been held in high esteem. On the basis of their prestige, they long resisted the naked force of money; closely related to political authorities, at the same time they have been autonomous from them. In both these respects, of course, European cultural agencies and cultural workmen are undergoing decisive change.

—in the One-party State

The Soviet Union, despite "revisionism," now represents one rather pure type of Stage Three. The source of money is the one-party state; masses of people are the managed public for culture; cultural activities are official activities. Opposition is traitorous, and exists mainly as a more or less hidden literary mood. In the absence of opposition parties, cultural activities become the only available form of opposition.

The physical terror and psychic coercion of The Purge seemed necessary to an official establishment of this type. For its very basis is a fusion of the special skills of cultural workmen and special tests of political loyalty; it is dominated by a political management of status, reputation, and public shaming. Suddenly the official line changes; then the only innocent man is the man who has accomplished nothing—because he is too young or because he has quietly withdrawn from work. Since any mature and active cultural workman has a quotable past, the very history of the intelligentsia leaves in its way a cumulative guilt. The disgraced man's past is publicly turned against him; so his one opportunity is to out-compete those who vilify him—he must vilify his own past and his own work. Such self-accusation and recanting may be an expedient adjustment to authority, or a genuine reversal of values. To understand which it is in any given case one must realize the totality of allegiance to The Party, and one must think in terms of traumas, and of activities well known in the religious sphere as penance and conversion.

In the Soviet bloc, the cultural apparatus is established by an authority that *post-dates* capitalism: an official apparatus of psychic domination, it is quiet fully a part of political authority. In the leading nations of Western Europe, the cultural apparatus is established out of a tradition that *pre-dates* capitalism; in it the authority of tradition and the prestige of culture have been intricately joined. Both cultural tradition and political authority are involved in any establishment of culture, but in the United States the cultural apparatus is established in a third way: there, culture, above all, is part of an ascendant capitalist economy, and this economy is now in a condition of seemingly permanent war. Cultural activities, on the one hand, tend to become a commercial part of an overdeveloped capitalist economy, or, on the other, an official part of the Science Machine of the Garrison State.

—and in the U.S.A.

Many an American intellectual, artist, scientist is becoming an important adjunct of a very peculiar kind of economy. His work is a business, but his business is with idea, image, technique. He is caught up, first, in the shift in economic emphasis from production to distribution, and, along with this, the joining of the struggle for existence with the merchandized panic for status

The virtual dominance of commercial culture is the immediate ground of America's cultural confusion, banality, excitement, sterility. What has happened in the last two centuries to work in general is now rapidly happening to artistic, scientific and intellectual endeavor: now these too become part of society as a set of bureaucracies and as a great salesroom.

The cultural workman has little control over the means of distribution of which he becomes a part. The distributor—along with his market researcher—"establishes a market" and monopolizes access to it. Then he claims to "know what they want." The orders he gives, even to the freelance, become more explicit and detailed. The price he offers may be quite high—perhaps too high, he comes to think, and perhaps he is right. So he begins to hire and in varying degree to manage a stable of cultural workmen. Those who thus allow themselves to be managed by the mass distributor are selected, and in time formed, in such ways as to be altogether proficient, but not quite compelling in their attractions. Accordingly, the search goes on for "fresh ideas," for exciting notions, for more luring models; in brief: for the innovator.

But in the meantime, back at the studio, the laboratory, the research bureau, the writer's factory, the distributor manages many producers who become rank-and-file workmen of the commercially established cultural apparatus.

Commercial Hack or Star

There is increasing bureaucracy but also there is the frenzy for new fashions; and in this situation, the cultural workman tends to become either a commercial hack or a commercial star. By the star, I refer to a person whose productions are so much in demand that, to some extent at least, he is able to use distributors as his adjuncts. This role has its own conditions and its own perils: the star tends to be culturally trapped by his own success. He has painted, for example, one sort of thing and he gets $5,000 a throw for it. However affluent, he often becomes culturally bored by this style and wants to explore another. But often he cannot: he is used to $5,000 a throw and there is demand for "his style." As a leader of fashions he is himself subject to fashion. Moreover, his success as a star depends upon his "playing the market": he is not in any educative interplay with publics that support him as he develops and which he in turn cultivates. By virtue of his success, the star too becomes a marketeer.

Some cultural workmen do remain independent. Perhaps three to four men actually earn a living in the fabulously wealthy United States merely by composing serious music; perhaps twenty-five or so, if we relax our standards a little, merely by writing serious novels. But generally the star system tends to kill off the chance of the cultural workman to be a worthy and independent craftsman. One is a smash-hit or one is nothing at all.

Behind these developments, there is the important fact that between the Jeffersonian era and the second world war no cultural establishment of the European type has existed in the United States. Underlying this fact, in turn, is the unopposed ascendancy of capitalism and liberalism. The bourgeoisie from its national beginnings has been unhampered by feudal power and prestige—by any pre-capitalist strata or powers or institutions. Accordingly, its members have easily monopolized both social prestige and political power as they have created and occupied the top positions of the class structure.

The very rich in America have not been notable as a self-cultivating elite. No nationally significant class of rentier gentlemen sat in the nineteenth-century countryside writing books, plays, histories, or painting pictures; nor, after the early days of the Republic, have American politicians been prone, as the French are said to be, to literary production. Even their own utterances are typically shaped by hired ghosts. Neither the very rich nor the politically powerful have generally been a suitable public for live artists and intellectuals. Their sons have become lawyers, not sculptors; graduates of business schools, not writers; and these sons, the daughters of the very rich have married.

Rise of European Bourgeoisie

All this stands in contrast to the rise of the European bourgeoisie. In Europe, to gain mere economic position has not been also to gain prestige and power. In Europe, the pomp of state, the dignity of Church, the honour of violence—and the halo of cultural sensibility—have rested upon feudal powers, which have monopolized strategic positions of authority—and of culture. Only slowly and after much struggle have the sons of the bourgeoisie come to rise alongside these strata, and in the course of generations to displace them. In its struggle, the bourgeoisie was itself transformed; to some extent, it was made over in the honorific ways of pre-capitalistic kinds of cultural sensibilities and political opinion.

Men Who Have Met Pay-rolls

Upon the American bourgeoisie—continuously predominant in wealth, power, and prestige—upon this bourgeoisie, as patron and as public, cultural workmen have been conspicuously dependent. It is the businessman who has established and run colleges, libraries, museums. And cultural workmen themselves have often felt considerable gratitude towards the "men who have produced" the "men who have met payrolls."

The capitalist producer has been felt to possess and even to create the ascendant American values: usefulness and efficiency. Even the most independent cultural critics have honored these same values. America's foremost critic in the period of America's most deep-going criticism—Thorstein Veblen in the Progressive Era—assumed these values as indubitable. He was opposed to the power of business precisely because he felt that business men did not truly serve these values, but rather those of waste and idleness. In short, the notion—brilliantly argued by Joseph Schumpeter—that under capitalism they inevitably become critics of consequence, does not generally hold true of the United States.

In conclusion, I should like to suggest to you that it is just the sort of establishment that Europe has known that many American intellectuals (as well as sophisticated circles of the ruling elite) want to bring about in the United States. I do not believe that they will make it, any more than I believe that these kinds of "establishments" prevail in Europe. For now Europe too is increasingly subject to those tendencies which now affect all cultural establishments as they enter the Fourth Epoch. You of England, I think, are living off a capital you are not replenishing. The form toward which your establishment now drifts may of course already be seen in a more pronounced, even flamboyant way in the United States of America.

"T HAT FINAL TALK of yours was absolutely splendid," E.P. Thompson wrote to Mills soon after listening to the third of three University Lectures in Sociology at the London School of Economics (LSE). Mills drew the lecture-series from a manuscript entitled *The Cultural Apparatus, or the American Intellectual*. These three LSE lectures, reprinted here in the order he delivered them, best represent this unfinished project, all the more so because he heartily approved of the editing.

"The Decline of the Left" was given in London on January 15, 1959, then broadcast on the BBC's Third Programme on March 16, then published in the April 2 issue of its magazine, *The Listener*. Mills read "The Decline of the Left" again on April 15, at Stanford University. Pacifica Radio broadcast it on May 13, and the magazine *Contact*, reprinted it in its 1959 issue. On August 7, 1961, WBAI Radio in New York City rebroadcast it at 9:00 A.M.

Opposition to The Establishment often consists merely of scattered groups, working in small-circulation magazines, dealing in unsold cultural products. Often but not always. Outsiders may also be members of an oppositional establishment of their very own. Such "left establishments" have often been as confining in their values, and as snobbish in their assignment of prestige, as any national establishment. In fact, often they have seemed more restrictive, first because of their usual pretensions not to be, and second because dogmatic gospel is often more needed by minority circles than by those secure in major institutions.

That is one reason why I think it naive to assume that the major divisions among the cultural workmen of a nation are those who are established and accordingly somehow unfree and those who are of an advanced guard, creative in culture and radical in politics. People who call themselves "left," or "advanced guard" or "high-brow" are often as fully routinized—although usually they are not so durable—as those who are in and of a national establishment. The left establishment also creates and sustains a cultural and political climate, sets the key tasks and the suitable themes, and establishes the proper canons of value and taste.

In our time, there is nowhere any left establishment that is truly international, or in fact truly left and at the same time consequential.

In the Soviet Union today there is no legal basis for any opposition: opposition is disloyalty; political and cultural activities are embraced by the establishment of the Communist Party, which is nationalist, official, and on due occasion coercive.

In the United States today there is no left: political activities are monopolized by an irresponsible two-party system; cultural activities—although formally quite free—tend to become nationalist or commercial, or merely private.

In Western Europe, what remains of the older left is weak; its remnants have become inconsequential as a cultural and political center of insurgent opposition. "The Left" has indeed become "established." Moreover, even if the left—as in Britain—wins state power, often it does not seem to its members to have much room for manoeuvre, in the world or in the nation.

There are, I think, two major explanations of this condition in Western Europe and in the United States: specifically, the nationalization of communism, which was the seat of the old left; and, more generally, the expropriation from cultural workmen of their means of distribution, and, increasingly, of cultural production as well.

Nationalization of the International Left

During the 'thirties in the Western societies, the main cultural and political seat of the left was communist. People on the left—in and out of the party—had to define their position and their outlook with primary reference to the party and to its doctrines. The history of oppositional establishments in almost all nations is closely linked with the cultural and political history of the Soviet Union. That history is well known: in brief, it is the story of how the international left became nationalized; of how it came to be seated in the new establishment of one nation; and of how Marxism itself became a rhetoric of rigid cultural defense and political abuse.

Up to the end of the second world war, all this could be overlooked by many intellectuals. Cultural as well as political struggles still seemed internationalist—within and between nations—as the encounter in Spain made evident. Right and left could be defined as fascism and anti-fascism. But for many people, the nationalization of communism soon became obvious, and unbearable. Although still world-wide in its efforts, communism had come to be the instrument of one nation, and its political force within various nations was often as reactionary as that of any other Great Power. No longer could socialism, in its viable meanings, be identified with the Soviet Union, nor the Soviet Union acknowledged as the carrier of the values of the left. Communism in fact was no longer unambiguously "left."

Yet in the West, many leftward circles were so closely identified with communism that when communism was reduced to Stalinism, left establishments declined or collapsed. They had become too dependent on this one centre to survive intact, much less to flourish.

U.S. Intellectuals in the 'Thirties

The case of America in these respects is of special significance because of the enormity of that nation's means of power, because of the *formal* freedom that political and cultural activities enjoy, and because inside the United States Communism has never been a real political force.

In the 'thirties many American intellectuals made believe they were revolutionaries. Came the second world war, and rather suddenly they became patriots. To be sure, at this decisive turn in the history of American life and thought, they did grouse a bit, in a literary way, but, it was a grousing about a society with which in actual practice they were well satisfied. Now, after the second world war, they have come to celebrate this society. In reality, they know very little about it; in reality, they are not trying very hard to find out.

The remnants of the left circles of the 'thirties have often become what I should like to call "'The Old Futilitarians." In their United States version, these ex-fighters are often quite shrill: they have stood up in another fashion in another era, but now they are done with fighting. They have not carried forth into the 'fifties any traditions of the left. Rejecting these altogether, they have come to embody and to display a kind of weariness with any politics of moral concern; for it—as is well known—they have substituted The American Celebration.

What is interesting about the ex-communists turned professional is psychological (although of course it has political meanings too): the fact is—I believe—their anti-communism is quite similar in psychological form to anti-semitism. At least I find it rather difficult to tell the difference between the anti-communism of some of my ex-friends and the anti-semitism of those who have always been my enemies. Both assume the immutability of communists or of Jews: once a communist (or a Jew) always a communist (or a Jew). Both assume that any contact is polluting: they assume that in any attempted co-operation with "them." the communists (or the Jews) will energetically exploit the chances offered and clannishly win out. Both admit that "by the nature of the case *It* cannot really be proved"—except by one's own feelings and intimate experience. Both assume that anyone who may doubt this is simply naive, or perhaps secretly—or anyway unconsciously—a communist (or a Jew). There is the same choked-up exasperation with detached reasoning about communism and communists, the same esoteric interpretation of texts to reveal "Stalinist mentality" or influence; the identification of any detachment from unconditional nationalism as merely treason.

In the United States today, the ex-communist turned professional is not as shrill as he was several years ago, but he has certainly played an important part in creating the sour and disillusioned atmosphere in which younger cultural workmen have grown up since the end of the second world war.

The Young Complacents

The complacency of the young is a counterpart of the futility of the old. It is difficult to find pure types of The Young Complacents. They represent more an underlying mood than a stable type of man, and they are very much subject to fashion.

Perhaps the clue to this mood is The Young Complacent's feeling that after all he has been treated rather well; behind that of course is the glorious and vulgar fact of economic prosperity. Political passions and moral convictions "leave them cold." Perhaps this posture results from the strain to be bright and interesting—and of course fashionable. Perhaps it results from the fact that he tends to judge the society in which he lives on the basis of his personal career within it, thus confusing his own modest personal success—of a modest sort—with the quality and conditions of social justice. To base one's political mood and moral judgment upon modest success is—and it is still a good phrase—the Philistine mood of the petty bourgeoisie.

Scientific Posture of Social Investigators

In the West, especially in the U.S.A., apart from the postures of sophisticated weariness and the curious complacency of the literary young, there are many further attitudes that stop political reflections as an active force—for example, there is The Scientific Posture of Social Investigators. So many intelligent academic people, both in Western Europe and in America, won't talk seriously about the politics of war and peace, slump and boom, democracy and tyranny. They are fully rational but they refuse to reason. Anything outside their particular methods they call speculation or scholarship—which they define as "writing books out of other books"—and which they think quite a low form of activity. They are often dogmatic, less about any set of beliefs than about the limits of reason itself. Many of them today are administrative intellectuals—head deep in war relevant "social research." Too sophisticated to attempt explicit argument for their politically weak alternatives they are in fact practising; they simply refuse explicit comment. Surely this is a numb retreat into a purely technical, and subservient, sphere.

The collapse of the left, and the more general attempt to divorce intellectual activities from politics of any sort, is based, then, upon the dogmatic and sour anti-communism of The Old Futilitarians; the uninformed boredom of The Young Complacents with politics and their ignorance of its human meanings today; the merely literary fads and personal prosperity of The Philistine as Thinker; and upon the unexamined conservatism and scientific pretentions of The Behavioral Scientists. As a loosely knit coalition, all these types are attempting to establish a nationalist mood to which conformity is demanded.

The nationalization of left establishments is only one explanation of the collapse of the left. There is another. The real "treason of Western intellectuals" today is based upon the bureaucratic establishment of their very cultural existence. It is not—as Julien Benda would have it—that they are "useful" but that they do not themselves control the uses made of them and their work. The fact cannot be understood without understanding the commercial and administrative realities that lie back of the changing roles intellectuals have in fact come to play in the Overdeveloped Society.

What intellectuals now confront is the expropriation of their cultural apparatus itself. We do not have access to the means of effective communication, but more than that, many of us are losing control of the very means of cultural production itself. The situation of the serious movie-maker—is not this the prototype for all cultural workmen? We are cut off from possible publics and such publics as remain are being turned into masses by those businessmen or commissars who do control and manage the effective means of communication. In their hands, these are often less means of communication than means of mass distraction.

Similarities in U.S. and U.S.S.R.

I argued before that in several structural trends and official actions, the U.S. and the U.S.S.R. are becoming increasingly alike. I remarked several cultural features of these two superpowers which I think mean that in cultural affairs, as well as in basic structure, similarities are becoming apparent. In the United States, we must remember there is no long-standing traditional establishment of culture on the European model; in Russia, we must remember such an establishment was destroyed by the Revolution.

The "'materialism" of the Soviet Union is no more important a religious and spiritual fact than the "Christianity" of the West—especially of the United States, where religion itself is now a quite secular activity. The official atheism of the Russians, the official Christianity of the Americans—does either mean very much today for national policy, for cultural endeavour, for the quality of everyday life? In the Fourth Epoch, religious—as well as educational— institutions tend to become mass media, tend to be shaped by major economic, military, and political forces. They do not originate; they adapt.

In neither the United States nor the U.S.S.R. is education necessarily a truly liberating experience. In both, it tends to become part of economic and military machines, as men and women are trained to fulfill technical functions in bureaucracies, with the ends and the meanings of which they have little to do.

In underdeveloped countries, of course, we witness a movement from mass illiteracy to formal education; in the overdeveloped nations, from mass education to educated illiteracy. In their classic period, liberal observers expected and assumed that universal education would no doubt replace ignorance by knowledge, and so indifference by public alertness. But in the overdeveloped nations things educational have not turned out this way. Nowadays, precisely the most "liberal" educators feel that something has gone wrong.

"Media Markets"

Like religion, education in the U.S.A. competes with, and in due course, takes its place alongside, the other mass means of distraction, entertainment, and communication; These fabulous media do not often truly communicate; they do not connect public issues with private troubles; they do not often make clear the human meaning of impersonal and often atrocious events and historic decisions. They trivialize issues, and they convert publics into mere "media markets."

The image of self-cultivating man as the goal of the human being has everywhere declined. It is the specialist who is ascendant both in Russia and America. He whose field is most specialized is considered most advanced.

Many cultural workmen, especially social investigators, try to imitate the supposed form of physical science. One result is that they tend to abdicate the intellectual and political autonomy of the classic traditions of their disciplines. Much social science nowadays is pretentious triviality; it is a set of bureaucratic techniques inhibiting social inquiry by methodological pretentions; congesting the work at hand by the obscurity of altogether grand theory; trivializing itself by concern with minor problems that have no connexion with issues of public relevance or troubles of individuals.

Underlying the ascendancy of the specialist in both the U.S. and the U.S.S.R., there is of course the ascendancy of physical science as military and economic facts, as well as the cultural model with the greatest prestige. Now "science" is regularly identified with its more lethal or its more commercially relevant products. The secrets of nature are made secrets of state, as science itself becomes a managed part of the machinery of the third world war, and in the U.S. also a part of the wasteful absurdities of capitalism.

In neither the U.S. nor the U.S.S.R. is there a set of free intellectuals, inside as well as outside the universities, which carries on the big discourse of the Western world and whose work is influential among parties and movements and publics. In neither, in brief, are there truly independent minds which are directly relevant to powerful decisions.

In neither the U.S. nor the U.S.S.R. are there media of genuine communication, freely and regularly open to such intellectuals, and with the aid of which they translate the private troubles of individuals into public issues, and public issues and events into their meanings for the private life: accordingly, in both there prevails a higher and irresponsible ignorance, and an isolation of the free intelligence from public life.

I do not wish to minimize the important differences between the establishment of culture in the Soviet Union and in the United States. I wish neither to excuse the brutal facts of Soviet cultural tyranny, nor to celebrate the formal freedom of cultural workmen in the West. Surely there is enough such celebration of self and denunciation of enemy.

The formal freedom of the West rests upon cultural traditions of great force; it is very real—this freedom; and it has been, and is immensely valuable. But must we not now ask to what extent the continuation of this freedom today is due to the fact that it is *not* being exercised? Certainly in America today there is much more celebration and defense of civil liberties than insurgent and effective use of them.

Intellectuals' Pseudo-withdrawal

The withdrawal of intellectuals from political concerns is itself a political act. Which is to say that it is at best a pseudo-withdrawal. To withdraw from politics today can only mean "in intent"; it cannot mean "in effect." For its effect is to serve whatever powers prevail, even if only by distracting public attention from them. Such attempts may be the result of fear or fashion; or of sincere conviction—induced by success. Regardless of the motive, the attempted withdrawal means to become subservient to prevailing authorities and to allow the meaning of one's own work to be determined, in effect, by other men.

"Bad men," John Adams wrote in 1790, "increase in knowledge as fast as good men, and science, art, taste, sense and letters are employed for the purposes of injustice and tyranny, as well as those of law and liberty; for corruption as well as for virtue."

If this is so, intellectuals cannot expect to maintain cultural freedom without waging a political as well as a cultural struggle, without realizing that just now these two struggles must be joined. They are still free to consider the decisions they are making. No other grouping or type of man is so free in just these ways; no other group, just now, is so strategically placed for possible innovation as those who belong by their work to the cultural apparatus.

Given our condition, I am persuaded of the following: A direct party struggle is today not open to intellectuals either in America or in the Soviet bloc. Whether it is open to intellectuals of Western Europe you would know better than I. In America, today there is no movement or party or organization that has a real chance to influence decisions of consequence and at the same time is open to the work of intellectuals. Given this, I think it is a waste of time and of talent better used in intellectual work for American intellectuals to busy themselves with merely local and ineffective "politics" in the name of independent political action.

We must work for political as well as cultural ideals in intellectual and moral ways, rather than in any more direct political ways. I do not believe, for example, that it is only "labour" that can transform American society and change its role in world affairs, and certainly I do not think that labour alone can do it.

Are you not learning this in Britain?

Intellectuals have created standards and pointed out goals. And then, always, they have looked around for other groups, other circles, other strata who might realize them. Is it not now time for us to try to realize them ourselves?

It is easy for intellectuals to talk generously of the need for workers to control the factories in which they work. It is somewhat more difficult for them to begin to take over their own means of work. What we ought now to do is repossess our cultural apparatus, and use it for our own purposes.

I mean this personally and literally. It is a mistake for us to swallow ourselves in a vague political "we." As creators and upholders of standards, of course, we do want to generalize for other men the ideals for which, as public men, we stand. But we ought not to do so in a merely optative mood. We ought to do so first of all by acting in our own immediate milieux.

I grow weary of the writers among us who bemoan the triviality of the mass media and yet allow themselves to be used in its silly routines. We should write and speak for these media on our own terms or not at all.

We should reveal our pride in our heritage as free men by taking it seriously. The thing to do with civil liberties is stop defending them long enough to use them.

The thing to do with our own alienation is to stop whining about it long enough to use it in the formulation of radical critiques, and audacious programmes.

If we do not do these things, who will? We should conduct a continuing and uncompromising criticism, and we should do so from the standpoint of explicitly utopian ideals, if need be.

Unless we do this, we have no chance to offer alternative definitions of reality. And that of course is our major business. If we as intellectuals do not define and re-define reality, who will?

What we must now do is become international again. But what does this mean for us, today? Does it not mean, first, that we personally must refuse to fight the Cold War? And second, that we personally must attempt to get in touch with our opposite numbers in all countries of the world—above all, those in the Sino-Soviet zone of nations?

With them we should make our own separate peace. Then as intellectuals, and so as public men, we ought to act and work as if this peace—and the exchange of values, programs, and ideas of which it consists—is everybody's peace, or surely ought to be.

What we must do, in summary, is to define the reality of the human condition and to make our definitions public; to confront the new facts of history-making in our time, and their meanings for the problem of political responsibility; to release the human imagination, in order to explore all the alternatives now open to the human community, by transcending both the mere exhortation of grand principles and the mere opportunist reaction.

I know that there are those among us who will say to all this: "'If I do not do this or that, others will, so what's the difference?" To them I must say that this is less an argument than a mannerism of the irresponsible. It is based upon a conception of yourself as an altogether private man, upon the acceptance of your own impotence, upon the idea that the act in question, whatever it be, is part of fate and so not subject to your decision.

My answers to this mannerism are: if you do refuse to do it, you at least are not responsible for its being done. If you refuse to do it, others may refrain from doing it, and those who still do it may then do it only with hesitation and with guilt. To refuse to do it is an affirmation of yourself as a moral centre of responsible decision; it is an act which recognizes that you, as an intellectual, are now a public man—whether or not you want to be; it is the act of a man who rejects "fate," for it reveals the resolution of at least one human being to take at least his own fate into his own hands.

TWENTY

On Latin America, the Left,
and the U.S.

THIS INTERVIEW WAS DRAWN out of a roundtable discussion sponsored by the Faculty of Social Sciences, National University of Mexico,
in March 1960. Of the four men putting questions to Mills one was sociologist Pablo Gonzales Casanova. Two others, Victor Flores Olea and Enrique
Gonzales Pedrero, were editors at the radical journal *El Espectador*, where Mills
was "the guiding light," according to the fourth interviewer, Carlos Fuentes.
"There was the most extraordinary sensation around his writings in Mexico,"
Fuentes recalls. *White Collar, The Power Elite, The Causes of World War Three*,
and *The Sociological Imagination* circulated briskly in translation from the
Fondo de Cultura Econ'omica; and Mills's ideas were debated in magazines
such as "La Cultura en Mexico," a supplement to *Simpre!,* and *Politica*, the
organ of the National Liberation Movement, a loose coalition of writers and
artists dedicated to revitalizing the left wing of the ruling PRI.

The initial publication of this interview in Mexico City drew a sharp letter
from Mills: "In the version you sent they have me practically saying that I am
a Leninist. Of course I have never been and am nothing of the sort." Revised
on November 4, 1960, it was republished in English in the January–February
1961 issue of the *Evergreen Review*.

QUESTION: *Do you believe the Left movement throughout the world has experienced a
decline and if so, what are the causes for it?*
PROF. MILLS: Whether or not one believes that there is a decline of the Left
depends upon one's view of the Soviet bloc. The question is whether—or to

what extent—one can identify the historic values of the Left with the Soviet Union. Under Stalinism I believe that these values were sacrificed. So I have to answer that there has been a decline of the Left. This is true not only of "Marxism," which has collapsed into Stalinism; but also of social democratic movements, which have generally collapsed into liberalism; and of liberalism itself, which has generally collapsed into an empty rhetoric.

Ten years ago there would have been no question—at least I would take that view—that the methods being used by Stalin were sacrifices of Left values. Ten years, though, is a long time. But now the Soviets have gotten over the hump of their industrialization. So what we must now ask about the Soviet Union is, first, whether the tendencies toward democratization mark a new beginning in the Soviet Union. And, second, whether these new beginnings add up to enough to let us believe that, maybe, the secular and humanist values of classic Marxism may still be available—despite everything—in the future of the Soviet Union.

In short, what we of the non-communist Left must do is continually to re-think our attitudes towards the Soviet regime. The whole "Left," from liberals through ex-communists, is either confused or dogmatic on this issue. My own views on this are still quite uncertain; during the coming year or so, I am going to try to formulate some theses on the whole question. At this point, in general, I follow the ideas of Isaac Deutscher and E. H. Carr.

Of course, all this is tied in with the nature and outcome of The Cold War. Let me put it, if I may, like this: What is going to happen in the world in the next decade or two?

First of all, it is impossible for one thing to happen, namely that the Soviet system and the capitalist system both continue just as they are now. We know that's not going to happen. Both of them are going to change, in interaction with one another, and inside themselves.

Second, it is possible to think that the capitalist world, especially the United States—the cornerstone of this world—is going really to lose the cold war. What would this mean? Ultimately, it would mean, presumably, that it would cease to be capitalist and, either through a revolution—which I don't think likely —or an evolutionary development, would become more communist, in economic and in political senses.

Third, the reverse of that might happen: you could conceive of the Soviet Union and the whole Soviet bloc really losing the cold war. What would that mean? Again, ultimately, it would mean that it would become more capitalist in some sense—through a revolution in the satellite countries, or what not.

As for numbers two and three—I do not see anything inherent in either the capitalist or in the Soviet system to make us believe that either [is] going to "lose" in the senses indicated.

A fourth possibility is that there will be World War III. In that case there's no use talking about it, because then we wouldn't be in a position to ask questions about the future of liberalism, socialism, capitalism or communism, or any other system.

I don't think any of these things are *necessarily* going to happen. What is more likely is that the changes within Soviet society and the United States will bring the two together in such a way that they will converge. History is going to bury both of them, as it does all societies. Maybe they're both going to be changed so that in due course the rhetoric of the cold war, the ideological conflicts, are going to diminish. The kinds of conflict that now exist between them may well become as irrelevant as, let us say, religion now is in the relationship between the big nations.

That's not necessarily an optimistic view! It depends upon what direction *both* these systems will take—the Soviet bloc and the capitalist bloc. I see many parallels between the Soviet Union and the United States. Beneath all the rhetoric and ideology dividing the two, there are the demands of industrialization which both societies satisfy—each in different ways, of course. This is already leading to the ascendancy of a type of human being in both societies, which, frankly, I don't particularly care for. And it is because of that possibility—and I state it just as a possibility—that I am most interested in exploring the Soviet, as well as the North American, possibilities of development.

Now think of the following possibilities—first, that these two systems now at such loggerheads, may end up in the same boat, and second, that we don't particularly care for this boat to be the *only* one in the world. Now that is why I look very much to various countries in the underdeveloped or pre-industrial world —as they try to get into some "third pattern." I am for international policies that would increase the chance for genuine neutralism; and I am for internal policies that would make for a genuine variety of political and economic forms of society in the world.

QUESTION: *What are the conditions, in your opinion, under which an independent Left could work out an effective revolutionary movement?*
PROF. MILLS: You mean by independent, I take it, independent of the Soviet bloc. I think that the real possibility on an international scale of a deep-going non-communist Left development depends very much upon one country:

India. We now think almost entirely in terms of the U.S. vs. U.S.S.R. as the central contestants. If I am right in what I have said earlier, it may well be that the real confrontation in the world today—the real competition, peaceful or otherwise—is between China and India. Not only because of the millions of people in those two countries, but because China represents the clearest example of an extreme kind of communist-type revolution, going much further and much faster than the Russian; and India, a country which, if it did develop industrially and politically in some independent Left manner, would of course be fabulously important because of its size, resources and its people.

It is not within advanced capitalism or within the Soviet bloc, but within the underdeveloped countries perilously outside both blocs that I see the best possibilities for an independent Left. As for the *probabilities* of it, quite frankly I don't estimate them being very high. I am rather pessimistic. There are, to be sure, peculiarities in every society, but the basic or generic model still tends to be *either* capitalist or communist. I don't know of any country which has yet displayed for us a really new beginning—a third model of industrialization, which, of course, would be the basis for any international new Left. Maybe Cuba will turn out that way; I haven't been there yet.

QUESTION: *What has happened because of the revolution in weapons?*
PROF. MILLS: I think it means that "victory" by war has become meaningless. There is not a single cold warrior in the United States or the Soviet Union that can tell you what it would mean for the United States or the Soviet Union to win an all-out war today. The meaning of such a "victory" is now empty.

But if you get behind that, beyond war, then you must say that the major meaning of "the victory" of the Soviet Union or the U.S.A. is to become the model for the industrialization of that part of the world not yet industrialized. This is the positive meaning of the cold war. What our strategy as Left-wing people should always be is to try to translate all the rhetoric, all the fearful bluff, all the mutual idiocy of The Cold War, into concrete proposals for the proper industrialization of the underdeveloped world. Those are the only constructive terms of this cold war. And in that sense, the cold war can really function as a progressive, international force—if only we can channel it in that way.

QUESTION: *Which of the models now offered to the underdeveloped countries of the world do you believe is more likely to be followed—the capitalist or the communist?*
PROF. MILLS: Skipping for a moment the Western Hemisphere—where Latin America is tied pretty firmly to the United States—the possibility of the Soviet pattern is more likely to be followed. I base that dire expectation on all

sorts of things, but above all, on the simple fact that in the United States—where the technical aid, for example, would have to come from if some capitalist pattern were to be followed—there is neither the will nor the actual capacity today to lead the underdeveloped countries at as fast a rate as the people in those countries are demanding. But suppose, through some political fluke, the United States were to start giving aid to Asia, or Africa, or Latin America, *not* for military purposes—(which has been what most of the aid has been for in the past)—and *not* just to rehabilitate capitalism in Western Europe. Suppose the United States wanted to give aid not for those reasons, but simply to help these hungry peoples to get on their own feet. In that case, do the North Americans have enough trained manpower really to put through agrarian reform? Do they have the technicians who know the foreign languages? The Russians do. The Russians have instituted —and, increasingly, so have the Chinese—fabulous programs in this connection. Even if the political decision were made by the United States really to make something of Point Four—which is now ludicrously inadequate—I don't think we have the personnel, much less the will actually to do it. This is not due to any technical incapacity, because as of now, the United States and the capitalist bloc are in a much better position than is the Soviet Union to provide assistance. It is due to lack of capitalist will, and the whole superstructure of capitalist society.

For example, as my British friend Ralph Miliband once remarked, perhaps two or three years from now, the Soviet Union can declare to the world: "From now on bread is free in the Soviet Union." (If the United States did that, the associated bakers of Cleveland etc. would be most upset!) But there is nothing inherent in the economy of the Soviet Union which prevents this from being done. Such things are not just utopian dreams, they are soon going to be perfectly possible for the Soviet Union, and I see no reason to believe that in the next decade or two they may not do just such things. Imagine the world effect if they were to say that from now on bread is a "natural human right," or whatever way they wish to put it!

QUESTION: *Is it possible for the underdeveloped countries to follow a pattern of a planned Marxist economy without falling into the Stalinist aberrations which occurred in the Soviet Union?*
PROF. MILLS: I do not really know; no one does; the evidence isn't in yet. But the immediate issue lies in this: Since the populations in many of these countries are mostly illiterate, it is the intelligentsia that is immediately relevant. I'm using this word "intelligentsia" in the East European sense to mean the whole white-collar pyramid, as well as artists, scientists and "intellectuals" in

our sense. The appeal of Marxism to them is much greater than the kind of appeal the United States, for example, is setting forth. This is especially evident in such places as Southeast Asia and in the most educated province of India which, let us not forget, has *voted* Communist.

It is precisely the intelligentsia that is the strategic [stratum] in many underdeveloped countries. One value of Marxism as a propaganda weapon, as an appeal, is of course the idea of planning it holds out. I think, however, that we should certainly be stupid to *identify* "planned economy" with the Stalinist way, and think that there is no other planning. So you're asking me whether you can engage in central planning—which we know must be done in an underdeveloped country—and yet avoid the Stalinist horror in the process. Here's my answer: it depends, first of all, on the tempo. If you go fast, then probably you cannot avoid it. Also you must remember that Stalin turned out to be correct on one point; had he not done what he did in the thirties, Nazi Germany would have conquered the Soviet Union. Now, that's hindsight, to be sure, but still it's the case. So I would answer the question of whether Stalinism is inevitable by posing the question of how fast do you want to go or feel you have to go? If you want to go *very* fast, then I would say yet, you are going to get something like Stalinism—*unless, of course, you get massive aid, in short, original accumulation by another people who give some of their surplus as aid.* But if you have to go very fast, and there is no such aid, then Stalinism is the major possibility for many countries.

QUESTION: *If capitalism works for the U.S., is the reason for this not the economic domination of the U.S. over underdeveloped countries who act as suppliers of raw materials?*

PROF. MILLS: I don't believe that the prosperity of the United States capitalism can be accounted for only by reference to a theory of imperialism. The statistics, such as I am acquainted with, do not bear that out. From, let us say, the Civil War up to World War II, the amount of U.S. economic growth due to the exploitation of foreign territories, for raw materials or anything else, has been quite small. This is in part due to the continental domain over which the U.S. spread. Since World War II, the foreign stuff, has, indeed, increased. But it is still not enough to account for the tremendous boom that has occurred in the United States. As an economic fact, the adequate reasons for U.S. economic prosperity cannot be found in any theory of imperialism of which I know. It has many other sources, that may be one of them, but it is not the major one, in my opinion. The permanent war economy, for example, is probably more important.

QUESTION: *Is it not true, nevertheless, that even though economic exploitation of foreign territories has not been a big factor in U.S. prosperity, U.S. economic domination of underdeveloped countries has still be a major factor in holding back the development of underdeveloped countries, especially in Latin America?*

PROF. MILLS: Political and economic domination—yes, that may be so. I would certainly be the first to admit that something which means very little to U.S. economic development could be disastrously great in another country which is smaller and is a primary producer. That is the problem of a country whose whole economy depends on one or two commodities which it exports for the world market, or mainly to the U.S. market. It is a question of magnitude; a question of determining to what extent U.S. prosperity, and in turn the continued misery of the underdeveloped societies, is due to economic and political relations with the United States. I don't know of any book which really persuades me that this is altogether the case. This is a question, I would insist, of factual evidence, of a quantitative nature. I don't even know if economists have the techniques and data to find out for sure. I don't think that Paul Baran's book proves it, though that is one of his theses. (Paul A. Baran, *Political Economy of Growth,* Monthly Review Press). He does not, it seems to me, have the data really to prove it.

Another point I want to make, you probably won't like. It is this: one of the chief obstacles to the development—the modernization and the industrialization—of many Latin American countries does not lie *outside* those countries at all. Nor does it lie in the "ignorance," "laziness," "apathy," and so on of the populations of these countries. It lies with the ruling groups of those countries. I think that a country like Brazil becomes very relevant in this connection. Brazil is not really "one country" economically, as Prof. Lambert has shown; Brazil is a Dual Society. It is really two countries—along the south coast, and in the capital, in Sao Paulo, there is a booming (perilously so) capitalist society. What motive do those on top there have for really industrializing Brazil? Why should they? Many of them are far better off than people of similar status in the United States.

But most of the rest of the country *is* underdeveloped and much of it is in abject misery. It is the Latin American country itself that is "an imperialist power" over their own hinterland, as it were. They spend millions for a fancy Brasilia, but little or nothing for the 20 million people of their hungry Northeast.

What I am trying to say is this: were I a Latin American in any given country I would first of all try to explain why my country was not further developed, or not developing faster, by exhausting all the internal factors that I possibly could. Only then would I search for the external mechanics. I think that this is not only good methodology, but it is also, if I may say so, politically more effective, for the simple reason that the Chilean intellectual, for example, can do very little *directly* about United States policies. But he can declare political or economic war on his own ruling groups in so far as they are deterring real development. You see what I mean?

QUESTION: *Here in Mexico there is freedom for the intellectual to express himself. But if we head south, the intellectual, if he raises some of the questions we have brought up, is physically threatened and loses his life.*
PROF. MILLS: I know, I know, and I grieve for them every day, for my country has been supporting some of those tyrannies.

It's been my observation, in such little comparative studies as I have so far done, that to the degree to which freedom—the real *use* of it—makes a difference to that extent it tends to be repressed. It is only when freedom doesn't make any real difference in the power sense, or when it isn't used, that one is quite free. U.S. intellectuals, for example, are very free people, in the formal sense of being able to write anything. I think that any book with any kind of quality, regardless of what it says, or what it condemns in the U.S., will find a publisher. I truly believe that. In that sense the intellectual is free. But it doesn't seem to make much difference. Why? Because my omnivorous society is so politically apathetic and so clownish in its cultural and political tastes that it will celebrate, and even make rich, a writer who has utterly condemned its very foundations.

This is a very hard thing to face. I'm not sure that it is not harder to face this (although it may seem brutal to say so) than to face a situation such as in the Soviet Union or that of Latin American countries in which to utter a word of protests may mean you are thrown in jail. There is one good point about the repression of freedom from the standpoint of the intellectual; somebody in power believes *that ideas do matter.* Maybe they are right.

QUESTION: *What is the reason for this? Why don't ideas matter in the U.S.?*
PROF. MILLS: That *is* a very long story. I do have a theory about it which I hope to publish in a few years under the title *The Cultural Apparatus.* This will be an examination of the roles of intellectuals, artists, technicians in the United States as well as in other countries. I'd rather not go into it in detail just now, for it is still rather involved. But briefly, it is due, I think, to the ascendancy of a commercial ethic in cultural production and distribution, so that in a real sense of the word, what has been happening to physical labor—

in a word, alienation—is now happening quite fully to cultural production, distribution and to cultural consumption as well.

The type of man and woman, the type of human being, that is selected and formed by a cultural apparatus such as the United States is something I'm going to try to develop under the term "The Cheerful Robot." We know that men can be turned into robots—by chemical means, by physical coercion, as in concentration camps, and so on. But we are now confronting a situation much more serious than that—a situation in which there are developed human beings who are cheerfully and willingly turning themselves into robots.

I wonder if you realize how deep-going that statement is? If it is half-way true, then we must reconsider the entire tradition of secular, humanist aspiration— a tradition virtually identical with "western civilization" including, certainly, classic Marxism. Both in Marxism and in psychoanalysis— the two big intellectual models we have—it is always assumed that deep down in the nature of man-as-man there is the urge to real freedom. I am not so sure that that is a valid assumption. It may well be that it is metaphysical nonsense and that, first, the urge to freedom and the cherishing of freedom, as we have known it in the West, is an historically specific trait, value, quality of human beings; and second, that it has always been confined, apart from a few very fortunate circumstances, to rather small circles of the population. I wish to God I could get real information about China.

Do you see what all this points to? To a profound moral crisis, a crisis of our basic morality, which goes way beneath a crisis of the left or of Marxism. It surely includes liberalism in all its varieties.

But however all that may be, it's a conscious problem now mainly for a few people in the overdeveloped societies. In the hungry-nation bloc, certainly in Latin America, the problem of freedom at least seems much simpler and more stark. Under conditions of economic misery and abysmal backwardness, with mass illiteracy and disease, and under an autocratic, military government, where there is no freedom but naked coercion—that is when an intelligentsia becomes ultra-left and revolutionary.

In the hungry nations of the world, two conditions seem to make for revolution: a disaffected intelligentsia with no place to go; and continued mass misery—a misery without hope. If you want to avoid revolution—in favor of peaceful change—then you must speak and act to those conditions. You must help eliminate the misery, and fast; you must in some way help provide really effective political and economic roles for the intelligentsia. You can't put down revolutions merely by supplying those in tyrannical power with military force. That is an illusion. That is the way to make a revolution.

Another illusion unfortunately fostered by my own country's official re-action to events in the hungry nations is that "the communists" have a monopoly on revolution as a way of making history under tyranny. They don't. As I've said, I haven't been there yet, so I don't know, but maybe Cuba is showing that they don't.

QUESTION: *What will be the response in the United States to revolutionary move-ments in Latin America and to what quarters in the United States can we look for support of these movements?*
PROF. MILLS: I think that at the back of your question there lies a kind of political strategy which I noticed in Brazil last fall and, if I may say so, here in Mexico. This is a strong tendency to try to excuse one's own lack of political activity by reference to what the United States will do or won't do. I think that's an error. I think that a profound book has to be written about Latin America and North America. It ought to be called *The Americas*. (Perhaps it is written, but if it is I don't know of it.)

Such a book would do two things: First, it would be a penetrating account of the ruling structures in each Latin American country, a real sociological characterization. Second, it would be an account, a measurement, of the extent to which these ruling structures, and the whole lack of development of these countries, could be conscientiously imputed to United States policies—economic, political, and military. Such a study would enable us to find, in the case of any given country, the answers to those two questions. Then *you* would not be in a position to excuse your own political inactivity by imputing it to this monster in the North. I think all of you know me well enough to know that I am certainly not an apologist for U.S. policies. I am very much opposed to many of them, especially to the international policies of the cold war. But that has nothing to do with it. It is too easy to impute everything in Latin America to relations with the United States.

QUESTION: *But have not the tactics of the United States changed in relationship to Latin American countries? Are they not now establishing "ghost governments," as, for instance, in the case of Venezuela, where a revolution was suppose to have occurred?*
PROF. MILLS: Maybe you are right, we've not got that book yet, but think of a concrete case. Let us suppose there was a real revolution in Venezuela which, in the course of a year to two, would expropriate the oil companies, or perhaps as a first step, take 75 per cent or 85 per cent of all profits from the oil companies for Venezuela's own development. What would the United States do? Do you really think they would send the Marines and put down the revolution? I can't quite imagine that. What they would do is to act eco-

nomically: The "revolutionary government of Venezuela" would not have ships to transport the oil and they couldn't use all the oil in Venezuela. But that is not as much of a problem as it would have been twenty years ago. There are other kinds of boats in the world; moreover, in time Venezuela could build her own ships. In short, the economic answer for Venezuela is to *diversify* its industries, to *diversify* its buyers, to *diversify* its sellers. In the meantime, I do not see why they have to depend wholly on the U.S. market. As a neutralist, I would exploit other possibilities, and I would deny that U.S. power is the only obstacle to Venezuelan development and economic independence. It is also due to the impotence on the part of any movement within Venezuela. To say that "they" are powerful means that "you" are powerless.

QUESTION: *What about the control of public opinion through the press and the radio?*
PROF. MILLS: You mean that Latin American newspapers echo so much the U.S. line? I am quite convinced that in the underdeveloped world the expropriation and use of the cultural apparatus can be as important as the expropriation of the means of economic production, which are rather rudimentary anyway, apart from the land. My own idea of a New Left (which I am now trying to develop, but which I have not yet gotten straight) to replace the old Left which has collapsed or become ambiguous, is going to center, first of all, upon the cultural apparatus and the intellectuals within it.

M ILLS RETURNED TO the United States in April 1960, after two months in Mexico, and found a cable from The Soviet Society for Friendship and Cultural Relations inviting him to visit. Arriving in Moscow on April 21, he spoke before a large crowd at the Soviet Academy of Science. The rest of his four weeks in the Soviet Union he spent interviewing intellectuals in Moscow, Leningrad, Tashkent (in Uzbekistan), and Tbilisi (in Georgia). His *Soviet Journal* came to 290 typed pages of reportage, interviews, notes, and reflections.

"I am not a Trotskyist," he wrote in the *Journal*. "But for Russia now, Trotsky is just the thing for you people to read." The Soviet intellectuals appeared to him blinded by their convictions, unwilling to recognize, much less to discuss, "antagonistic contradictions" within socialist society. Ruefully he noted that he had asked the same series of questions to established intellectuals in the United States, Mexico, Poland, Yugoslavia, and Western Europe, "and in no place but the Soviet Union does everyone answer the same, like parrots who mouth a formula."

The excerpt reproduced here, a minor exception to the rule, is an interview conducted in Moscow on May 5, 1960, with Alexander Chakovski, editor-in-chief of the Foreign Literature Publishing House; Raisa Orlova, section editor of the magazine *Inostrannaya literatura* and specialist on Foreign Literature; and Ms. Kulakovskaya, translator for the magazine.

Raisa Orlova resigned from *Inostrannaya literatura* the following year. Later, she quit the Party and lost her Soviet citizenship, for reasons recounted in her *Memoirs* (1983), trans. Samuel Cioran.

Foreign Literature publishes literature from all over the world in Russian, including articles and non-fiction; there's a section on the film and on the graphic arts and fine and performing arts. They publish about a hundred thousand copies each issue. It was founded in 1955. It is administered and sponsored by the Writers Union Congress. They have published Ernest Hemingway, John Steinbeck, Mitchell Wilson. The countries from which they publish—number one, Britain and the Commonwealth countries, about fifty authors, seven big novels have been serialized—number two, USA, 53 authors, also seven big novels—three, West Germany, nine authors, three big novels; four, China, they have 49 authors and two big novels and a couple of plays. The staff consists of some forty persons. The budget is about 300,000 rubles; they're autonomous financially.

CWM: How do you make a decision on the novels?
Chakovski: First we take literary newspapers from all over the world. Second, we take the catalogues and bulletins from most publishing houses. Third, the editorial board and staff go abroad and meet leading writers of publishing organizations, so we know their plans as well as their publications. Fourth, delegations visit us and visit our editorial office, such as yourself now, and we ask them about possible books. Then the staff reads materials, screening it, and they make suggestions to the editorial board. The editorial board finally decides.

CWM: What is the composition of the board?
Chakovski: The director of the Institute of World Literature of the Academy of Science; a Writers Union man; a well-known Cossack writer; the head of the Oriental Institute; a famous film director; another writer; a professor of Western literature; Mikhail Sholokhov, a literary critic; a public figure, etc.

CWM: What are the decisive factors in selecting what you print?
Chakovski: First, works by authors who adhere to the same ideological principles as ourselves. Second, however, we also public works which are aloof from politics, or shall I say, do not share our political view yet nevertheless still in their work objectively mirror realities and trends.

CWM: In other words, those who are with you, and second, those who are nevertheless worthwhile.
Chakovski: Yes, of course!

CWM: I'm rather clear on the notion of pessimism and optimism in your literature, but not on the meaning of individualistic and the canon of socialist realism. Would you explain it?

Chakovski: We don't use the word "canon." That has a dogmatic air. It's too narrow and unchanging.

CWM: Well, then, what do you want to call it?

Chakovski: I want to call it socialist realism as a method. It is a changing idea, and all of it is changing, the idea itself. The idea of the individual, for example, has been and is a changing one.

Q: Well, then, what stages has it gone through?

Chakovski: Now you are asking questions as if you'd read Marx! First, at the beginning of the Revolution, the concept of "I" was seen as negative, as bourgeois, as of the old order. Even the conception of individual authorship was seen as somehow not so good. The people as a collective—that was the hero. The mass as hero.

Second, this notion, however, was soon seen as infantile, as something that you grow out of. So quite early there appeared books with individual heroes. Fadeev, *The Debacle*, and also, what could be called *The Route* are examples. Yet these books were against individualism.

CWM: What is that? What is individualism?

Chakovski: This is the key to it: the man for whom his own well-being is more important than the group's welfare. "We are for the person but against individualism." That means, we are for individuality but not for the philosophy of individualism, for the life of every society is obviously richer when it is many-sided, and the life of every person also when he is working for and with his society.

Q: Since Stalin's death, what have been changes in socialist realism?

Chakovski: No drastic changes have been made in the principles of socialist realism. In general, there has been a further democratization of literary life, among readers, above all, and also among writers and critics. Dogmatic writers who abused the method under Stalin have now seen matters in a more correct light. More books are read now and compared with other books. Now, everywhere, there is a freedom of discussion. More public action in the literary sphere, as well as elsewhere. This month, for example, we have here at this magazine three readers' conferences. These are composed of people who have written letters to our magazine, and they are coming to talk with some members of our editorial board and staff.

I then explained to them that I had the impression that the optative mood was the basic factor in socialist realism. I explained it by talking about a collective farmer in the Soviet Union as he is and then as he ought to be. They answered me as follows:

Chakovski said: Please don't use this publicly, but there is a United States conception of liberty and freedom that is quite different in FDR's time and in Joseph McCarthy's time. So the question is, has the conception of US democracy changed in those two phases? I should say, no, that's a wrong question; the principle is the same but the implementation of it is different.

Chakovski said: But you asked for changes in socialist realism since Stalin's death. This shows that you think of socialist realism as a policy, not as philosophy or as a method. When you ask, now, about first, changes in practical policies of literature—yes, of course, that has been true. When you ask for changes in literature—that also is easy to answer. But thirdly, when you ask about socialist realist principles, that is a senseless question. It shows you're not clear, or that you identify it with the literary policy of the state, or of some group in control.

[Chakovski]: Since I am not a theoretician, let us switch over to examples. I am a writer as well as an editor. Suppose I want to describe this scene, our meeting with you. First, if I am a photographic naturalist, I can describe only the impressions and feelings of our very brief time together. But second, as soon as I try to visualize your further reactions when you leave here—for example, in writing about our meeting yourself, or in a press release—then I become a socialist realist. I anticipate your actions only—that is not correct socialist realism—but to base my anticipations of you on what we see as the future of you, and your environment, not upon what we want—that is socialist realism. Socialist realism, in short, is nothing else but the ability to see things in all their developments, connections and their contradictions.

CWM: Truly a wonderful gift.
Chakovski: It is the talent of the writer. Different writers possess it to different degrees. Take another example. A man foresees his own death. A prophet discusses with this man about this, and that is conditioned by the knowledge the prophet has. It would be primitive to regard socialist realism as a set of canons and norms.

CWM: How about the happy ending?

Chakovski: Ah, yes, the happy ending. That is often asked of us. And yet it is an illogical question. We are asked why we've so many happy endings. Well, please think of what I've already said, and also this. In World War II, about one-third of this country was razed. We writers naturally came to feel an ardent desire to explain all of our readers that not all was lost, that we could rebuild. Nowadays we do pay more attention to our own shortcomings and contradictions—to tragedies, for example—because are now at another stage in the development of our society. This is being lived through and so we are writing about it.

CWM: Now here's a really big question, but you can easily answer it in five or six hours. In brief, what I want to know is your model of the ideal man of communism. I hope you'll agree that the institutions of every society select various types of men and women who become the ascendant models of character. They become models of aspiration and of imitation. Now, the ultimate moral basis of everything Karl Marx wrote, the way he judged a society, was in terms of the kinds, the qualities of men and women who flourished in it. Right? Also, as writers, the method you claim to follow relates literature very closely to social development. Well, then: relate it: Here you stand saying "Now we begin the transition to communism." What then is the ideal image, the model of character, of the communist man?

Chakovski says to Orlova: This would take three months to answer.

CWM: I know, I know, but you must have thought about it a good deal.

Chakovski: Do you mean, first, our impression of the ideal contemporary image of the hero of our society today? Or, do you mean the man of the future epoch, the epoch of communism?

CWM: I'd like your views of both.

Orlova: There is no such gulf between them!

Chakovski: Wait a minute, I can't answer the second part, the ideal man of the new epoch, because I don't want to be merely schematic about such a complex human affair.

CWM: That's not good enough. Don't you see that for old Marx, writing a hundred years ago, or even Lenin 50 years ago, the question might be utopian and all that, but it's become less so, very much less so, according to you, for you claim to be beginning the transition from socialism to communism, and you are planning it in a hundred areas. So you've got to know the answer to this question and to say it out. What are you planning for? You are a writer, and isn't that a very important job of a socialist realist writer today?

Orlova: The man of communism will have some traits of the characters in, let us say, Gogol's *The Marriage*, other traits from Ostrovsky's will be available, also from Fadeev, *The Young Guard*. Ostrovsky's book is called *How the Steel Was Tempered*. Moreover, in our life, in books as well, war exploits are particularly important, because in the deeds of these heroes we perhaps see the future. These qualities are displayed in many people, in the Soviet people as they develop.

Kulakovskaya: Our epoch has created a type of revolutionary which has been the idea for several generations, or at least I hope so.

CWM: You mean a Leninist man?

Chakovski: Yes, a Leninist man. A good early example of such a man was Dzerzhinsky, who was chairman of counter-revolutionary activities and the very incarnation of the early period of the Revolution. His prison diary is very important.

CWM: There's another aspect that bothers me, in a way it's above politics although not altogether so. It's the problem of the cheerful robot.

Orlova interrupts: Yes, yes, we've read your BBC lectures of last year about that.

CWM: But let me put it somewhat differently, for I've thought a lot about it since then. Models of character in the past societies and in many societies today are spontaneous. Now, with the growth of mass media, centrally controlled, such models can be selected, accentuated, planned. From both sides, spontaneously and deliberately. And moreover, the planning of men's character itself may, for the first time in world history, at least on a mass scale, now be possible. Doesn't this worry you? Doesn't it worry you like hell?

Orlova: You know about our discussion going on in *Komsomol* and other publications, the engineer versus the poet?

CWM: Yes, I've heard something of it.

Orlova: It bears on this problem of the cheerful robot, and it shows that we are very much aware of the problem. One student said that Bach and Bloch are not necessary for society; art and all of that is old sentimental stuff. In our society only the technical and scientific skills and those kinds of men and women are needed. About this, we have been having an enormous and controversial discussion. It is the question of the man of the future. Most of the discussants have been against the engineer's viewpoint, the view of the cheerful robot, that is. We've built and are building a society with great privations and sacrifices, and we are not doing that for sputniks alone, but for man, a fully rounded man. Here is another example that may interest you:

There is an art teacher in a Siberian village who wrote a letter to the *Literary Gazette*. In Siberia in that little village, she wrote, it is difficult to carry out aesthetic education, for there are no products of culture there to use in this work. But now many many letters are written to her, and she received reproductions etc. from all over the Soviet Union.

CWM: Where does your passion for learning come from?
Chakovski: It is in the national character.
CWM: But surely that is no answer.
Orlova: I think this would be the same in Africa. I believe it would. And China and India. Any long underdeveloped country that's coming into quick development would experience this.
Chakovski: How good it is to have such clever ladies here: There is nothing for me to do. Please go on.

CWM: The time is getting close, and I don't wish to impose upon you any longer. I've been selfish, monopolizing the questions. Now, will you ask me what you will?

They then asked me questions, all concerned with possible choices for their publication in fiction and non-fiction and estimations of US and British writers. Yes, they now do Fitzgerald's *Great Gatsby*. I suggested the *Crack-Up* articles might be interesting. They do Salinger's *Catcher in the Rye*. The translator lady is especially enthusiastic about Salinger. "Does it describe young Americans?" they asked. I refused to answer, saying I just did not know, etc. "In the general estimation and in your own, who are the four or five leading critics?" They knew everyone mentioned. "How about American historians?" I mentioned people, but they were not aware of them. They're not too interested in US historians. Sociologists, yes. I mentioned three, two of whom they did not know. They copied names and titles. In all of this discussion I used the Soviet hierarchy of medals, their official honorific system, to estimate the people whose names came up, and this they greatly enjoyed. For example, I would say, "This critic would be only a merited critic. Only this one, Edmund Wilson, would have the Order of Lenin," and so on.

I explained my theory of why U.S. publishers do not do more Soviet writings and said, "If you give me a hundred pages or so on socialist realism in

English, I'll place it readily with any one of half a dozen publishers in the U.S." They said, "Is that a bargain?" "Yes."

A very jolly and nimble two or three hours, like the Georgian writers. Definitely, writers and editors are the most interesting, lively, open and generally knowledgeable type of intellectuals with whom I've talked.

TWENTY-TWO

Listen, Yankee!

The Cuban Case against the U.S.

T HIS EXCERPT FROM *Listen, Yankee: The Revolution in Cuba* made the cover of the December 1960 *Harper's*. The editors featured it against the background of the new Cuban flag. Inside, before Mills's preface, they inserted disclaimer that read, in part: "The message Mr. Mills puts in the mouth of the Cubans is, in effect, a piece of propaganda—uncritical, emotional, oblivious to the faults of the Castro regime. But, while criticism of that regime is widely published in America, the revolutionary elan which brought it into power and supports it is little understood; and it is something we must confront if we are to deal responsibly with Cuba and Latin America."

———⊷⊷⊷———

This article reflects the mood and the contents of my discussions with revolutionaries in Cuba during August. But it is about more than Cuba. For Cuba's voice today is a voice of the hungry-nation bloc, and the Cuban revolutionary is now speaking—most effectively—in the name of many people in that bloc. In Asia, in Africa, as well as in Latin America, the people behind this voice are becoming articulate; they are becoming strong in a kind of fury they've never known before. As nations, they are young. To them, the world is new.

No matter what you may think of it, no matter what I think of it—Cuba's voice is a voice that must be heard in the United States of America. Yet it has not been heard. It must now be heard because the United States is too powerful, its responsibilities to the world and to itself are too great, for its people not to be able to listen to every voice of the hungry world.

If we do not listen to them, if we do not hear them well, we face all the perils of ignorance—and with these, the perils of disastrous mistakes. Some of the mistakes of ignorance have already been made, in our name, by the United States government— and with disastrous consequences everywhere in the world, for the image and for the future of the United States. But perhaps it is not too late for us to listen—and to act.

My major aim is to present the voice of the Cuban revolutionary; I have taken up this aim because of its absurd absence from the news of Cuba available in the United States today. You will not find here The Whole Truth about Cuba, nor "an objective appraisal of the Cuban revolution." I do not believe it is possible for anyone to carry out such an appraisal today. The true story of the Cuban revolution, in all its meaning, will have to wait until some Cuban, who has been part of it all, finds the universal voice of his revolution. In the meantime, my task has been to try to ask a few of the fruitful questions, and then to seek out and to listen well to as full a variety of answers as I could find.

I believe that much of whatever you have read recently about Cuba in the U.S. press is far removed from the realities and the meaning of what is going on in Cuba today.

Unlike many Cubans, I do not believe that this fact is entirely due to a deliberate campaign of vilification—co-ordinated advertising pressure, official handouts, and off-the-record talks. Yet it is true that if U.S. business interests adversely affected by the revolution do not co-ordinate your news on Cuba, they may none the less be a controlling factor in what you know, and don't know, about Cuba. More generally, business as a system of interests, which includes the media of communication, certainly does play a role in such matters.

It is also true that the news editors' demand for violent headlines does restrict and shape the copy journalists produce. They print what they think is the salable commodity.

Our ignorance is also due to the fact that the revolutionary government in Cuba does not yet have a serviceable information agency for foreign journalists. Those Cubans in a position to help are very busy with the revolution. But more than that: they are increasingly unwilling to help, for they feel that their trust has been betrayed.

"To report" a real revolution involves much more than the ordinary journalist's routine. It requires that the journalist abandon many of the clichés and habits which now make up his very craft, and that he know something in detail about the great variety of left-wing thought and action in the world today. Most North American journalists know very little of that variety. To most of them it appears as all just so much "Communism." Even those with the best will to understand, by their very training and the habits of their work, are not able to report fully enough and accurately enough the necessary contexts, and so the meanings, of revolutionary events.

But one thing is clear: We are not getting sound information about the hungry-nation bloc.

Having said that, I must immediately add that whatever may be truthful or useful in this article is due less to any skill on my part than to my good fortune in having been given complete access to information and experience by Cubans close to events and who, once trust is established, are eager to express everything they feel. That trust was given to me, not because of any viewpoint I held toward them or toward their revolution, but simply because of their acquaintance with previous books of mine.

In writing about Cuba, I have tried not to allow my own worries for Cuba —and for the United States—to intrude upon my presentation of the Cuban voice, nor have I attempted either to conceal or to underline such ambiguities as I happen to find in this argument. My aim, I repeat, is to see to it that the Cuban Revolutionary is given a hearing.

C. Wright Mills

We write to you because we believe that you have lost touch with us. As human beings, it is true, we Cubans have never had any close relations with you. But as peoples, each with its own government, now we are so far apart that there are Two Cubas—ours, and the one you picture to yourselves. And Two North Americas, too. Perhaps this wouldn't matter so much, were it not that we know our Cuba has become a new beginning in the Western Hemisphere, and maybe even in the world. It could be a new beginning for you, too.

To most of us—and we want you to know this above all else—our new beginning is the very best thing that has ever happened to us. To some of us— and we suppose to most of you—much of it is uncertain, obscure, bewildering. But aren't new beginnings always like that? We Cubans are traveling a road no people of the Americas have ever traveled before. We don't know, we can't know, exactly where it leads. But we do fear that what you do and what you fail to do might well affect the question. And that does worry us; for you see, it's *our* destiny. To us, the question of Cuba is first of all the question of how we are going to live—or even for how long. And you are involved in this. We don't think you do understand who we are, how we got this way, what we are now trying to do, and what the obstacles along our road may be.

Consider for a moment how it's been that we've known each other.

Some of you came down to Havana—tens of thousands, in fact, during the 'fifties. Some of you came down just to lie in the sun or on the beaches we Cubans were not allowed to use. But some of you came down to gamble and to whore. We stood on our street corners and watched you in your holiday place in the sun, away from your bleak, Yankee winter. We Cubans, like everyone else, we know all about sin, being Catholics of a sort. But in the old Havana, organized sin meant big money for the few, and every filthy practice of the brothel for girls, twelve and fourteen years old, fresh from the *bohios*, the huts where they lived with their families.

Maybe you don't know two facts about the gambling and the whoring. A lot of that money ended up in the pockets of a corrupt Cuban government, which your government and some of your businessmen supported and helped. Also much of it ended up in the pockets of your gangsters from Chicago and New York and Los Angeles. Nobody knows how many of our sisters were whores in Cuba during the last years of the Batista tyranny. As for the gambling, it was not convenient for anyone to keep records, but slot machines in the tens of thousands were everywhere on the Island. It was a thorough and complete racket, controlled, directly or indirectly, by the big men of the tyranny.

And whatever Cuba has been in all these respects, you helped make it that: by your support of "our" government, by your gangsters who were in on it, and by the patronage and the whims of your rich tourists. Well, that's over, Yankee, please know that: we've made laws and we're sticking to them, with guns in our hands. Our sisters are not going to be whores for Yankees any more. So anyway—you knew us as tourists know people—and that's not knowing very much.

For the rest, how have you known us? By what your newspapers and magazines have said about us. And about this, we Cubans are very sure of one fact: Most of your newspapers and magazines, they have lied to you, and they are lying to you now.

A lot of people in the world who aren't limited to *Time* magazine and the Hearst papers, and listening to your networks and all the rest of it, are getting to know something of the truth about Cuba today. They're getting to know that your press on Cuba is about as real as your quiz programs have been. They are both full of outrageous lies which may fool Yankees but don't fool anyone else.

Anyway, off and on, you've been hearing about Latin America since you were in high school, and we know how boring it's been to you. But you can't afford to ignore us any longer. For now our history is part of your present. And now some of the American future is ours, too, as well as yours.

You say, or you think, "We haven't done anything to you Cubans." Well, that is just not true: look at the history of our two countries, how they've been involved with each other.

First, in 1848, you tried to buy Cuba outright for $100 million. You tried again a few years later. But Spain wouldn't sell, and the U.S. was not satisfied. The Old South wanted Cuba for slavery. And when they couldn't buy it, some U.S. envoys issued the "Ostend Manifesto." Cuba, it said, was geographically part of the United States; if the United States could not buy it, "by every law, human and divine, the United States has the right to take it by force."

It didn't come off: Cuba remained under the Spanish yoke; and against that yoke we kept on revolting. In the late 1860s we began an uprising that lasted for the next ten years; we demanded that the slaves be freed and that Cubans govern their own island. But still the slaves were not freed—until twenty years later—and Cuba was not independent.

Then finally in 1895, inspired by José Martí, Cubans made an insurrection and tens of thousands of soldiers sent from Spain couldn't cope with our guerrillas. The next year, the Spanish sent a big general—he "turned Cuba into a series of concentration camps," and in them we suffered.

But also many Spanish soldiers died. True, for a long time, Cubans failed; true, our countryside was laid waste; true, out of our misery Yankee businessmen made money. They bought land cheap after our devastation. In the last twenty years of the nineteenth century, Yankee bankers went all out for sugar plantations. By 1896 they had about $30 million of our property. Also, they bought up Cuban mines—iron, nickel, manganese. Bethlehem Steel and the Rockefeller interests—they began to buy us up. By the time this century began, the Yankees owned $50 million worth of Cuban sugar land, and tobacco, and mines.

Meanwhile, what were we Cubans doing?

Working, as usual, when we could get the work.

But also fighting Spain for our independence, and dying for that. The rest of Latin America, most of it, had already thrown off the old Spanish yoke, decades before, but Cubans were still rising against them at the turn of the twentieth century.

And then came—the Yankee marines. Our revolutions in Cuba—first against Spain, then against the —they've come closer together than in most of Latin America. We are the last of the nineteenth-century revolutions and, maybe, the first of the twentieth-century ones, unless you count Mexico. But back to our history for a moment. At first we thought you were going to help us to be really free—but it didn't turn out that way. In 1901, the U.S. forced upon us something called the Platt Amendment, which simply took away our sovereignty. It gave Yankees "the right" to come into Cuba with guns in their hands if they wanted to, to intervene to see to it that the government here was protecting Yankee property. And that's just what they did.

The first time was before the Platt Amendment, in 1899. One of your generals and his troops occupied our island—after we had just about whipped the Spanish who had been occupying us before you. The Yankee soldiers left in 1902, leaving behind the right to have a naval base—for $2,000 or $3,000 a year!—at our Guantánamo Bay; as we write to you, in August 1960—the base is still here.

But you did it again and again: Yankee troops came in 1906. Again in 1912. Again in 1917. And in 1920 you controlled our government directly, without even using your own troops.

Violence and cash, cash and violence. Can you understand why we might believe they are all Yankees think about?

The dollar and the flag, they were all mixed up together. In the late 'nineties only 10 per cent of our sugar production came through mills owned by Yankees. Just before the first world war, about one-third. By the middle 'twenties, the figure was two-thirds. Corrupted Cuban politicians and your absentee capitalists, they got together. Our politicians were grafters and lackeys; your capitalists were upright, honorable men in New York, who paid off the grafters and took out the big money. And we Cubans? We were the vassals of both. It wasn't what *we* did or what *we* didn't do that was making our history and our way of life. It was what was decided in the Directors' Rooms on lower Manhattan.

And we didn't even know those men.

We never saw them.

Just before our revolution, those men in the Directors' Rooms on lower Manhattan controlled more than 90 per cent of our electricity and telephones; about half of what was called our "public service" railroads; some 40 per cent of our sugar land; and practically all our oil. They dominated two-thirds of our imports.

And the Cuban government?—well, your government and corporations had much to do with that and at times ran it outright. Sometimes the truth *is* simple: those who ruled us were mainly incompetent despots, venal grafters—and often, especially toward the end, bloody butchers. Revolutions usually exaggerate the evils of the old order. We Cubans have not had to do that.

Fulgencio Batista seized power of the army in 1933, and with it he seized the government of Cuba. Your government "recognized" him as the true government of Cuba almost immediately. The Yankees didn't intervene then, you can be sure, and he ruled over us, with the power of the army, for ten years. Then again, in 1952, after the war of the Four Freedoms was all over and done with, Batista came back into power. Very soon then his blood-bath began. Before we threw Batista out, late in 1958, this butcher and his gangsters, trained by your military missions, using weapons your government gave to him, had murdered some 20,000 Cubans.

To Batista, anyone who was against him, anyone who complained out loud about anything, was A Dirty Communist. And always his answer was the same: torture them, mutilate them, kill them all. In Havana alone, God only knows how many men and boys were castrated; and when women were raped, their husbands were made to look upon it. And always the same excuse: "The Dirty Communists, they are trying to take over our fine little democracy."

While all this was going on, in the 1950s—just yesterday, it seems to us—for four and a half years, the Eisenhower-Nixon government sold bombs and war planes and bullets and guns to this gangster and dictator. They always said it was for Hemispheric Defense. But those weapons were used to kill Cubans. And that's one reason why it is that whenever we Cubans hear talk about "Hemispheric Defense," we shudder.

Your Ambassadors—hear their names, Yankee, and send them to disgrace—Mr. Arthur Gardner and Mr. Earl E. T. Smith—did they tell you what was going on? Did they tell you about the inhuman outrages, or did they just watch the sugar quotations? Did your radios, your newspapers, all your TVs, did they tell you all about how bombs made in the U.S.A. were used to kill thousands of Cubans in the city of Cienfuegos in September of 1957? Did they tell you that shortly after those bombings, the United States Air Force decorated the Cuban general of Batista who directed those air attacks? And if they did tell you, Yankee, what did you do?

If we Cubans have "gone to extremes," know this: so have you Yankees. We've been involved with each other in *extremist* ways. The abuses printed in Cuba against the Yankees have been all overbalanced by the abuses printed in the United States against us Cubans. On both sides, some of these statements are extreme, maybe even absurd. But much that we've said against you is simply the plain, miserable truth, and we know it is because we have lived it; and you don't know it because you have not lived it.

Our country, our Cuba, it *was* simply an economic colony of the U.S. corporations until our revolution.

And all the time, Cuba was a place of misery and filth, illiteracy and exploitation and sloth—a caricature of a place for human habituation. (Between 1902 and 1958 only one new school was built in Havana.) And it is out of all that, the Cuban revolution is struggling. Keep that big fact in mind, Yankee, write it into your conscience, when you read about what's happening in Cuba today.

We Cubans have had a highly visible standard of living—and of starving and dying, too—but you didn't see that. We did. And that's what our revolution is all about. Our revolution is not about your fight with Russia, or about Communism, or Hemispheric Defense, or any of all that: all those words came later, partly forced down our throat by your government and your monopolies.

Point number one, Yankee, is that our revolution is about our old Cuban standard of living. Of course, it's about more than that, much more. We are building, at breakneck speed, an entirely new society, and we didn't inherit much to build it with from the old order in Cuba. From that we inherited disorder and grief. We're in a fluid moment and everything's at stake; like the men in the Sierra Maestra, now a whole nation of Cubans, we're camping out.

Our soil and climate are among the best in the world; you can grow almost anything. But we couldn't even grow enough to feed ourselves. The reason is simple: we couldn't use our land for the kind of diversified agriculture we needed. We had to import 70 per cent of all we ate at high prices we couldn't afford. Why? Less than one-tenth of all the farms in Cuba held over two-thirds of the land. But again, why? Sugar.

Until 1934, the United States companies that bought Cuban sugar paid the same price as the companies of all other countries. But in that year your quota system was established—in order to protect your producers of beet sugar. A tariff was not enough: your producers couldn't compete on the world market. So the U.S. withdrew from the world market, setting up special prices higher than this market.

Many people think that the U.S. was making a present to Cuba by this quota price. But that's not true. You have to look not only at the traffic in sugar, but at *all* the economic transactions between Cuba and the U.S.A.

When you do that, you see at once that in return for your sugar quota, as it were, U.S. exporters to Cuba got such an advantage that no one else could compete with them. Producers of sugar in Cuba were given a higher import price, but because of an advantageous tariff, U.S. exporters to Cuba were able to take back any benefit the quota system might have produced. In the last ten years of the tyranny, despite its tiny economy, Cuba lost some one billion dollars to the United States.

To this must be added the fact that about 40 per cent of Cuba's sugar production was in the hands of the U.S. monopolies. *Now* of course, all sugar is produced in *Cuban* mills, and so the economic benefit of all Cuban sales is Cuba's. We're coming out from under, Yankee.

Our revolution is already economic construction. For the first time in the history of Cuba, the rural population is going to have—this is just an example—plenty of chicken to eat at prices they can afford. Who is raising these chickens? People who just yesterday were squatting in miserable *bohios* between the highway and the cane fields. We've built houses for these people with floors and toilets in them, and they've helped build the long sheds of pole and straw matting for the baby chickens.

Who's for the revolution? Those people who are now raising chickens. Who's for the revolution? The people who are eating the chickens these people are raising. You see how it's working? We are going to do the same with our fishing industry. And we are cutting down on the lard we import for you and raising our own peanuts for the good oil in them.

We Cubans, we're a do-it-yourself outfit. We're not capitalists and we're not building a capitalist society in Cuba today. Neither are we building a Stalinist society. We ourselves don't know quite what to call what we are building, and we don't care. It is, of course, Socialism of a sort. We're not a bit afraid of that word—and why ever should you be?

There is one more thing that you must understand about us young intellectuals who've led this Cuban revolution:

Since we did not belong to the old left intelligentsia who had gone through Communism and been disillusioned with Stalinism and with the purges and the trials and the thirty-five years of all that, we've had one enormous advantage as revolutionaries: We've not gone through all that terribly destructive process; we have not been wounded by it. We've never had any "God That Failed." We don't have all that cynicism and futility about what we're doing and about what we feel must be done.

That's the big secret of the Cuban revolutionary. We are new men, and we are not afraid to do what must be done in Cuba.

We're always acting with reference to one master aim: to make Cuba economically sovereign and economically prosperous. We don't want to be *anyone's* satellite. So we're increasing and diversifying our production and our consumption—especially in our agriculture; we're doing the same with our export markets and our sources of supply from abroad; and we're beginning to industrialize our island at the same time as we are immediately improving our standard of living.

Think about our economic way like this: At one extreme—say, Stalin's old way—the agricultural problem wasn't solved and there was very little consumer-goods industry; everything went into big heavy industry—for the future. And there were no friends to help the Soviet Union economically.

At the other extreme—perhaps it was Perón's way in Argentina—agriculture was left in a stale condition; there was no heavy industry and no real planning for it. Practically everything went into the consumer-goods industry. Also, Perón had no friends to help him economically.

In Cuba, we've just about solved the agricultural problem by our land reform: we've increased production and greatly diversified what we are growing. For instance, we're going to get cellulose from our wasted sugar cane, and we're going to make paper. We're putting great energies into consumer-goods industries. Already the benefits are showing up in our everyday lives. At the same time, we're doing some work on heavier industry, and we're planning it carefully with an eye to our own resources and markets. And in this respect, we do have friends who are helping us.

So we don't have to be in such a hurry that we'll sacrifice a generation to get industry; we don't have to do that, and that's not our Cuban way.

If you want to make up your own mind about Cuba, here are some things you've got to know:

First of all, we Cubans are part of Latin America—not North America. We speak Spanish, we are mainly rural, and we are poor. Our history is part of Latin American history. And Latin America is over 180 million people, growing faster than you are growing, and scattered over territory more than twice as large as the U.S.A.

Second, unlike most of Latin America, we Cubans have done something about exploiters from your country in Cuba and about our own Cuban exploiters of Cubans too. We mean business, your kind of business first of all: economic business for us. Your corporations and your government, they don't like what we've done and what we're doing.

But—here's our third point—we are not alone.

Today the Revolution is going on in Cuba. Tomorrow it is going to go on elsewhere. A revolution like ours does not come about just because anyone wants it—although it takes that, too. Revolutions in our time come out of misery, out of conditions like those of the old Cuba. Where such conditions continue and there's a mountain nearby, there'll be revolutions. That is why this continent is going to become the scene of convulsions you've never dreamed of. You can't buy off revolutions with $500 million of aid. You can only buy off some Latin American governments—and for that, its far too much money; they can be bought much cheaper!

What will happen when the people of all those South American countries realize their enormous wealth and yet find themselves poor; then looking across to tiny Cuba, they see that Cubans are not poor? What will happen then?

We are all part of "Western Civilization"—so we've always been told. But are we really? All of us?

Today we Latin Americans die at the average age of thirty-five. You Yankees live until you're past sixty-five. Our illiterate, disease-ridden, hungry peasant masses in Bolivia and Peru and Venezuela, and yesterday in Cuba—are they part of the same "Western Civilization" as you? If so, isn't it a curious kind of a civilization in which such things go on?

As long as they do go on, perhaps we Latin Americans had better realize that the people of whom we are a part are not part of whatever civilization you North Americans belong to.

Hunger is hunger. To die before you reach thirty-five in Central America while working for the Fruit Company is not so different from dying in South Africa while working in a diamond mine. Disease is disease. And not to be able to read is the same in any language: it is to be a people without history; it is to be only half a man. Almost half of us Latin Americans are such primitive creatures—we are illiterate. What does "The Free World" of the Yankees mean to us?

If you still think that we are members of the same Western Civilization with you, and if you value that civilization—whatever it means to you—then perhaps you'd better find out what is going on within what you take to be its confines. Many of us know only the confines.

Your power and wealth, Yankee—that's why it seems so crazy to us when your government says to us, as it has been saying, that our Cuban government is following "... a pattern of relentless economic aggression ... against the United States...." Now isn't that slightly ridiculous? We are about six million people, you are 180 million. You're approximately two hundred times richer than we. You spend more in a year for lipstick and things like that than all of us down here earn for a full year's work.

Anyhow, it's time you knew that all over the world there's been building up the hatred of what your government and your corporations have been doing. Most of that hate has had no chance to come to your indifferent attention. But some of it has, and a lot more will.

About two years ago—remember?—your Vice President tried to make a good-will tour of South America. In many countries, Mr. Nixon and his company were often jeered at and the questions put to him got sharper and sharper. In Caracas, capital of oil-rich, poor-people Venezuela, the rocks thrown at him got as big as melons; his limousine was attacked. Later that day, the army of Venezuela broke up demonstrations "with bayonets and tear gas." Then Yankee Marines and Paratroopers were dispatched to Caribbean bases.

There have been many more such incidents, some reported, others not. But in the spring and summer of 1960, the results of what you're doing and what you're leaving undone really began to show up—dramatically, violently. In South Korea, on Taiwan, on Okinawa, in Japan. That's not the complete list.

But why are we blaming you for all this? Because of your power, first of all, as we've already said. With such power as you have, if you do *not* act you *are* acting. Don't you see that? Now you are the main target of this trouble and this hate. All those tens of millions of people, they didn't just happen to pick on Yankees. They had some reasons, maybe wrong reasons—some of them—but do you even know what their reasons were?

Have you ever tried to find them out?

Tomorrow the returns from what you fail to do, everywhere in the hungry-nation bloc, will be even more evident. But will they be obvious enough to distract you from your energetic pursuit of your private affairs? That's a real question for us Latin Americans. It's also a question about world history—today and tomorrow—a world history of which we are all a part, whether we want to be or not.

So things are not under the easy old control, and your country—and so you, too, if it is your country any more—is becoming the target of a world hate such as easy-going Yankees have never dreamed of.

But listen, Yankee: Does it have to be that way? Isn't it up to you? Isn't at least some of it up to you? As you think about that, please remember this:

Because we have been poor, you must not believe we have lost our pride. You must not believe we have no dignity, no honor, no fight. If you don't see this, it is going to be a very bad time of troubles for us all.

Don't you see that events all over the world demand that you think, feel, act? We Cubans don't take satisfaction in the fact that we are the center of the Cold War in the Caribbean. We don't like the Cold War anywhere—who does? We don't want to be the Western Hungary—who does?

But we are glad, we have to be glad, that finally many things that must be done are now being done in Cuba.

So what can we say to you to make you understand?

Can we say: Become aware of our agonies and our aspirations? If you do, it will help you to know what is happening in the world. Take Cuba as the case— the Case in which to establish the way you are going to act when there are revolutions in hungry countries everywhere in the world. In terms of Cuba, think again about who *you* are, Yankee. And find out what Cuba, our Cuba, means. We are one of the vanguards of the hungry peoples. Like all vanguards, what we've done, what we're dong, what we're going to do—it puts us on a perilous road. We may fail. We don't yet know where it will all end. But do you?

What does Cuba mean?

It means another chance for you.

M ILLS DRAFTED THIS LETTER on July 4, 1960, and saw it published in the September–October issue of a new British journal, *New Left Review*. On September 25, he revised it for reprinting in the second volume of a new American journal, *Studies on the Left*, where it took a slightly different title: "On the New Left."

Daniel Bell, one of Mills's targets in the letter, quickly returned fire with "Vulgar Sociology," an article in *Encounter*. "A first reading of the article, and a second, leaves one a bit bewildered," Bell complained. "The style is explosive, detonative rather than denotative, leading in all directions at once." Bell denounced Mills's stance as "rock-throwing from the podium." But the "Letter to the New Left" became a pivotal statement in the revival of Anglo-American radicalism.

When I settle down to write to you, I feel somehow "freer" than usual. The reason, I suppose, is that most of the time I am writing for people whose ambiguities and values I imagine to be rather different than mine; but with you, I feel enough in common to allow us "to get on with it" in more positive ways. Reading your book, *Out of Apathy*, prompts me to write to you about several problems I think we now face. On none of these can I hope to be definitive; I only want to raise a few questions.

It is no exaggeration to say that since the end of World War II in Britain and the United States smug conservatives, tired liberals and disillusioned radicals have carried on a weary discourse in which issues are blurred and potential debate muted; the sickness of complacency has prevailed, the bi-partisan banality flourished. There is no need—after your book—to explain again why all this has come about among "people in general" in the NATO countries; but it may be worthwhile to examine one style of cultural work that is in effect an intellectual celebration of apathy.

Many intellectual fashions, of course, do just that; they stand in the way of a release of the imagination—about the cold war, the Soviet bloc, the politics of peace, about any new beginnings at home and abroad. But the fashion I have in mind is the weariness of many NATO intellectuals with what they call "ideology," and their proclamation of "the end of ideology." So far as I know, this began in the mid-fifties, mainly in intellectual circles more or less as2-sociated with the Congress for Cultural Freedom and the magazine *Encounter*. Reports on the Milan Conference of 1955 heralded it; since then, many cultural gossips have taken it up as a posture and an unexamined slogan. Does it amount to anything?

Its common denominator is not liberalism as a political philosophy, but the liberal rhetoric, become formal and sophisticated and used as an uncriticised weapon with which to attack Marxism. In the approved style, various of the elements of this rhetoric appear simply as snobbish assumptions. Its sophistication is one of tone rather than of ideas: in it, the *New Yorker* style of reportage has become politically triumphant. The disclosure of fact—set forth in a bright-faced or in a dead-pan manner—is the rule. The facts are duly weighed, carefully balanced, always hedged. Their power to outrage, their power truly to enlighten in a political way, their power to aid decision, even their power to clarify some situation—all that is blunted or destroyed.

So reasoning collapses into reasonableness. By the more naive and snobbish celebrants of complacency, arguments and facts of a displeasing kind are simply ignored; by the more knowing, they are duly recognized, but they are neither connected with one another nor related to any general view. Acknowledged in a scattered way, they are never put together: to do so is to risk being called, curiously enough, "one-sided."

This refusal to relate isolated facts and fragmentary comment with the changing institutions of society makes it impossible to understand the structural realities which these facts might reveal; the longer-run trends of which they might be tokens. In brief, fact and idea are isolated, so the real questions are not even raised, analysis of the meanings of fact not even begun.

Practitioners of the no-more-ideology school do of course smuggle in general ideas under the guise of reportage, by intellectual gossip, and by their selection of the notions they handle. Ultimately, the-end-of-ideology is based upon a disillusionment with any real commitment to socialism in any recognizable form. *That* is the only "ideology" that has really ended for these writers. But with its ending, *all* ideology, they think, has ended. *That* ideology they talk about; their own ideological assumptions, they do not.

Underneath this style of observation and comment there is the assumption that in the West there are no more real issues or even problems of great seriousness. The mixed economy plus the welfare state plus prosperity—that is the formula. US capitalism will continue to be workable; the welfare state will continue along the road to ever greater justice. In the meantime, things everywhere are very complex, let us not be careless, there are great risks. . . .

This posture—one of "false consciousness" if there ever was one—stands in the way, I think, of considering with any chances of success what may be happening in the world.

First and above all, it does rest upon a simple provincialism. If the phrase "the end of ideology" has any meaning at all, it pertains to self-selected circles of intellectuals in the richer countries. It is in fact merely their own self-image. The total population of these countries is a fraction of mankind; the period during which such a posture has been assumed is very short indeed. To speak in such terms of much Latin-America, Africa, Asia, the Soviet bloc is merely ludicrous. Anyone who stands in front of audiences—intellectual or mass—in any of these places and talks in such terms will merely be shrugged off (if the audience is polite) or laughed at out loud (if the audience is more candid and knowledgeable). The end-of-ideology is a slogan of complacency, circulating among the prematurely middle-aged, centered in the present, and in the rich Western societies. In the final analysis, it also rests upon a disbelief in the shaping by men of their own futures—as history and as biography. It is a consensus of a few provincials about their own immediate and provincial position.

Second, the end-of-ideology is of course itself an ideology—a fragmentary one, to be sure, and perhaps more a mood. The end-of-ideology is in reality the ideology of an ending: the ending of political reflection itself as a public fact. It is a weary know-it-all justification—of the cultural and political default of the NATO intellectuals.

All this is just the sort of thing that I at least have always objected to, and do object to, in the "socialist realism" of the Soviet Union.

There too, criticism of milieux are of course permitted—but they are not to be connected to criticism of the structure itself: one may not question "the system." There are no "antagonistic contradictions."

There too, in novels and plays, criticisms of characters, even of party members, are permitted—but they must be displayed as "shocking exceptions":

they must be seen as survivals from the old order, not as systematic products of the new.

There too, pessimism is permitted—but only episodically and only within the context of the big optimism: the tendency is to confuse any systematic or structural criticism with pessimism itself. So they admit criticism, first of this and then of that: but engulf them all by the long-run historical optimism about the system as a whole and the goals proclaimed by its leaders.

I neither want nor need to overstress the parallel, yet in a recent series of interviews in the Soviet Union concerning socialist realism I was very much struck by it. In Uzbekistan and Georgia as well as in Russia, I kept writing notes to myself, at the end of recorded interviews: "This man talks in a style just like Arthur Schlesinger Jr." "Surely this fellow's the counterpart of Daniel Bell, except not so—what shall I say?—so gossipy: and certainly neither so petty nor so vulgar as the more envious status-climbers. Perhaps this is because here they are not thrown into such a competitive status-panic about the ancient and obfuscating British models of prestige." The would-be enders of ideology, I kept thinking, "Are they not the self-coordinated, or better the fashion-coordinated, socialist realists of the NATO world?" And: "Check this carefully with the files of *Encounter* and *The Reporter*." I have now done so; it's the same kind of . . . thing.

Certainly there are many differences—above all, the fact that socialist realism is part of an official line; the end of ideology is self-managed. But the differences one knows. It is more useful to stress the parallels—and the generic fact that both of these postures stand opposed to radical criticisms of their respective societies.

In the Soviet Union, only political authorities at the top—or securely on their way up there—can seriously tamper with structural questions and ideological lines. These authorities, of course, are much more likely to be intellectuals (in one or another sense of the word—say a man who actually writes his own speeches) than are American politicians (about the British, you would know better than I). Moreover, such Soviet authorities, since the death of Stalin, *have* begun to tamper quite seriously with structural questions and basic ideology—although for reasons peculiar to the tight and official joining of culture and politics in their set-up, they must try to disguise this fact.

The end-of-ideology is very largely a mechanical reaction—not a creative response—to the ideology of Stalinism. As such it takes from its opponent something of its inner quality. What does it all mean? That these people have become aware of the uselessness of Vulgar Marxism, but not yet aware of the uselessness of the liberal rhetoric.

But the most immediately important thing about the "end of ideology" is that it *is* merely a fashion, and fashions change. Already this one is on its way out. Even a few Diehard Anti-Stalinists are showing signs of a reappraisal of their own past views; some are even beginning to recognize publicly that Stalin himself no longer runs the Soviet party and state. They begin to see the poverty of their comfortable ideas as they come to confront Khrushchev's Russia.

We who have been consistently radical in the moral terms of our work throughout the postwar period are often amused nowadays that various writers—sensing another shift in fashion—begin to call upon intellectuals to work once more in ways that are politically explicit. But we shouldn't be merely amused—we ought to try to make their shift more than a fashion change.

The end-of-ideology is on the way out because it stands for the refusal to work out an explicit political philosophy. And alert men everywhere today do feel the need of such a philosophy. What we should do is to continue directly to confront this need. In doing so, it may be useful to keep in mind that to have a working political philosophy means to have a philosophy that enables you to work. And for that, at least four kinds of work are needed, each of them at once intellectual and political.

In these terms, think—for a moment longer—of the end-of-ideology:

(1) It is a kindergarten fact that any political reflection that is of possible public significance is *ideological*: in its terms, policies, institutions, men of power are criticized or approved. In this respect, the end-of-ideology stands, negatively, for the attempt to withdraw oneself and one's work from political relevance; positively, it is an ideology of political complacency which seems the only way now open for many writers to acquiesce in or to justify the *status quo*.

(2) So far as orienting *theories* of society and of history are concerned, the end-of-ideology stands for, and presumably stands upon, a fetishism of empiricism: more academically, upon a pretentious methodology used to state trivialities about unimportant social areas; more essayistically, upon a naïve journalistic empiricism—which I have already characterized above—and upon a cultural gossip in which "answers" to the vital and pivotal issues are merely assumed. Thus political bias masquerades as epistemological excellence, and there are no orienting theories.

(3) So far as the *historic agency of change* is concerned, the end-of-ideology stands upon the identification of such agencies with going institutions; perhaps upon the piecemeal reform, but never upon the search for agencies that might be used or that might themselves make a structural change of society. The problem of agency is never posed as a problem to solve, as our

problem. Instead there is talk of the need to be pragmatic, flexible, open. Surely all this has already been adequately dealt with: such a view makes sense politically only if the blind drift of human affairs is in general beneficent.

(4) So far as political and human *ideals* are concerned, the end-of-ideology stands for a denial of their relevance—except as abstract ikons. Merely to hold such ideals seriously is in this view "utopian."

But enough. Where do *we* stand on each of these four aspects of political philosophy? Various of us are of course at work on each of them, and all of us are generally aware of our needs in regard to each. As for the articulation of ideals: there I think your magazines have done their best work so far. That is *your* meaning—is it not?—of the emphasis upon cultural affairs. As for ideological analysis, and the rhetoric with which to carry it out: I don't think any of us are nearly good enough, but that will come with further advance on the two fronts where we are weakest: theories of society, history, human nature; and the major problem—ideas about the historical agencies of structural change.

We have frequently been told by an assorted variety of dead-end people that the meanings of Left and of Right are now liquidated, by history and by reason. I think we should answer them in some such way as this:

The Right, among other things, means—what you are doing, celebrating society as it is, a going concern. Left means, or ought to mean, just the opposite. It means: structural criticism and reportage and theories of society, which at some point or another are focused politically as demands and programmes. These criticisms, demands, theories, programmes are guided morally by the humanist and secular ideals of Western civilization—above all, reason and freedom and justice. To be "Left" means to connect up cultural with political criticism, and both with demands and programmes. And it means all this inside *every* country of the world.

Only one more point of definition: absence of public issues there may well be, but this is not due to any absence of problems or of contradictions, antagonistic and otherwise. Impersonal and structural changes have not eliminated problems or issues. Their absence from many discussions—that *is* an ideological condition, regulated in the first place by whether or not intellectuals detect and state problems as potential *issues* for probable publics, and as *troubles* for a variety of individuals. One indispensable means of such work on these central tasks is what can only be described as ideological analysis. To be actively Left, among other things, is to carry on just such analysis.

To take seriously the problem of the need for a political orientation is not of course to seek for A Fanatical and Apocalyptic Vision, for An Infallible and

Monolithic Lever of Change, for Dogmatic Ideology, for A Startling New Rhetoric, for Treacherous Abstractions—and all the other bogeymen of the dead-enders. These are of course "the extremes," the straw men, the red herrings, used by our political enemies as the polar opposite of where they think they stand.

They tell us, for example, that ordinary men can't always be political "heroes." Who said they could? But keep looking around you; and why not search out the conditions of such heroism as men do and might display? They tell us we are too "impatient," that our "pretentious" theories are not well enough grounded. That is true, but neither are they trivial; why don't they get to work, refuting or grounding them? They tell us we "don't really understand" Russia—and China—today. That is true; we don't; neither do they; we are studying it. They tell us we are "ominous" in our formulations. That is true: we do have enough imagination to be frightened—and we don't have to hide it: we are not afraid we'll panic. They tell us we "are grinding axes." Of course we are: we do have, among other points of view, morally grounded ones; and we are aware of them. They tell us, in their wisdom, we don't understand that The Struggle is Without End. True: we want to change its form, its focus, its object.

We are frequently accused of being "utopian"—in our criticisms and in our proposals; and along with this, of basing our hopes for a New Left *politics* "merely on reason," or more concretely, upon the intelligentsia in its broadest sense.

There is truth in these charges. But must we not ask: what now is really meant by utopian? And: Is not our utopianism a major source of our strength? "Utopian" nowadays I think refers to any criticism or proposal that transcends the up-close milieux of a scatter of individuals: the milieux which men and women can understand directly and which they can reasonably hope directly to change. In this exact sense, our theoretical work is indeed utopian—in my own case, at least, deliberately so. What needs to be understood, and what needs to be changed, is not merely first this and then that detail of some institution or policy. If there is to be a politics of a New Left, what needs to be analyzed is the *structure* of institutions, the *foundation* of policies. In this sense, both in its criticisms and in its proposals, our work is necessarily structural—and so, *for us*, just now—utopian.

Which brings us face to face with the most important issue of political reflection—and of political action—in our time: the problem of the historical agency of change, of the social and institutional means of structural change. There are several points about this problem I would like to put to you.

First, the historic agencies of change for liberals of the capitalist societies have been an array of voluntary associations, coming to a political climax in a parliamentary or congressional system. For socialists of almost all varieties, the historic agency has been the working class—and later the peasantry; also parties and unions variously composed of members of the working class or (to blur, for now, a great problem) of political parties acting in its name— "representing its interests."

I cannot avoid the view that in both cases, the historic agency (in the advanced capitalist countries) has either collapsed or become most ambiguous: so far as structural change is concerned, *these* don't seem to be at once available and effective as *our* agency any more. I know this is a debatable point among us, and among many others as well; I am by no means certain about it. But surely the fact of it—if it be that—ought not to be taken as an excuse for moaning and withdrawal (as it is by some of those who have become involved with the end-of-ideology); it ought not to be bypassed (as it is by many Soviet scholars and publicists, who in their reflections upon the course of advanced capitalist societies simply refuse to admit the political condition and attitudes of the working class).

Is anything more certain than that in 1970—indeed this time next year— our situation will be quite different, and—the chances are high—decisively so? But of course, that isn't saying much. The seeming collapse of our historic agencies of change out to be taken as a problem, an issue, a trouble—in fact, as *the* political problem which *we* must turn into issue and trouble.

Second, is it not obvious that when we talk about the collapse of agencies of change, we cannot seriously mean that such agencies do not exist. On the contrary, the means of history-making—or decision and of the enforcement of decision—have never in world history been so enlarged and so available to such small circles of men on both sides of The Curtains as they now are. My own conception of the shape of power—the theory of the power elite—I feel no need to argue here. This theory has been fortunate in its critics, from the most diverse points of political view, and I have learned from several of these critics. But I have not seen, as of this date, any analysis of the idea that causes me to modify any of its essential features.

The point that is immediately relevant does seem obvious: what is utopian for us is not at all utopian for the presidium of the Central Committee in Moscow, or the higher circles of the Presidency in Washington, or—recent events make evident—for the men of SAC and CIA. The historic agencies of change that have collapsed are those which were at least thought to be open to *the left* inside the advanced Western nations: those who have wished for structural changes of these societies. Many things follow from this obvious fact; of many of them, I am sure, we are not yet adequately aware.

Third, what I do not quite understand about some New-Left writers is why they cling so mightily to "the working class" of the advanced capitalist societies as *the* historic agency, or even as the most important agency, in the face of the really impressive historical evidence that now stands against this expectation.

Such a labor metaphysic, I think, is a legacy for Victorian Marxism that is now quite unrealistic.

It is an historically specific idea that has been turned into an a-historical and unspecific hope.

The social and historical conditions under which industrial workers tend to become a-class-for-themselves, and a decisive political force, must be fully and precisely elaborated. There have been, there are, there will be such conditions; of course these conditions vary according to national social structure and the exact phase of their economic and political development. Of course we can't "write off the working class." But we must *study* all that, and freshly. Where labor exists as an agency, of course we must work with it, but we must not treat it as The Necessary Lever—as nice old Labor Gentlemen in your country and elsewhere tend to do.

Although I have not yet completed my own comparative studies of working classes, generally it would seem that only at certain (earlier) stages of industrialization, and in a political context of autocracy, etc., do wage-workers tend to become a class-for-themselves, etc. The "etcs." mean that I can here merely raise the question.

It is with this problem of agency in mind that I have been studying, for several years now, the cultural apparatus, the intellectuals—as a possible, immediate, radical agency of change. For a long time, I was not much happier with this idea that were many of you; but it turns out now, in the spring of 1960, that it may be a very relevant idea indeed.

In the first place, is it not clear that if we try to be realistic in our utopianism—and that is no fruitless contradiction—a writer in our countries on the Left today *must* begin there? For that is what we are, that is where we stand.

In the second place, the problem of the intelligentsia is an extremely complicated set of problems on which rather little factual work has been done. In doing this work, we must—above all—not confuse the problems of the intellectuals of West Europe and North America with those of the Soviet Bloc or with those of the underdeveloped worlds. In each of the three major components of the world's social structure today, the character and the role of the intelligentsia is distinct and historically specific. Only by detailed comparative studies of them in all their human variety can we hope to understand any one of them.

In the third place, who is it that is getting fed up? Who is it that is getting disgusted with what Marx called "all the old crap"? Who is it that is thinking and acting in radical ways? All over the world—in the bloc, outside the bloc and in between—the answer's the same: it is the young intelligentsia.

I cannot resist copying out for you, with a few changes, some materials I've just prepared for a 1960 paperback edition of a book of mine on war:

"In the spring and early summer of 1960—more of the returns from the American decision and default are coming in. In Turkey, after student riots, a military junta takes over the state, of late run by Communist-Container Menderes. In South Korea too, students and others knock over the corrupt American-puppet regime of Syngman Rhee. In Cuba, a genuinely left-wing revolution begins full-scale economic reorganization—without the domination of US corporations. Average age of its leaders: about 30—and certainly a revolution without any Labor As Agency. On Taiwan, the eight million Taiwanese under the American-imposed dictatorship of Chiang Kai-shek, with his two million Chinese grow increasingly restive. On Okinawa—a US military base—the people get their first change since World War II ended to demonstrate against US seizure of their island: and some students take that chance, snake-dancing and chanting angrily to the visiting President: "Go home, go home—take away your missiles." (Don't worry, 12,000 US troops easily handled the generally grateful crowds; also the President was "spirited out the rear end of the United States compound"—and so by helicopter to the airport.) In Great Britain, from Aldermaston to London, young—but you were there. In Japan, weeks of student rioting succeed in rejecting the President's visit, jeopardize a new treaty with the USA, displace the big-business, pro-American Prime Minister, Kishi. And even in our own pleasant Southland, Negro and white students are—but let us keep that quiet: it really *is* disgraceful.

"That is by no means the complete list; that was yesterday; see today's newspaper. Tomorrow, in varying degree, the returns will be more evident. Will they be evident enough? They will have to be very obvious to attract real American attention: sweet complaints and the voice of reason—these are not enough. In the slum countries of the world today, what are they saying? The rich Americans, they pay attention only to violence—and to money. You don't care what they say, American? Good for you. Still, they may insist;

things are no longer under the old control; you're not getting it straight, American: your country—it would seem—may well become the target of a world hatred of the like of which the easy-going Americans have never dreamed. Neutralists and Pacifists and Unilateralists and that confusing variety of Leftists around the world —all those tens of millions of people, of course they are misguided, absolutely controlled by small conspiratorial groups of trouble-makers, under direct orders straight from Moscow and Peking. Diabolically omnipotent, it is *they* who create all this messy unrest. It is *they* who have given the tens of millions the absurd idea that they shouldn't want to remain, or to become, the seat of American nuclear bases, those gay little outposts of American civilization. So now they don't want U-2's on their territory; so now they want to contract out of the American military machine; they want to be neutral among the crazy big antagonists. And they don't want their own societies to be militarized.

"But take heart, American: you won't have time to get really bored with your friends abroad: they won't be your friends much longer. You don't need *them*; it will all go away; don't let them confuse you."

Add to that: In the Soviet bloc, who is it that has been breaking out of apathy? It has been students and young professors and writers; it has been the young intelligentsia of Poland and Hungary, and of Russia too. Never mind that they've not won; never mind that there are other social and moral types among them. First of all, it has been these types. But the point is clear—isn't it?

That's why we've got to study these new generations of intellectuals around the world as real live agencies of historic change. Forget Victorian Marxism except whenever you need it; and read Lenin again (be careful)—Rosa Luxemburg, too.

"But it's just some kind of moral upsurge, isn't it?" Correct. But under it: no apathy. Much of it is direct non-violent action, and it seems to be working, here and there. Now we must learn from their practice and work out with them new forms of action.

"But it's all so ambiguous. Turkey, for instance. Cuba, for instance." Of course it is; history-making is always ambiguous; wait a bit; in the meantime, *help* them to focus their moral upsurge in less ambiguous political ways; work out with them the ideologies, the strategies, the theories that will help them consolidate their efforts: new theories of structural changes of and by human societies in our epoch.

"But it's utopian, after all, isn't it?" No—not in the sense you mean. Whatever else it may be, it's not that: tell it to the students of Japan.

Isn't all this, isn't it something of what we are trying to mean by the phrase, "The New Left"? Let the old men ask sourly, "Out of Apathy—into what?" The Age of Complacency is ending. Let the old women complain wisely about "the end of ideology." We are beginning to move again.

Yours truly,
C. Wright Mills

Like Thorstein Veblen, who died in 1929, C. Wright Mills died at the dawn of a decade whose most flamboyant features his vision was the first to illuminate. Yet neither his epigones nor his enemies have generated anything to compare with Joseph Dorfman's *Thorstein Veblen and His America* (1934), no comprehensive biography in the absence of which informed disagreement miscarries. Mills admired Dorfman's book in college. Later, he added Ernest Jones (on Freud) and Isaac Deutscher (on Trotsky) to his short list of model biographers. But no equivalent has stepped forward to relate his life to the issues he articulated and advanced, and the evidential basis for received opinion remains today a maw of apocrypha, partial truth, and provincial falsification.

Around Mills's biography has grown a logic of venerating and debunking. The apparent discrepancy between his criticism of American exceptionalism and his exceptional success as an American critic has attracted culture warriors in search of *lessons*. The moralists ignore his humor, his sensitivity to the ironies of success, the nuances and difficulties of his attempt to write as both defender of humanist aspiration and witness to its eclipse. Sociologists, unfortunately, have done little but measure Mills against the norms of the academic professional.

In my judgment the following articles and short books are the best readings for any large-scale reassessment. For a fuller range of titles, consult *C. Wright Mills*, a three-volume set compiled by Stanley Aronowitz and published in 2004 by Sage.

Gillam, Richard. "*White Collar* from Start to Finish: C. Wright Mills in Transition." *Theory and Society*, v. 10 (1981): 1–30.

————. "Richard Hofstadter, C. Wright Mills, and 'the Critical Ideal.'" *The American Scholar* (Winter 1977/78): 69–85.

————. "C. Wright Mills and the Politics of Truth: *The Power Elite* Revisited." *American Quarterly*, v. 27 (October 1975): 461–475.

————. "C. Wright Mills and Lionel Trilling: 'Imagination' in the Fifties." *The Gettysburg Review*, v. 2 (Autumn 1989): 680–689.

Hayden, Tom. *Radical Nomad: C. Wright Mills and His Times*. Boulder, CO: Paradigm Publishers, 2006.

Miller, James. "Democracy and the Intellectual: C. Wright Mills Reconsidered." *Salmagundi*, 70-71 (Spring/Summer 1986): 82–101.

Oakes, Guy, and Arthur J. Vidich. *Collaboration, Reputation, and Ethics in American Academic Life: Hans H. Gerth and C. Wright Mills*. Urbana: University of Illinois Press, 1999.

Summers, John H. "No-Man's-Land: C. Wright Mills in England." In *Penultimate Adventures with Britannia: Personalities, Politics, and Culture in Britain*, edited by Wm. Roger Louis, 185–199. London: I.B. Tauris, 2008.

————. "The Epigone's Embrace: Irving Louis Horowitz on C. Wright Mills." *Minnesota Review*, n.s. 68 (Spring 2007): 107–124.

————. "The Epigone's Embrace, Part II: C. Wright Mills and the New Left." *Left History*, v. 13, no. 2 (Fall/Winter 2008), in press.

————. "Perpetual Revelations: C. Wright Mills and Paul Lazarsfeld." *Annals of the American Academy of Political and Social Science*, v. 608 (November 2006): 25–40.

————. "James Agee and C. Wright Mills: Sociological Poetry." In *Agee Agonistes: Essays on the Life, Legend, and Works of James Agee*, edited by Michael Lofaro, 199–216. Knoxville: University of Tennessee Press, 2007.

————. "The Deciders." *New York Times Book Review* (May 14, 2006): 39.

————. "The Cultural Break: C. Wright Mills and the Polish October." *Intellectual History Review*, v. 18, no. 2 (July 2008).

Tilman, Rick. *C. Wright Mills: A Native Radical and His American Intellectual Roots*. University Park: Pennsylvania State University Press, 1984.

1934

"Personal Notes #1," journal, April–Oct. 14, 1934.

"Some Early Observations," journal, July 25, 1934.

"Viewpoint of Science," letter to the editor of *Dallas Morning News* (Aug. 10, 1934): sec. 2, p. 2; in response to W.C. Stovall, "Scientists So-Called," letter to the editor of *Dallas Morning News* (Aug. 4, 1934) sec. 2, p. 2.

"The Place of Athletics," paper for Rhetoric and Composition, Department of English, Agricultural and Mechanical College of Texas, Fall 1934.

1935

"Camouflage," poem, Feb. 1935.

"Rain Melody," poem, Feb. 25, 1935.

"Usages of Leisure," paper for Rhetoric and Composition, Department of English, Agricultural and Mechanical College of Texas, March 5, 1935.

"The Small Potted Plant," poem, March 29, 1935.

"Powder Puff," poem, Spring 1935.

"Jug," poem, Spring 1935.

"Dirt-work," poem, Spring 1935.

"Digressions on College Life," *The Battalion* (April 3, 1935): 8.

"Weights," poem, April 25, 1935.

"At a Railroad Station," poem, April 28, 1935.

"Another Viewpoint," *The Battalion* (May 8, 1935): 8.

"Snake," poem, May 9, 1935.

"Bio Final," poem, May 14, 1935.

"Unnatural," poem, May 25, 1935.

"Personal Notes #3," journal, June 1935.

"Tourist Philosophy," poem, June 1, 1935.

"Dust," poem, June 7, 1935.

"Social Order," poem, Summer 1935

"Park," poem, June 5, 1935.

"Women," poem, Aug. 1935

"Educational Need," paper for English Composition, Department of English, University of Texas, Nov. 5, 1935.

1936

"Room-to-Rent," paper, Feb. 1936.

"Elizabeth Goodman," paper, April 17, 1936.

"A Study of the Role of the Intellectual and Romantic Values in the Determination of Personality: Personal Life-History," 101-page journal for Social Attitudes, Department of Sociology, University of Texas, Dec. 4, 1936.

1937

"Contemporary Thought on Man," journal, Jan. 1937.

"Concerning the Integration, or So-Called Unity of the Self," paper, April 25, 1937.

"D.H. and Me," journal, May 9, 1937.

"The Function of Moral Judgements," paper, 1937.

1938

"Men, Women, and Thinkers," journal, Jan. 23, 1938.

"Character and Loci of the Problematic," paper, Spring 1938.

"The Role of Concepts in Research," paper for Nineteenth Annual Meeting of the Southwestern Social Science Association, Oklahoma City, April 16, 1938.

"Science and Religion," paper for Seminar on Scientific Method, Department of Philosophy, University of Texas, April 1938.

"Language: Its Social Setting, Character and Incidence," paper for Seminar on Scientific Method, Department of Philosophy, University of Texas, May 16, 1938.

"Science and Society," paper for Seminar on Scientific Method, Department of Philosophy, University of Texas, May 19, 1938.

"The Value Situation and the Vocabulary of Morals," paper for Seminar in the Theory of Value, Department of Philosophy, University of Texas, Fall 1938.

"Pivot," short story, Sept. 7, 1938.

"Language, Logic, and Culture," paper, Sept. 28, 1938.

"Functions for Philosophers," paper for History of Philosophy, Department of Philosophy, University of Texas, Fall 1938.

"Schematic Note on the Sociologistic Perspective," paper, Dec. 18, 1938.

"The Academic," short story, 1938; revised Aug. 11, 1940, and Sept./Oct. 1943.

1939

Untitled 18-page autobiographical statement, journal, Jan. 30, 1939.

"Reflection, Behavior, and Culture: An Essay in the Sociology of Knowledge," Master's Thesis in Philosophy, University of Texas, submitted April 15 and accepted June 1939.

"Types of Rationality," paper, 1939.

"Politics and Me," journal, summer 1939.

"Self-Examination: Of Politics and Me," journal, June 1939.

"Honey in the Village," short story, June 1939.

"Knight Errant" (with David Rose), short story, Aug. 8, 1939.

"Local Trouble," journal, Aug. 20, 1939.

"Education in Love" (with David Rose), short story, Aug. 1939.

"Pick Up," short story, Aug. 1939.

"Portrait of a Young Liberal," short story, Aug. 1939.

"Language, Logic and Culture," *American Sociological Review*, v. 4 (Oct. 1939): 670–680.

"A Note on the Classification of Social Psychological Sciences," paper on Ruth Benedict and Margaret Mead, Nov. 7, 1939.

1940

"Bibliographical Appendix" in *Contemporary Social Theory*, by Harry Elmer Barnes, Howard Becker, and Frances Bennett Becker (New York: D. Appleton-Century Co., 1940): 889–912.

Booknote on *Reality*, by Paul Weiss, *American Sociological Review*, v. 5 (Feb. 1940): 150.

Booknote on *Toward a Dimensional Realism*, by C. M. Perry, *American Sociological Review*, v. 5 (Feb. 1940): 150.

Review of *Ideas Are Weapons*, by Max Lerner, *American Sociological Review*, v. 5 (April 1940): 267–269.

Booknote on *The German Ideology*, by Karl Marx and Frederick Engels, *American Sociological Review*, v. 5 (June 1940): 466.

Booknote on *Culture and the People*, by Maxim Gorky, *American Sociological Review*, v. 5 (June 1940): 466.

Booknote on *The Philosophy of Physical Science*, by Sir Arthur Eddington, *American Sociological Review*, v. 5 (Aug. 1940): 685.

Review of *The Human Enterprise, An Attempt to Relate Philosophy to Daily Life*, by Max Otto, *American Sociological Review*, v. 5 (Aug. 1940): 681.

"The Language and Ideas of Ancient China: Marcel Granet's Contribution to the Sociology of Knowledge," paper for Cultures and Styles of Thought and Sociology of Knowledge, Department of Sociology and Anthropology, University of Wisconsin, Oct. 1940.

Review of *Ideas Are Weapons* and *It Is Later Than You Think*, by Max Lerner, *Journal of Social Philosophy*, v. 6 (Oct. 1940): 88–93.

Review of *The Technique of Theory Construction*, by J. H. Woodger, *American Sociological Review*, v. 5 (Oct. 1940): 807–808.

Booknote on *The Journal of Unified Science*, eds. Rudolf Carnap and Hans Reichenbach, *American Sociological Review*, v. 5 (Oct. 1940): 843.

"Methodological Consequences of the Sociology of Knowledge," *American Journal of Sociology* v. 46 (Nov. 1940): 316–330.

"Situated Actions and Vocabularies of Motive," *American Sociological Review*, v. 5 (Dec. 1940): 904–913. First given as a paper for Society for Social Research, University of Chicago, Aug. 16–17; condensed version published in *Bulletin of the Society for Social Research* (Dec. 1940): 18–19.

Review of *Man and Society in an Age of Reconstruction*, by Karl Mannheim, trans. Edward Shils, *American Sociological Review* v. 5 (Dec. 1940): 965–969.

"Sociological Methods and Philosophies of Science," unpublished essay-review of *Foundations of Sociology*, by George Lundberg. Portions published in Howard Becker, "The Limits of Sociological Positivism," *Journal of Social Philosophy*, v. 6 (July 1941): 362–369.

"American Pragmatism: A Socio-Historical Examination of an Intellectual Movement," fellowship application to Social Science Research Council, 1941.

"Language and Culture," unpublished 8-page paper for Anthropology 214, University of Wisconsin, 1941.

1941

"Methodological Consequences: Three Problems for Pathologists," paper, 1941.

Booknote on *Karl Marx*, by Karl Korsch, *American Sociological Review*, v. 6 (Feb. 1941): 153.

"The Metropolis and Mental Life" (with Hans H. Gerth), mimeographed translation of "Die Grosstadte und das Geistesleben" by Georg Simmel. Department of Sociology and Anthropology, University of Wisconsin, Spring 1941; published in *The Sociology of Georg Simmel*, trans., ed. Kurt H. Wolff (Glencoe, IL: Free Press, 1950), 409–424.

"General Memorandum for Howard Becker," proposal for a textbook on social psychology with Hans Gerth, 1941.

Booknote on *Development of Contemporary Civilization*, by W. J. Bossenbrook et al., *American Sociological Review*, v. 6 (June 1941): 461.

Booknote on *The Pecan Shellers of San Antonio: The Problem of Underpaid and Unemployed Mexican Labor*, by Selden C. Menefee and Orin C. Cassmore, *American Sociological Review*, v. 6 (June 1941): 460.

"Some Uses of Philosophy of Science," paper (undelivered) for Sixth International Congress for the Unity of Science, Chicago, Sept. 1–6, 1941.

"Adventures of a Young Man," journal, Sept. 1941.

Booknote on *The Earlier Writings of Karl Marx*, by H. P. Adams, *American Sociological Review*, v. 6 (Oct. 1941): 771.

Booknote on *The Foundations of Empirical Knowledge*, by A. J. Ayer, *American Sociological Review*, v. 6 (Oct. 1941): 770.

"Locating the Enemy: Problems of Intellectuals during Time of War," unpublished essay, Dec. 9, 1941; revised Jan. 2, 1942.

1942

"A Marx for the Managers" (with Hans H. Gerth), review-essay of *The Managerial Revolution*, by James Burnham, *Ethics: An International Journal of Legal, Political and Social Thought*, v. 52 (Jan. 1942): 200–215.

Review of *Vectors in Group Change*, by L. H. Rohrbaugh, *American Journal of Sociology*, v. 47 (Jan. 1942): 653.

Review of *What Reading Does to People*, by Douglas Waples, Bernard Berelson and Franklyn R. Bradshaw, *American Sociological Review*, v. 7 (Feb. 1942): 154.

Essay-review of *The Social Life of a Modern Community*, by W. Lloyd Warner and Paul S. Lunt, *American Sociological Review*, v. 7 (April 1942): 263–271.

Review for *American Journal of Sociology* (written May 11, 1942 but not published) of "Symposium on the Significance of Max Scheler for Philosophy and Social Science," *Philosophy and Phenomenological Research*, v. 2 (March 1942).

"Ideology, Economics and Today," review of *The Making of Tomorrow*, by Raoul J. J. F. de Roussy de Sales, *The New Leader*, v. 25 (June 27, 1942): 3.

Review of *The Academic Man*, by Logan Wilson, *American Sociological Review*, v. 7 (June 1942): 444–446.

Booknote on *In Quest of Morals*, by Henry Lanz, *American Sociological Review*, v. 7 (June 1942): 463.

"The Orientation of Dewey's *Quest for Certainty*," paper for Department of Philosophy, University of Wisconsin, summer 1942.

"A Sociological Account of Some Aspects of Pragmatism," PhD diss, University of Wisconsin, submitted Aug. 3 and approved on Aug. 21, 1942.

Letter to the editor, *Journal of Philosophy*, v. 39 (Aug. 27, 1942): 503–504; responding to Thelma Z. Lavine, "Sociological Analysis of Cognitive Norms," *Journal of Philosophy*, v. 39 (June 1942): 342–356.

"Pragmatism, Politics and Religion," two part review-essay on *The Paths of Life*, by Charles W. Morris, *The New Leader*, v. 25 (Sept. 12, 1942): 8; 25; and (Sept. 19): 8.

"Locating the Enemy: The Nazi Behemoth Dissected," review-essay on *Behemoth: The Structure and Practice of National Socialism*, by Franz Neuman, *Partisan Review*, v. 9 (Sept.–Oct. 1942): 432–437.

"Collectivism and the 'Mixed-Up' Economy," *The New Leader*, v. 25 (Dec. 19, 1942): 5–6.

1943

"What Died?" review of *Postmortem on Malaya*, by Virginia M. Thompson, *The New Leader*, v. 26 (Feb. 20, 1943): 1.

Review of *The Evolution of Social Classes*, by John W. McConnell, *American Sociological Review*, v. 8 (Feb. 1943): 108.

"Conversation in Capetown," dialogue (withdrawn) for *The New Leader*, March 1943.

"The Political Gargoyles," essay-review of *Business as a System of Power*, by Robert A. Brady, *The New Republic*, v. 109 (April 12, 1943): 482–483.

"Political Man: Personal and Political Morality," book project statement, May 22, 1943.

"The Case for the Coal Miners," *The New Republic*, v. 108 (May 24, 1943): 695–698; reply by the editors, "Mr. Lewis Pro and Con," *The New Republic*, v. 108 (May 24, 1943): 688.

Booknote on *The Wright Brothers*, by Fred C. Kelly, *The New Republic*, v. 108 (May 31, 1943): 742.

"A Bibliography of War," review of *A Study of War*, by Q. Wright, *Partisan Review*, v. 10 (May–June, 1943): 301–302.

Booknote (unpublished) on *The War against God*, ed. Carl Cramer, summer 1943.

Booknote (unpublished) on *The Union of South Africa*, by Lewis Sowden, June 1943.

"Prometheus as Democrat," review of *The Hero in History*, by Sidney Hook, *The New Republic*, v. 108 (June 21, 1943): 834–835.

"The Sailor, the Sex Market and the Mexican," *The New Leader*, v. 26 (June 26, 1943): 5, 7.

"Item for Bandwagon," review of *The God of the Machine*, by Isabel Paterson, *The New Republic*, v. 109 (July 5, 1943): 28–29.

Booknote on *Duel for the Northland: The War of Enemy Agents in Scandinavia*, by Kurt Singer, *The New Republic*, v. 109 (July 26, 1943): 118.

"The Professional Ideology of Social Pathologists," *American Journal of Sociology*, v. 49 (Sept. 1943): 165–180.

"In Tolerance," review of *History of Bigotry in the United States*, by Gustavus Myers, *The New Republic*, v. 109 (Sept. 6, 1943): 344–345.

"Probing the Two-Party State," essay-review of *American Political Parties*, by Wilfred E. Binkley, *The New Leader*, v. 26 (Oct. 30, 1943): 3, 7.

Booknote on *Food and Farming in Post-war Europe*, by P. Lamartine Yates and D. Warriner, *The New Republic*, v. 109 (Nov. 22, 1943): 726.

Booknote on *Preview of History*, by Raymond Swing, *The New Republic*, v. 109 (Nov. 29, 1943): 757–758.

1944

"The Horror of Peace," review of *The Unemployed*, by Eli Ginzberg, *The New Leader*, v. 27 (Jan. 1944): 3.

"Freedom and Security," unpublished six-page essay, Feb. 14, 1944.

Note on "The Chinese Draft Constitution," *Politics*, v. 1 (Feb. 1944): 31.

Review of *Socialism and Ethics*, by Howard Selsam, *Politics*, v. 1 (Feb. 1944): 28.

Review of *Society and Nature: A Sociological Inquiry*, by Hans Kelson, *Political Science Quarterly*, v. 59 (March 1944): 102–104.

"The Boy Scout World: Military Planning for the Peace," unpublished essay responding to speech by Secretary of the Navy, Frank Knox, in Cleveland on Jan. 14, 1944.

"C.W.M.," comment under "Typical Reactions to Vol. 1, No. 1," *Politics*, v. 1 (April 1944): 94.

Note on "Is China's Economy to be Modelled on Japan's?" *Politics*, v. 1 (April 1944): 93.

"The Powerless People: The Role of the Intellectual in Society," *Politics*, v. 1, no. 3 (April 1944): 68–72; reprinted in the *American Association of University Professors Bulletin*, v. 31, no. 2 (Summer 1945): 231–243.

"Christian Crisis," review of *The University and the Modern World*, by Arnold S. Nash, *The New Leader*, v. 27 (April 29, 1944): 12.

Review of *The Spirit of American Economics: A Study in the History of Economic Ideas in the United States Prior to the Great Depression*, by J. F. Normano, *Journal of Legal and Political Sociology*, v. 2 (April 1944): 151–152.

Review of *The Russian Enigma*, by William H. Chamberlain, *Maryland Quarterly*, v. 1 (Spring 1944): 85–87.

Review of *The Origins of American Sociology: The Social Science Movement in the United States*, by L. L. Bernard and Jessi Bernard, *Scientific Monthly*, v. 58 (May 1944): 399–400.

"Three Styles of Exhortation," essay-review of *American Unlimited*, by Eric A. Johnston; *The Practice of Idealism*, by Alfred M. Bingham; and *What Is Our*

Destiny? by Norman Thomas, *Partisan Review*, v. 11 (Summer 1944): 353–355.

"The 'Morale' of the Public," review of *Gauging Public Opinion*, by Hadley Cantril et al., *The New Leader*, v. 27 (July 15, 1944): 13.

Review of *Symposium on the Significance of Max Scheler for Philosophy and Social Science*, ed. Marvin Farber, *American Journal of Sociology*, v. 50 (Sept. 1944): 171.

"A Note on Max Weber" (with Hans H. Gerth), *Politics*, v. 1 (Oct. 1944): 271–272.

"Class, Status, Party" (with Hans H. Gerth), translation of parts of *Wirtschaft und Gellschaft*, by Max Weber, *Politics*, v. 1 (Oct. 1944): 272–278.

"Research and Training," fellowship application to the John Simon Guggenheim Memorial Foundation, Nov. 7, 1944.

1945

"The Politics of Truth," unpub essay, 1945.

"The Trade Union Leader: A Collective Portrait" (with assistance from Mildred Atkinson), *Public Opinion Quarterly*, v. 9 (Spring 1945): 158–175; condensed versions in "A Who's What of Union Leadership," *Labor and Nation*, v. 1 (Dec. 1945): 33–36; and "Who Are Our Labor Leaders?" *Read* (Feb. 1946): 9–14. Findings reported in *Newsweek*, Nov. 5, 1945, and *New York Mirror*, Dec. 31, 1945.

Review of *The Sociology of Religion*, by Joachim Wach, *Political Science Quarterly,* v. 60 (March 1945): 151–152.

"The Conscription of America," *Common Sense*, v. 14 (April 1945): 15–18. Condensed in *Conscription News* (June 7, 1945): 3.

Review of *Foundations of the Social Sciences*, by Otto Neurath, *American Journal of Sociology*, v. 51 (July 1945): 75.

Review of *The Sociology of Literary Taste*, by Levin L. Schucking, *Politics*, v. 2 (Sept. 1945): 281.

Review of *Methodology of the Social Sciences*, by Felix Kaufmann, *Political Science Quarterly*, v. 60 (Sept. 1945): 470–472.

"The Barricade and the Bedroom" (with Patricia J. Salter), *Politics*, v. 2 (Oct. 1945): 313–315; in response to "The Political Meaning of Some Recent Revisions of Freud," by Paul Goodman, *Politics*, v. 2 (July 1945): 197–203.

"Confidential Memorandum" to Margaret Nicolson, Oxford University Press, about *Twilight of Reason*, by Max Horkheimer, Oct. 10, 1945.

"What Women Think of U.S. Highway 36 Plan," *Sunday Herald and Review* (Decatur, IL) (Nov. 25, 1945): 4.

"The American Business Elite: A Collective Portrait," *Journal of Economic History*, v. 4, Supplement 5, *The Tasks of Economic History* (Dec. 1945): 20–44.

Review of *Problems of the Postwar World*, ed. Thomas T. C. McCormick, *American Sociological Review*, v. 10 (Dec. 1945): 818.

"Proceedings of Meeting of Inter-Union Institute," discussion with Elizabeth Baker, Broadus Mitchell, Ben B. Seligman, M. Marseille, and P.W. Fox, Dec. 20, 1945.

"The Public's View of Research in the State Department of Labor" (with Marjorie Fiske), project report for the Bureau of Applied Social Research, Dec. 31, 1945.

1946

From Max Weber: Essays in Sociology, translated (with Hans H. Gerth), New York: Oxford University Press, 1946.

"Memorandum to Philip Vaudrin" about *White Collar*, submitted to Philip Vaudrin, Oxford University Press, Jan. 7, 1946.

"Proceedings of Meeting of Inter-Union Institute," discussion with J. B. S Hardman and Mark Starr, New York City, Jan. 18, 1946.

"An Early Labor Leader," review of *William Sylvis, Pioneer of American Labor: A Study of the Labor Movement during the Era of the Civil War*, by Jonathan Grossman, *Labor and Nation*, v. 2 (Feb.–March, 1946): 57.

Small Business and Civic Welfare (with Melville J. Ulmer, under the direction of John Blair), report of the Smaller War Plants Corporation to the Special Committee to Study Problems of American Small Business, *Senate Document* no. 135, 79th Cong., 2d sess., Feb. 18, 1946. Field report on Nashua, New Hampshire; Rome, New York; and Flint, Grand Rapids, Pontiac, and Kalamazoo, Michigan. Submitted as "Big Business and the Middle Class: A Report on Six Cities," May 1945.

"The Fourth Edition," review of *Our Inner Conflicts: A Constructive Theory of Neurosis*, by Karen Horney, *Briarcliffe Quarterly*, v. 3 (April 1946): 84–85.

"The Intellectual and the Labor Leader," April 8, 1946, from remarks made Jan. 18 at the Inter-Union Institute in New York; revised and published as "No Mean-Sized Opportunity" in *The House of Labor: Internal Operations of American Unions*, ed. J.B.S. Hardman and Maurice F. Neufeld (New York: Prentice-Hall, 1951), 515–520.

"A Line-Up of Movie Leaders," report for Bureau of Applied Social Research on movie attendance in Decatur, Illinois, April 1946; findings reported in Paul Lazarsfeld, "Audience Research in the Movie Field," *Annals of the American Academy of Political and Social Science*, v. 254 (Nov. 1946): 160–168.

"Consumption: Leaders, Relayers, and Followers," report for Bureau of Applied Social Research, 1946.

"Leaders of Political Opinion," 54-page discussion draft for Bureau of Applied Social Research, May 18, 1946.

"The Politics of Skill," *Labor and Nation*, v. 2 (June–July 1946): 35.

"What Research Can Do for Labor," *Labor and Nation*, v. 2 (June–July 1946): 17–20.

"The Love Life of the Young Intellectual," journal, Aug. 24, 1946.

"The Competitive Personality," publication A-79, Bureau of Applied Social Research; published in *Partisan Review*, v. 13 (Sept.–Oct. 1946): 433–441.

"The Middle Classes in Middle-Sized Cities: The Stratification and Political Position of Small Business and White Collar Strata," *American Sociological Review*, v. 11 (Oct. 1946): 520–529. From an address to the American Sociological Society in Cleveland, March 1–3. Translated as "La clase media en las ciudades medias" and republished in *Antología sobre estratificación social*, ed. Eduardo Hamuy (Santiago, Chile: Editorial Universitaria, S. A., 1958): 239–262.

"What the People Think: Review of Selected Opinion Polls" (with Hazel Gaudet), *Labor and Nation* 2 (Nov.–Dec. 1946): 11–13.

"The Influence Study: Some Conceptions and Procedures of Research," address to the American Association for the Advancement of Science, Boston, Dec. 29, 1946.

"Memorandum to Paul F. Lazarsfeld," Dec. 30, 1946.

1947

"The New Middle Class" and "The Defeat of Socialism 1920-1947 and the Need for Reorientation," addresses to the Labor Action School, Hotel Diplomat, New York, Jan. 5, 1947.

"Memorandum: Opportunities for Research in the Navy, and Other Related Matters," submitted to Paul F. Lazarsfeld, Jan. 1947.

"Memorandum: The Labor Research Division," submitted to Paul F. Lazarsfeld, Jan. 28, 1947.

"Man Exuberant," review of *Balzac*, by Stefan Zweig, *Labor and Nation*, v. 3 (Jan.–Feb. 1947): 58.

"What the People Think: The People in the Unions" (with Thelma Ehrlich), *Labor and Nation*, v. 3 (Jan.–Feb. 1947): 28–31. Condensed version published as "People in the Unions" (with Thelma Ehrlich Anderson) in *The House of Labor: International Operations of American Unions*, ed. J. B. S. Hardman and Maurice F. Neufeld, prepared under the auspices of the Inter-Union Institute (New York: Prentice-Hall, 1951), 48–51.

"A Spot Survey of a Naval Research Community," 65-page report submitted to A. H. Hausrath, Director, Scientific Personnel Branch, Office of Naval Research, U.S. Navy, Feb. 1, 1947.

"A Proposal for a Study of the Social Structure and Personnel of Naval Research Establishments," submitted to A.H. Hausrath, Director, Scientific Personnel Branch, Office of Naval Research, U.S. Navy, Feb. 1, 1947.

"A Proposal for a Study of the Character and Motives of the Research Scientist in the United States," submitted to A. H. Hausrath, Director, Scientific Personnel Branch, Office of Naval Research, U.S. Navy, Feb. 1, 1947.

"What the People Think: Anti-Labor Legislation" (with Hazel Gaudet Erskine), *Labor and Nation*, v. 3 (March–April 1947): 25–28.

"Goodbye Blues: Songs of the Working Man," journal, April 3, 1947.

"All That And—A Survey of the Left," *Labor and Nation*, v. 3 (March–April 1947): 41–42.

Review of *Industry and Society*, ed. William F. Whyte, *Annals of the American Academy of Political and Social Science*, v. 251 (May 1947): 200–201.

"Five 'Publics' the Polls 'Don't Catch': What Each of These Think of and Expect from the Labor Leaders," *Labor and Nation*, v. 3 (May–June 1947): 22–27.

"The Political Complexion of Union Leadership" (with Helen Schneider), *Labor and Nation*, v. 3 (July–August 1947): 10–15.

"The Labor Leader: Who He Is and What He Believes," Publication A-81, Bureau of Applied Social Research, 1947; published as "Leaders of the Unions" (with Helen S. Dinerman) in *The House of Labor: Internal Operations of American Unions*, ed. J. B. S. Hardman and Maurice F. Neufeld, prepared under the Auspices of the Inter-Union Institute (New York: Prentice-Hall, 1951), 24–47.

"Memorandum Re: Survey of the U.S. Left," submitted to Robert Lynd, Oct. 30, 1947.

"What Chances of Organic Trade Union Unity?" (with Helen Schneider), *Labor and Nation*, v.3 (Sept.–Oct. 1947): 14–16.

"Comment on Paper," discussion of "Recent Developments in the Field of Personality Studies," American Sociological Society, Dec. 29, 1947.

"General Instructions for the 'Everyday Life in America' Guide: *White Collar Study*," 1947.

"Walter Reuther's Coalition," 41-page journal about the United Automobile Workers convention, Atlantic City, Nov. 9–14, 1947.

"The Politics of Truth, and Other Essays, 1939–1947," book proposal, 1947.

1948

"Edward Alexander Westermarck and the Application of Ethnographic Methods to Marriage and Morals," in *An Introduction to the History of Sociology*, ed. Harry E. Barnes (Chicago: University of Chicago Press, 1948), 654–667.

"Rationality Without Reason," dialogue, 1948.

"Grass-Roots Union with Ideas: The Auto Workers—Something New in American Labor," *Commentary*, v. 5 (March 1948): 240–248.

"Doctors and Workers: A Pilot Report to the UAW on Health Problems and Medical Care," submitted to the UAW's Research and Social Security Department, April 21, 1948. Excerpts read into the record of the United Auto Workers–General Motors contract negotiations in the Spring. Findings reported in "The Auto Workers' Blues," *Fortune,* v. 38 (Nov. 1948): 210, 214.

"Sociological Poetry," review of *Let Us Now Praise Famous Men*, by James Agee and Walker Evans, *Politics*, v. 5 (Spring 1948): 125–126.

"International Relations and Sociology: Discussion," *American Sociological Review*, v. 13 (June 1948): 271–273; in response to W. Rex Crawford, "International Relations and Sociology," *American Sociological Review*, v. 13 (June 1948): 263–268. From a discussion at a joint meeting of the American Sociological Society, American Statistical Association, Institute of Mathematical Statistics, the Sociometric Institute, and the Biometric Society, New York, December 28, 1947.

The New Men of Power: America's Labor Leaders (with the assistance of Helen Schneider), New York: Harcourt, Brace, 1948. Publication date Sept. 23. Excerpted as "What Kind of Men Run Our Trade Unions Today?" *New York Star*, magazine section (Sept. 5, 1948): 15.

"Free Enterprise: Is It Working?" television forum with Lawrence Fertig, Leo Wolman, Representative Clifford P. Case, Norman Thomas, and I. Howard Lehman, broadcast on WABD Television (Channel 5) in New York at 9:30 A.M., Oct. 4, 1948.

"Public Affairs," radio forum with Wellington Roe, broadcast on WNBC Radio in New York at 1:45 P.M., Oct. 9, 1948.

"Labor Arbitration," radio forum with Samuel R. Zack and Ashley L. Totten, broadcast on WMCA Radio in New York at 9:30 P.M., Nov. 4, 1948.

"Comments on 'The Challenge to Free Inquiry,'" New School for Social Research, Nov. 21, 1948.

"Liberal Perspectives and Radical Facts," journal, post-November 1948.

"The Meaning of the Election," journal, post-November 1948.

"A Third Camp in a Two-Power World" (with Louis Clair and Irving Sanes), unpublished 16-page essay, Dec. 1948.

1949

"The Contribution of Sociology to Industrial Relations," *Proceedings of the First Annual Conference of the Industrial Relations Research Association*, no. 4, ed. Milton Derber (Urbana, IL: IRRA Press, 1949): 199–222; from a paper read to the Industrial Relations Research Association, Cleveland, Dec. 30, 1948. Translated as "Note sur l'idéologie sur des relations humaines dans l'industrie." Pts. 1 and 2, *La Revue*

Socialiste, v. 84 (Feb. 1955): 191–201; and v. 85 (March 1955): 303–313.

"Proceedings of Meeting of Inter-Union Institute," New York City, January 8, 1949.

"Types of Academic Men: Chicago Memorandum Number One, Some Problems of the College Staff," 27-page memorandum, Spring 1949.

"Dogmatic Indecision," *Labor Zionist*, v. 4 (April 15, 1949): 3; in response to Mark Starr, "Labor through Polls," *Labor Zionist*, v. 4 (March 18, 1949): 2.

"Notes on White Collar Unionism," two-part essay in *Labor and Nation*, v. 5 (March–April 1949): 17–21; and (May–June 1949): 17–23.

"C.W.M.," editorial note, *Labor and Nation*, v. 5 (May–June 1949): 8.

"How Powerful Is Labor Leadership?" radio forum with Joel Seidman and Lee C. Shaw, NBC Radio Discussion, published as *University of Chicago's Roundtable*, no. 581 (May 8, 1949): 1, 15.

"The Pattern of Human Relations," paper read at the Social Sciences Today Seminar, Rand School of Social Science, Nov. 16, 1949.

"The Third Report of the College Committee in Sociology," submitted to the Dean of Columbia College and the Executive Officer of the Department of Sociology, Nov. 21, 1949.

1950

Review of *The Psychology of Social Classes*, by Richard Centers, *Annals of the American Academy of Political and Social Science*, v. 268 (March 1950): 241–242.

Moderator of debate between Max Shachtman and Earl Broader, sponsored by Eugene V. Debs Society, Brooklyn College, March 31, 1950; transcript, including Mills's remarks, published as "Is Russia a Socialist Community? The Verbatim Text of a Debate," *The New International*, v. 16 (May–June 1950): 145–176.

Review of *Trade Unions in the New Society*, by Harold J. Laski, *Canadian Journal of Economics and Political Science*, v. 16 (Aug. 1950): 440–441.

The Puerto Rican Journey: New York's Newest Migrants (with Clarence Senior and Rose Kohn Goldsen), Publication B-11, Bureau of Applied Social Research, New York: Harper, 1950. Publication date September 6.

"Public Opinion: Sociologists Assess the Effect of Mass Communications upon the Ways in Which Men Make Up Their Minds," unpublished essay for *Amerika*, publication of the U.S. Department of State, Nov. 29, 1950; barred by Soviet censor Aug. 1951.

"C. Wright Mills: Islander Exploring Main Street," interview, *Columbia Alumni News*, v. 42 (Dec. 1950): 18.

1951

"This Is the Answer," *American Magazine*, v. 151 (May 1951): 25, 132.

White Collar: The American Middle Classes. New York: Oxford University Press, 1951. Publication date September 6. Introduction excerpted as "The White Collar Takes Over" in *The World of History*, ed. Courtlandt Canby and Nancy E. Gross (New York: New American Library, Mentor edition, 1954), 123–128.

Review (unpublished) of *The Social System*, by Talcott Parsons, written for *New York Times Book Review*, Nov. 1, 1951.

"The American Political Elite: A Collective Portrait" (with Ruth Mills), paper, 1951.

"History of Schools of Social Psychology," paper, 1951.

1952

"Liberal Values in the Modern World: The Relevance of Nineteenth Century Liberalism Today," *Anvil and Student Partisan* v. 4 (Winter 1952): 5–7.

"The Sociology of Stratification," paper for Contemporary Civilization B1: Culture, Personality and Society, Columbia College, 1952.

"The Psychoanalysis of Truth and Culture," double review of *Psychoanalysis and Politics: A Contribution to the Psychology of Politics and Morals*, by R. E. Money-Kyrle; and *Psychoanalysis, Man and Society*, by Paul Schilder, arranged by Lauretta Bender, *The New Republic*, v. 126 (Jan. 14, 1952): 19–20.

"Why I Wrote *White Collar*," *Book Find News*, no. 136 (1952): 2, 5.

"Autopsy of Prometheus," review (unpublished) of *The Counter-Revolution in Science*, by F. A. Hayek, for *New York Times Book Review*, 1952.

Review of *Higher Civil Servants in American Society*, by Reinhard Bendix, *American Journal of Sociology*, v. 57 (March 1952): 523.

"Freedom and Security in Our Garrison State," address at the Sixth Annual Dean's Day, co-sponsored by the Association of the Alumni of Columbia College and the Faculty of Columbia College, March 22, 1952.

"On Intellectual Craftsmanship: In Lieu of a Handbook for Students Beginning Independent Work," written April 1952 and mimeographed in Feb. 1955 for distribution to students in Columbia College.

"A Question of Degree," review of *They Went to College: The College Graduate in America Today*, by Ernest Havemann and Patricia S. West, *New York Times Book Review* (April 6, 1952): 5.

"Stendhal," journal, April 16, 1952.

"Labor in the United States," unpublished 29-page essay for *Encyclopedia Americana*, May 16, 1952.

Contribution to "Our Country and Our Culture," symposium in *Partisan Review*, v. 19 (July Aug. 1952): 446–450.

Review of *Men in Business: Essays in the History of Entrepreneurship*, by William Miller, *American Sociological Review*, v. 17 (Aug. 1952): 504–505.

"A Peek at Public Morality: Girls Using Vice to Help Careers," *New York Journal American* (Aug. 31, 1952): 4L. From "Plain Talk on Fancy Sex: A Peek at Public Morality," distributed by *International News Service*.

"A Look at the White Collar," *Office Management Series*, no. 131 (1952): 30–36. From an address at the Hotel New Yorker to the Office Management Conference of the American Management Association, Oct. 17, 1952.

"The Fifty Years That Made Us What We Are Today," review of *The Big Change*, by Frederick L. Allen, *New York Times Book Review* (Nov. 2, 1952): 3.

"Three Hundred Who Lost Their Way," review of *Report on the American Communist*, by Morris L. Ernst and David Loth, *New York Times Book Review* (Nov. 30, 1952): 26.

"What Helps Most in Politics?" (with Ruth Mills), *Pageant Magazine* (Nov. 1952): 156–168.

"Higher Civil Servants in American Society," letter to the editor, *American Journal of Sociology*, v. 58 (Nov. 1952): 304; in response to Reinhard Bendix letter to the editor, *American Journal of Sociology*, v. 58 (July 1952): 67–68.

"Knowing How to Wait," published in Paris as "Savoir Attendre," *Esprit*, no. 196, v. 27 (Nov. 1952): 693–698.

"We Are for Stevenson Because . . ." one of 324 signers for Columbia Faculty Volunteers for Stevenson, petition appearing in *New York Times*, Oct. 16, 1952.

"Official Liberalism and Its Centralization," journal, post election, 1952.

"A Diagnosis of Our Moral Uneasiness," *New York Times Magazine* (Nov. 23, 1952): 10, 55–57.

1953

Character and Social Structure: The Psychology of Social Institutions (with Hans H. Gerth). New York: Harcourt, Brace, 1953.

"Introduction," in *The Theory of the Leisure Class: An Economic Study of Institutions*, by Thorstein Veblen (1899; New York: New American Library, Mentor Edition, 1953): vi–xix.

"The American Elite," address to Smith College, 1953.

"Letter to a College Girl," journal, 1953.

Review of *The Counterfeit Revolution*, by Sidney Lens, *American Journal of Sociology* v. 58 (March 1953): 535.

Review of *The Organizational Weapon: A Study of Bolshevik Strategy and Tactics*, by Philip Selznick, *American Journal of Sociology*, v. 58 (March 1953): 529.

"The Symbol of Race," review of *Racial and Cultural Minorities: An Analysis of Prejudice*, by George E. Simpson and J. Milton Yinger, *New York Times Book Review* (April 26, 1953): 14.

"The Darling Little Slaves," review (unpublished) of *The Second Sex*, by Simone de Beauvoir, written for *The Nation*, 1953.

Review of *The Worldly Philosophers*, by Robert L. Heilbroner, *Book Find News* (1953): 1.

"For Ought," journal, Sept. 19, 1953.

"Leisure and the Whole Man," *New York Herald Tribune* (Oct. 25, 1953), sec. 9, p. 48. From an address at the third session of New York Herald Tribune Forum, Waldorf-Astoria Hotel, New York, Oct. 25, 1953. Reprinted as "The Unity of Work and Leisure," *Journal of the National Association of Deans of Women*, v. 42 (Jan. 1954): 58–61.

"Two Styles of Research in Current Social Studies," *Philosophy of Science*, v. 20 (Oct. 1953): 266–275.

"An Old School Custom," review of *Drinking in College*, by Robert Straus and Selden D. Bacon, *New York Times Book Review* (Oct. 4, 1953): 22.

Review of *Community Power Structure: A Study of Decision Makers*, by Floyd Hunter, *Social Forces*, v. 32 (Oct. 1953): 92–93.

1954

"The Labor Leaders and the Power Elite," in *Roots of Industrial Conflict*, ed. Arthur Kornhauser, Robert Dubin and Arthur M. Ross (New York: McGraw Hill, 1954), 144–152.

"Work Milieu and Social Structure," in *People at Work: A Symposium*. Proceedings of the Mental Health Society of Northern California, 1954. From an address at the Asilomar Conference of the Mental Health Society of Northern California, March 13, 1954. Expanded version addressed to the Psychological Association, Copenhagen, Denmark, Oct. 1956.

"Knowledge and Power," address at the Eighth Annual Dean's Day, co-sponsored by the Association of the Alumni of Columbia College and the Faculty of Columbia College, March 20, 1954.

"Nothing to Laugh At," review of Frederic Wertham, *Seduction of the Innocent* in *New York Times Book Review* (April 25, 1954): 20.

"Who Conforms and Who Dissents?" letter to the editor, *Commentary*, v. 17 (April 1954): 403–405; in response to "Philistine Leftism," by Nathan Glazer, *Commentary*, v. 17 (Feb. 1954): 201–206.

"IBM Plus Reality Plus Humanism = Sociology," *The Saturday Review*, v. 37 (May 1, 1954): 22–23, 54.

"Mass Society and Liberal Education," *Notes and Essays on Education for Adults*, no. 9 (June 1954): 1–17. From an address in New Orleans in April to the National Conference on Method for the Study of the Urban Community, sponsored by the Center for the Study of Liberal Education for Adults.

"Are We Losing Our Sense of Belonging?" *Food for Thought* (Sept./Oct. 1954): 11–16. From an address to the Couchiching Conference, on the shores of Lake Couchiching, Ontario, sponsored by the Canadian Association for Adult Education, Aug. 1954. Also broadcast by the Canadian Broadcasting Corporation.

Review of *Politics, Economics, and Welfare*, by Robert A. Dahl and Charles E. Lindblom, *American Sociological Review*, v. 19 (Aug. 1954): 495–496.

"Those Early Paradoxes," review of *Yankee Reformers in the Urban Age*, by Arthur Mann. *New York Times Book Review* (Oct. 17, 1954): 33.

Review of *Professional People in England*, by Roy Lewis and Angus Maude, *Harvard Law Review*, v. 68 (Nov. 1954): 198–199.

"The Conservative Mood," *Dissent*, v. 1 (Winter 1954): 22–31.

1955

"Introduction" to *History of European Morals from Augustus to Charelemagne*, by W. E. H. Lecky (New York: Braziller, 1955): v–viii; also used as introduction to *History of the Rise and Influence of the Spirit of Rationalism in Europe*, by W. E. H. Lecky (New York: Braziller, 1955): v–viii.

"Mills, Charles Wright," in *Twentieth Century Authors*, first supplement, *A Biographical Dictionary of Modern Literature*, ed. Stanley J. Kunitz (New York: H. H. Wilson, 1955), 674–675.

"Types of Eminent Americans and the Social Structure of the United States," unpublished paper, 1955.

"The American Scientist," address to the Seventh Annual Forum of Democracy, Columbia College, on the theme of "Science and Democracy," Feb. 24, 1955.

"Woman with a Mission," review of *The Margaret Sanger Story: And the Fight for Birth Control*, by Laurence Lader, *New York Times Book Review* (April 17, 1955): 10.

"Memorandum on Selected Types of American Intellectuals," submitted to Social Science Research Council, Columbia University, Spring 1955; approved April 22, 1955.

"Proposal for a book on 'The American Intellectual,'" submitted to William Oman, Oxford University Press, May 1, 1955.

"Instructions for Completing 'The Intellectuals': Schedule No. 1," for Dan Wakefield, summer 1955.

"The Cultural Economy," "The Big Split," "The Politics of Culture," "Future of the Apparatus," "On Being Political," "On Politics without Parties," "The US and the USSR," "Uses of Intellectuals in the Overdeveloped Society," "The American Attempt to Establish Culture Politically," and "Subservience on Three Levels" are (undated) essays or chapters toward *The Cultural Apparatus, or, The American Intellectual,* which Mills began in 1955 and continued until 1960. (Additional essays/chapters for which dates are known are listed accordingly).

"On Knowledge and Power," *Dissent,* v. 2 (Summer 1955): 201–212. From an address to a joint meeting of the William Alanson White and Harry S. Sullivan Societies in Feb. 1955.

"Bounteous New Man," review of *People of Plenty: Economic Abundance and the American Character,* by David M. Potter, *The Saturday Review,* v. 38 (July 16, 1955): 19.

Letter to President Eisenhower and Attorney General Herbert Brownell Jr. regarding Smith Act prosecutions, one of 73 signers, Aug. 7, 1955.

"The Growth of Administrative Structures and the Modern State," address at Air War College, Maxwell Air Force Base, Alabama, Aug. 25, 1955.

Review of *The Exurbanites,* by A. C. Spectorsky, *The Saturday Review,* v. 38 (Oct. 29, 1955): 11–12.

"Two Criteria for the Good Society," address to the National Conference of the Adult Education Association, St. Louis, Missouri, Nov. 11, 1955.

"A Note on Professor Perlman's Theory of Unionism," paper for the Conference on the Sociology of Labor and Work, Wayne University, Nov. 1955.

Review of *The American Lawyer: A Summary of the Survey of the Legal Profession,* by Albert P. Blaustein, Charles O. Porter and Charles T. Duncan, *Stanford Law Review,* v. 8 (Dec. 1955): 147–149.

"What, Then, Ought We To Do?," unpublished essay, 1955.

1956

The Power Elite. New York: Oxford University Press. Excerpted in translation as "Sobre los altos círculos," *La Gaceta,* Mexico City (Oct. 1957): 1; as "L'élite du pouvoir." Pts. 1 and 2, *Les Temps Modernes,* Paris, v. 135 (May–June, 1957): 1704–1731 and v. 136 (July–Aug. 1957): 1943–1971; and as "Las Celebridades," in *Sociología del Poder,* ed. Andres Bello (Santiago, Chile, 1960), 378–398.

"Sociologist on a Motorcycle," interview with Thomas E. Cooney, *Saturday Review,* v. 39 (April 28, 1956): 9.

"Power and Culture," address to PEN Club, New York, May 14, 1956.

"Substance and Shadow," review of *The American Business Creed,* by Francis X. Sutton et al. *New York Times Book Review* (Sept. 30, 1956): 7.

"Amerikanismen og de intellektuelles ansvar," *Berlingske Tidende* (Dec. 1, 1956): 10.

"Amerika og Kampen om den europaeiske Kultur," *Berlingske Tidende* (Nov. 18, 1956): 1, 3.

"Crawling to the Top," review of *The Organization Man*, by William H. Whyte Jr., *New York Times Book Review* (Dec. 9, 1956): 6, 26.

Review (unpublished) of *Crestwood Heights*, by John R. Seeley et. al., 1956.

1957

"Why I Write to You," autobiographical letter written toward a manuscript titled *Contacting the Enemy: Tovarich*, Sarajevo and Copenhagen, Winter 1957.

"The Power Elite: Military, Economic and Political," in *Problems of Power in American Democracy*, ed. Arthur Kornhauser (Detroit: Wayne State University Press), 145–183. From an address at the Detroit Institute of Art Lecture Hall, Fifth Annual Series, Leo M. Franklin Memorial Lectures, Wayne University, April 25, 1955.

"The Power Elite: Comment on Criticism," *Dissent*, v. 5 (Winter 1957): 22–34. Final draft dated Nov. 10, 1956.

"Why I Wrote *The Power Elite*," *Book Find News*, no. 188 (1957): 1.

"Who or What Causes War?" dialogue, Spring 1957.

Letter to the editor, *Commentary*, v. 23 (June 1957): 580–581, drafted April 12 in response to "Organization Men," by Robert Lekachman, *Commentary*, v. 23 (March 1957): 270–276.

"In Great Books of Old Is Found New Meaning," review of *Literature and the Image of Man: Sociological Studies of the European Drama and Novel, 1600–1900*, by Leo Lowenthal, *New York Times* (July 7, 1957): 156.

"Growing Up: Facts and Fancies," "On Guilt," "On Who I Might Be and How I Got That Way," and "On Injustice and Personal Trouble" were autobiographical letters written toward a manuscript titled *Contacting the Enemy: Tovarich*, Innsbruck, Austria, Autumn 1957.

"Program for Peace," *The Nation*, v. 185 (Dec. 7, 1957): 419–424.

1958

"The Complacent Young Men: Reasons for Anger," review of *Look Back in Anger*, by John Osborn; and *Lucky Jim*, by Kingsley Amis, *Anvil and Student Partisan*, v. 9 (Winter 1958): 13–15.

"The Structure of Power in American Society," *British Journal of Sociology*, v. 9 (March 1958): 29–41. From addresses to the Students' Union, London School of Economics, March 2, 1957, and to the University of Frankfurt, May 3, 1957.

"On War and Peace," Sidney Hillman Award Lectures, Andrew Rankin Memorial Chapel, Howard University, March 24, 26, and 28, 1958.

"A Pagan Sermon to the Christian Clergy," *The Nation*, v. 186 (March 8, 1958): 199–202. From "War Becomes Total: A Pagan Sermon for Christian Ministers," an address at Prince Arthur House to the Board of Evangelicalism and Social Service, United Church of Canada, Toronto, Feb. 27, 1958.

"The Causes of World War Three," address at the University of Illinois, Urbana, April 11, 1958.

"The Promise of Sociology," paper for the American Political Science Association, St. Louis, Missouri, Sept. 14, 1958.

"World War Three and Utopian Capitalists," address at the University of Texas, Austin, Oct. 24, 1958.

"State of the World: Propositions and Policies," Oct. 1958; first draft dated Feb. 1957.

"The Rise and Fall of the Left Establishment," essay written toward book manuscript, *The Cultural Apparatus, or The American Intellectual*, 1958.

"The Man in the Middle: The Designer," *Industrial Design*, v. 5 (Nov. 1958): 72–76. From "Social Forces and the Frustrations of the Designer," an address read to the Eighth Annual International Design Conference, Aspen, Colorado, June 22 and 28, 1958.

"On the Problem of Freedom," address to the American Studies Conference on Civil Rights, Cornell University, Oct. 16, 1958.

"Comparative Sociology," research plan and grant application submitted to Rabinowitz Foundation, Autumn 1958.

The Causes of World War Three. New York: Simon and Schuster and Ballantine, 1958. Publication date December 7. Excerpted as "Crackpot Realism," *Fellowship*, v. 25 (Jan. 1, 1959): 3–8.

"Characteristics of Our Times" address at the Annual Assembly, Division of Home Missions, National Council of the Churches of Christ in the United States of America, Atlantic City, New Jersey, Dec. 10, 1958.

"Some Thoughts on Creativity—The Politics of Culture," address to Cooper Union, New York, Dec. 1958.

1959

The Sociological Imagination. New York: Oxford University Press, 1959. Excerpted as "Psychology and Social Science," *Monthly Review*, v. 10 (Oct. 1958): 204–209.

"Culture and Politics: The Fourth Epoch," *The Listener*, v. 61, no. 1563 (March 12, 1959): 449–451. First of three University Lectures in Sociology, London School of Economics, Jan. 12, 1959; broadcast on the

BBC's Third Programme on March 6 and reprinted in Danish as "Den fjerde epoke," *Vindrosen: Gyldendal litteraere magasin*, v. 7, no. 6 (1960): 443–466.

"The Cultural Apparatus," *The Listener*, v. 61, no. 1565 (March 26, 1959): 552–553, 556. Second of three University Lectures in Sociology, London School of Economics, Jan. 13, 1959; broadcast on the BBC's Third Programme on March 13.

"The Decline of the Left," *The Listener*, v. 61, no. 1566 (April 2, 1959): 594–595, 598. Third of three University Lectures in Sociology, London School of Economics, Jan. 15, 1959; broadcast on the BBC's Third Programme on March 16. Also given at Stanford University on April 15, broadcast by Pacifica Radio on May 13, and republished in *Contact,* v. 1 (1959): 5–18. Rebroadcast by WBAI Radio, New York, at 9:00 A.M. on Aug. 7, 1961.

"On Politics and Culture," three addresses to a joint meeting of the Polish Sociological Society and the Institute of Philosophy and Sociology, Polish Academy of Sciences, Warsaw, Jan. first week 1959.

"The Causes of World War Three," Institute of International Affairs, Warsaw, Jan. first week 1959.

"The Big City: Private Troubles and Public Issues," address at The Troubled Metropolis: Fifth Annual Winter Conference of the Canadian Institute on Public Affairs, Toronto, Feb. 7, 1959.

"On Intellectual Craftsmanship," in *Symposium on Sociological Theory*, ed. Llewellyn Gross (Evanston, IL: Row and Peterson, 1959), 25–53.

"Creativity: How It Functions in the Arts and Sciences," address to the Advanced Study Group, Clarkstown High School, New York, sponsored by the Intellectual Resources Pool, Rockland Foundation, April 25, 1959.

"Intellectuals and Russia," *Dissent*, v. 6 (Summer 1959): 295–298; in response to Irving Howe, "C. Wright Mills's Program" *Dissent*, v. 6 (Spring 1959), 194.

"The History Makers," *Social Progress* (Oct. 1959): 5–16.

"The Intellectuals' Last Chance," *Esquire*, v. 52 (Oct. 1959): 101–102.

"What Does It Mean to Be an Intellectual?" autobiographical letter written toward a manuscript titled *Contacting the Enemy: Tovarich*, Rio de Janeiro, Brazil, between Oct. 18 and 29, 1959.

"Resistencias a Mudanca: Factores que impeden o Difficultan o Desenvolvimiento," *Centro Latinoamericano de Investigaciones en Ciencas Sociales*, v. 10 (1960): 281–287. From an address to the International Seminar on Resistance to Social Development, Latin American Center of Investigation in the Social Sciences, Rio de Janeiro, between Oct. 18–29, 1959.

"A Pagan Sermon to the Christian Clergy: Part II," unpublished essay, 1959.

"Were I President: Results of a Change in Elites," journal, 1959.

1960

Images of Man: The Classic Tradition in Sociological Thinking, edited and introduced. New York: Braziller, 1960.

The New Left, book manuscript dated Jan. 1960 and expanded in undated chapters throughout 1960 and 1961. Table of contents on Sept. 25, 1960.

"Dynamics of a Thinker," review of *Max Weber: An Intellectual Portrait*, by Reinhard Bendix, *New York Times Book Review* (Jan. 17, 1960): 16.

Interview on *We Dissent*, documentary film produced by Kenneth Tynan and directed by Michael Redington; broadcast on Associated Television in Britain, Jan. 24, 1960.

"On Marx and Marxism," lecture-series at the National University of Mexico, Feb.– March 1960.

"On Latin America, the Left and the U.S.," interview in Mexico City in March 1960 with Victor Flores Olea, Enrique Gonzales Pedrero, Carlos Fuentes, and Jaime Garcia Terres, *Evergreen Review*, v. 5 (Jan.–Feb. 1961): 110–122. Published in Mexico City, then corrected by Mills on Nov. 4, 1960.

"The Sociological Imagination," address at the Institute of Philosophy, Soviet Academy of Science, April/May 1960.

Soviet Journal, 295-page journal, April/May 1960.

"Up Closer," autobiographical letter written toward a manuscript titled *Contacting the Enemy: Tovarich*, Moscow, April/May 1960.

"The Balance of Blame: Further Notes on the Strategic Causes of World War III," *The Nation*, v. 190 (June 18): 523–531. Reprinted in *London Tribune* on July 10 and incorporated into second paperback ed. *The Causes of World War Three*, 1960.

Letter to the editor (unpublished), *New York Times*, June 21, 1960; in response to James Reston, "National Purpose," *New York Times* (June 20, 1960): 28.

"Specimen Days of My Life" and "Self-Images and Ambitions," and "On Race and Religion," autobiographical letters written toward a manuscript titled *Contacting the Enemy: Tovarich*, New York, summer 1960.

"A Personal Note to the Reader: Appendix to *The Cultural Apparatus*," summer 1960.

"Letter to the New Left," *New Left Review* v. 5 (Sept.–Oct. 1960): 18–23; drafted July 4, 1960, revised Sept. 25; reprinted as "On the New Left," *Studies on the Left*, v. 2 (1961): 63–72.

"C. Wright Mills Talks, Yankee Listens," interview with Michael B. Conant, *Columbia Owl*, v. 2 (Oct. 12, 1960): 1, 4.

"Trouble," journal, Oct. 24, 1960.

Listen, Yankee: The Revolution in Cuba. New York: McGraw Hill and Ballantine, 1960. Publication early November. Portions broadcast over WBAI Radio, New York, on March 28 and April 4, 1961.

"How to Improve Relations with Cuba and South America," address to the National Board, Americans for Democratic Action, New York City, Nov. 19, 1960.

"C. Wright Mills: Controversial Figure in Conforming Sociology," interview with Arnold Abrams, *Columbia Daily Spectator* (Nov. 29, 1960): 3.

"Listen Yankee: The Cuban Case against the United States," *Harper's Magazine*, v. 222 (Dec. 1960): 31–37.

1961

Statement Calling for the Abolition of the House Committee on Un-American Activities, one of 250 signers for the American Civil Liberties Union, March 19, 1961.

Telegram to President John Kennedy, one of 11 signers for the Fellowship of Reconciliation, April 17, 1961.

Telegram to San Francisco Fair Play for Cuba Committee, April 22, 1961; published in *The Militant* (May 1, 1961): 4; and *Fair Play* (June 5, 1961): 4.

"The Other Human Beings: Preface to *Tovarich*," May 1, 1961.

"The House That Jack Must Build: Modest Proposals for Patriotic Americans—A Satire" (with Saul Landau), *London Tribune* (May 19, 1961): 5.

"Escucha Otra Vez, Yanqui: 1961," appendix to *Eschucha Yanqui: La Revolucion en Cuba*, 3d ed. (Mexico and Buenos Aires: Fondo de Cultura Economica, 1961): 211–259.

"Letter to Spain," unpublished essay, July 1961.

"C. Wright Mills on Kennedy," interview by Juan Archoca in Moscow, published in *Fair Play*, v. 2 (Aug. 26, 1961): 2.

"Escucha Yanqui," telephone interview published in *Politica* (Sept. 19, 1961): 57.

"The Way to Necropolis," review of *The City in History*, by Lewis Mumford, *The Guardian*, Manchester (Oct. 6, 1961): 8.

1962

The Marxists. New York: Dell, 1962.

Posthumous

Power, Politics, and People: The Collected Essays of C. Wright Mills, ed. Irving Louis Horowitz. New York: Oxford University Press, 1963.

Sociology and Pragmatism: The Higher Learning in America, ed. Irving Louis Horowitz. New York: Oxford University Press, 1964/1966.

De Hombres Sociales y Movimentos Politicos, translated by Florentino del Torner and compiled by Irving Louis Horowitz. Mexico City: Siglo Veintiuno, 1969.

C. Wright Mills: Letters and Autobiographical Writings, ed. Kathryn Mills, with Pamela Mills. Berkeley: University of California Press, 2000.

The Charles Wright Mills Papers are located at the Center for American History, University of Texas, Austin.

INDEX